CONTESTING CITIZENSHIP

Contesting Citizenship

Irregular Migrants and New Frontiers of the Political

ANNE McNEVIN

 Columbia University Press *New York*

Columbia University Press
Publishers Since 1893
New York   Chichester, West Sussex
Copyright © 2011 Columbia University Press
All rights reserved
Library of Congress Cataloging-in-Publication Data

McNevin, Anne.
Contesting citizenship : irregular migrants and new frontiers
of the political / Anne McNevin.
p.   cm.
Includes bibliographical references and index.
ISBN 978-0-231-15128-3 (cloth : alk. paper) — ISBN 978-0-231-52224-3 (e-book)
1. Emigration and immigration—Government policy.   2. Citizenship.
3. Illegal aliens.   I. Title.
JV6271.M36 2011
325—dc22
2010042545

Columbia University Press books are printed on permanent
and durable acid-free paper.
This book is printed on paper with recycled content.
Printed in the United States of America

References to Internet Web sites (URLs) were accurate at the time of writing. Neither
the author nor Columbia University Press is responsible for URLs that may have
expired or changed since the manuscript was prepared.

CONTENTS

PREFACE AND ACKNOWLEDGMENTS

This book began as an idea in late 2001 against the backdrop of the *"Tampa* affair" when Australia refused to allow asylum seekers rescued by the Norwegian container ship *Tampa* entry into its territories. The incident remains symbolic of Australia's recent history of border policing against men, women, and children who for many complex reasons are compelled to seek a better life—or, indeed, a life at all—in states that are not their own. It marked a shift in strategy to evade responsibility for refugee protection by pushing the border offshore into places and jurisdictions where refugees would be treated as "illegal" bodies and pawns in political maneuvers. The *Tampa* affair ushered in a political culture that denied association between the boats appearing on Australia's shores and the journeys of European Jews fleeing Nazi persecution—the very (equally thwarted) journeys that inspired states to enshrine refugee protection in international law in the aftermath of World War Two. Instead, the boats and their occupants were actively linked to *the sources* of insecurity that threatened to erode our sovereign, liberal prosperity.

Ten years on, Australia's approach has not been confined to a single chapter in a nervous island's history. In 2010, Kevin Rudd's Labor government raised the specter of return to the worst of Howard-era policies, suspending claims for protection for Afghanis and Sri Lankans on the basis that their countries were safe to return to (or would be soon enough) and reopening remote detention centers to accommodate boat arrivals. As this book goes to print, asylum seekers are once again the focus of electioneering as a new Labor leader, Julia Gillard, comes to power. John Howard's hard-line stances made Australian policy the envy of governments around the world, and the Australian context continues to inspire strategic innovation in the geographic, temporal, and symbolic technologies deployed to instrumentalize the movement of people. The *Tampa* affair thus resonates with *global* trends in border policing against all kinds of outsiders whose deaths on various border-lines is the shocking legacy of our time.

Why is this happening now? Why have specific migration flows that have long been part of the history of an interconnected world only recently been called "illegal"? And why does the movement of certain kinds of people inspire so much fear and anxiety at a time when cosmopolitanism is the catch-cry of a global age? The shift toward global frames of reference for all manner of human endeavor is a crucial factor in understanding contemporary border policing. Irregular migrants have become scapegoats for a series of rapid transformations that rupture long-held certainties about where and with whom our political cleavages and affiliations lie. The morphing spaces through which we shape our political relation to others and the hardening of borders against irregular migrants are interlinked phenomena that this book attempts to unpack. What human geographies give form to hierarchies whereby some people are welcome everywhere and others nowhere? What constellation of power is underwritten by these arrangements, and how does it operate to make arbitrary distinctions seem like matters of common sense?

These questions are driven by my own grave disturbance at the "common sense" that has made it possible in Australia, my home, and elsewhere to justify a regime of border control that systematically shatters lives or suspends people in a state of limbo from which few emerge without the scars of profound and ongoing trauma. Yet such scenarios, which so often inspire a deep sense of despair, are only part of the story. A different set of questions is driven by an equally compelling starting point: that irregular migrants are more than passive victims shuttled from one place to another. They are also active agents in the transformation of political belonging. This book also asks about the ways in which irregular migrants contest their positioning as illegitimate intruders on sovereign communities and, in the process, reconstitute the social and spatial parameters of citizenship.

This book has been written in different forms over several years with the support of many people. I am grateful for the time and freedom given to me to devote myself to the task at both the School of Social Sciences at the Australian National University in Canberra and the Global Cities Research Institute at RMIT University in Melbourne. I am indebted to the encouragement, guidance, and intellectual generosity of mentors in both places, to thoughtful and critical feedback from old and new friends and colleagues, and to the good humor of loved ones who showed every confidence without letting me take myself too seriously. Thanks in particular to Jim George, John Dryzek, Kim Huynh, Katrina Lee-Koo, Fiona Browitt, Bina D'Costa, Judy Hemming, Barry Hindess, Heather Rae, Jane Stratton, Manfred Steger, Paul James, Lisa Slater, Andy Scerri, Erin Wilson, Vicki Squire, Peter Nyers, and Engin Isin. Heartfelt thanks to my family and partner, Andrew.

In the months leading up to completing the final version of the manuscript, one group of people influenced its human and intellectual development more than they probably realize. I had the great pleasure of sharing time and working with an unlikely bunch of asylum seekers and supporters who joined together in Melbourne to tell their stories on stage. The result of this collaboration—the theater production *Journey of Asylum-Waiting*—confirmed in my mind the power of everyday acts "from below" to resist what can sometimes feel like an overwhelming force "from above." This group's determination to find ways and means of being political shows me that the human spirit is always more than what can be captured by administrative categories, legal scenarios, and map-drawn spaces. This "excess" is precisely what holds the greatest potential to redraw and reinvigorate the most rewarding human solidarities. Although these particular stories have not made it into the pages of this book, the book is in many ways about them. To those who invited me so warmly into their journeys of asylum, I am deeply grateful, and this work is dedicated to them.

The discussion of the Australian neoblieral context in chapter 3 draws on an earlier version of the argument in my article "The Liberal Paradox and the Politics of Asylum in Australia," *Australian Journal of Political Science* 42, no. 4 (2007): 611–30, although the argument has been modified substantially. The discussion on border policing and a new terrain of sovereign practice in this same chapter draws on a section of my article "Border Policing and Sovereign Terrain: The Spatial Framing of Unwanted Migration in Australia and Melbourne," *Globalizations* 7, no. 3 (2010): 407–19.

The discussion of the Sans-Papiers in chapter 4 is a substantially modified version of sections of my article "Political Belonging in a Neoliberal Era: The Struggle of the Sans-Papiers," *Citizenship Studies* 10, no. 2 (2006): 135–51. An earlier and more abbreviated version of chapter 4's discussion on the three forms of contestation appeared in "Contesting Citizenship: Irregular Migrants and Strategic Possibilities for Political Belonging," *New Political Science* 31, no. 2 (2009): 163–81.

CONTESTING CITIZENSHIP

In 2008, Alejandro was studying nursing at a college in Los Angeles, where he had lived for the past seven years. He also worked as a marketer for a private ambulance company. Originally from the Philippines, Alejandro believed that after seven years working and paying taxes, he now had the right to have a say in how his adopted country should be governed. He felt that eight years of the George W. Bush administration had run the economy down and driven too many jobs offshore. He was also aware that presidential nominee Barack Obama had spoken in favor of comprehensive immigration reform that would give many immigrants like himself a pathway to U.S. citizenship. Alejandro spoke out to his fellow students, asking them to vote for Obama and making them aware of federal and state bills under debate that would provide financial aid to undocumented students to assist with their college expenses and grant them legal status for the duration of their studies.[1]

Alejandro is one of millions of irregular migrants whose ongoing presence is not formally sanctioned by the state in which they reside. Some have crossed borders illegally; others have overstayed valid visas. Many have traveled to work, and many send money home to families and communities abroad. Some, facing circumstances considerably different to Alejandro's, have fled conflict and disaster; others are seeking asylum from political persecution. Some in the latter category may be granted short-term visas, but their futures remain gravely uncertain. Most live with the ongoing prospect of deportation. Irregular migration provokes enormous anxiety within destination states. Stories like Alejandro's raise questions about the capacity of states to retain control not only over entry and exit, but also over the social relations that shape political communities. Migration in all its forms creates social change that challenges prevailing ideas about who we are as citizens. When Alejandro plays a role in shaping the society from which he is technically excluded, a new set of questions arises around the status of citizenship itself.

In this book, I examine how citizenship is constructed, policed, and contested in relation to irregular migration. I argue that under conditions of globalization, the terms in which citizenship is understood, and the privileges it guarantees are changing. This change is happening alongside the more general transformation of the state. Globalizing states increasingly prioritize a transnational sphere of market relations. As a consequence, the territorial frame according to which citizenship has traditionally been shaped is being disrupted. In the face of these changes, border policing against irregular migrants helps to enforce a territorial account of citizenship that is otherwise challenged by globalizing trajectories. In the chapters that follow, I investigate these processes via illustrative examples that focus in particular on Australia, France, and the United States. I also examine the political strategies that irregular migrants employ to stake claims to belong to the communities in which they live and work. I contend that irregular migrants' struggles for legitimate presence and political equality are contestations of citizenship that both undermine *and* reinscribe the conventional form of citizenship and the state's power to enforce it. This book thus seeks to challenge the reader to think differently about citizenship by reflecting on the constitutive acts of those who are cast as its outsiders. It interprets that outsider status as both a mode of subjectification and a site of active resistance.

Two perplexing conditions inform the rationale for this book. The first concerns the apparent contradictions of the globalizing state. On one hand, states willingly open their borders to global market forces and do so on the pretence that liberalizing borders is the only feasible option for economic growth and development. This opening of borders raises questions about the meaning of citizenship, which has heretofore been based on the notion of a sovereign territorial political community. On the other hand, states are also under increasing pressure to close their borders to certain types of migrants and to maintain a strong sense of bounded national identity. Irregular migrants are caught at the crossroads of these state practices. Many, as workers, respond to a transnational labor market that is part and parcel of global market forces. At the same time, they are brutally policed as transgressors of borders that are elsewhere compromised by states' neoliberal agendas.

These parallel trends suggest that simplistic readings of the contemporary global condition cannot account for the everyday realities that increasingly shape the experiences of citizens and migrants alike. Exaggerated notions of a deterritorialized and borderless world fly in the face of an extraordinary militarization of borders as key sites of defense against flows of unwanted people (irregular migrants and terrorists) and contraband goods (drugs and arms). Yet skeptics of globalization, who doubt the novelty of networks and circuits across transnational space, are likewise faced with the failure of borders to contain these various flows and new modes of communication and transit that challenge our assumptions about limits to time and space. The broader question, positioned between these two crude extremes, is how we are to understand the spatial framing of states, sovereignty, and citizenship in an age that defies "either/or" accounts of rupture or continuity with the spaces of the past.

From this starting point, the state that pursues both a globalizing *and* a border-policing agenda might be recognizable to us less in contradictory terms than in ways that reflect a complex rescaling of state space.[2] From this starting point, in turn, it is possible to discern a *logic* of globalization in its hegemonic neoliberal form whereby fast-tracked border crossings for certain commodities and persons are connected to heightened surveillance of others. These interlinked dynamics result in new subjectivities—new forms of citizenship based on global connectivity and new forms of alienage based on circumscribed access to mobility. From this perspective, the journeys of irregular migrants cannot be sufficiently explained by "push factors" that originate in isolation from destination states. Irregular migrants should be seen not as aberrant but as *immanent* subjects of contemporary global capitalism that come into being *on account* of the trajectories of globalizing states. Finally, from this starting point, we also find that irregular migrants are often located in sites more akin to a spatially rescaled conception of the state than to clear-cut distinctions between two sides of a territorial border. Whether working for transnational production circuits in special economic zones, detained in offshore and excised territories, or safeguarded—at least to some extent—in official city sanctuaries, irregular migrants do not always fit within the spaces defined by prevailing territorial categories. Different kinds of spaces are at work in both technologies of border policing and counterpractices of political belonging. This spatial transformation is a crucial factor in this broader inquiry into the dynamics of citizenship.

The second condition informing this book is the emergence of irregular migrants as political actors. In recent years, irregular migrants have marched, occupied buildings, rioted, gone on strike, petitioned, blogged, written manifestos, and generally brought attention to their long-term presence in states where they live with the constant threat of deportation. The Sans-Papiers, a coalition of irregular migrants based in France, have occupied churches, government offices, union headquarters, and restaurant chains in Paris. They have demanded that their status be regularized and have contested the very basis on which they are positioned as outsiders. In other cases, irregular migrants have won political privileges *despite* their lack of legal status. In the United States, irregular migrants have obtained drivers' licenses, the right to vote for school boards, and "in-state" college tuition, and they have mobilized in huge demonstrations. In each of these cases, irregular migrants are being recognized as a semilegitimate presence. Administrations sometimes respond to their presence with measures that create an ambiguous status between legal and illegal, inclusion and exclusion, belonging and not belonging.

How should citizenship be understood against this background of border transgressions and ambiguous forms of status? If the state is said to represent a bounded community of citizens, what happens when the boundaries defining that community no longer act as buffers to a range of global forces? If irregular migrants are policed as illegitimate outsiders, what happens when they seek and obtain political rights in places where they technically do not belong? The stories of people who do not fit into defined categories of citizenship threaten to rupture a particular configuration of global political power that gives the state its raison d'être. Hence, the tightening of borders against such people is as much a defense of the conceptual framework legitimizing those boundaries as it is a defense of material borders themselves. Irregular migrants' growing political activism generates new claims to citizenship that deploy alternative political geographies. These claims are made at a time when the fault lines of citizenship are very much unsettled and vulnerable to challenge. This timing accounts, at least in part, for the depth of emotion that surrounds the issue of migration and the status of irregular migrants in particular, for what is at stake are not only matters of material distribution—however important they may be—but also questions of life, death, and identity that shape our sense of who we are and how we determine our security into the future.

The theoretical groundwork for the book as a whole is established in chapter 1. Here, I ask, in more detail, who irregular migrants are and why this particular designation of status has so much to reveal about contemporary dynamics of citizenship. I argue that irregular migrants are brought into being in relation to particular constructions of citizenship. In recent decades, this co-constitution reflects a growing crisis of identity against the backdrop of globalization. As migration becomes more hierarchical, we are witnessing the *illegalization* of certain kinds of migrants as a bulwark against citizens' vulnerabilities. I contend that both border policing against irregular migrants and the strategies employed by irregular migrants to contest their "illegal" status add a crucial dimension to the question of citizenship's future. This question is central to a broad field of interdisciplinary scholarship that seeks to reimagine political communities in transnational, postnational, and cosmopolitan terms. Yet, as I show, irregular migrants' specific circumstances are largely absent within this field or insufficiently theorized.

My own approach is to interpret irregular migrants' acts of contestation as a new frontier of the political—that moment of confrontation and destabilization when one account of justice competes with another to shape what we think of as "common sense" justifications for particular status hierarchies. Citizenship in its conventional form has long been the marker of access to important rights and freedoms. Irregular migrants' claims make that relation controversial. They are implicated in new kinds of subjectivities that undermine citizenship as a clear-cut measure of status. In chapter 1, I introduce the notion of the political with respect to irregular migrants, drawing on the early work of Ernesto Laclau and Chantal Mouffe. I argue for an approach to the political that engages directly with the spatial dimension of contemporary citizenship struggles, and I outline some key spatial concepts that are central to this task.

Chapter 2 engages with the spatial dimension more concretely. I examine a new terrain of sovereign practice emerging under conditions of neoliberal globalization and manifesting, for example, in offshore markets, special economic zones, transnational production circuits, and global cities. I show how the globalizing state both responds to and generates these spaces. Such spaces call into question long-held assumptions about the significance and function of state borders. They therefore prompt a range of anxieties about the onset of globalization, the limits of sovereignty, and the privileges that citizenship guarantees. In this unsettling context, states swing between a transnational orientation and the domestic political compulsion to demonstrate territorial loyalties. Irregular migrants are caught between these twin imperatives. As flexible workers, they are incorporated into new terrains in which the state is active, yet their identities continue to be constructed in territorial terms, as unwanted intruders into sovereign, bounded communities. This chapter identifies border policing against irregular migrants as both a strategy of neoliberal governance and a performance of territorial closure.

Neoliberal governance also produces an alternative tier of citizen subjectivities, which are also the subject of chapter 2. Neoliberal hierarchies and subjectivities do not map directly onto territorial containers. If a new terrain of sovereign practice does not cohere with the inside/outside logic of territorial norms, then corresponding hierarchies of mobility, labor, and status in turn defy the conventional line between citizen and noncitizen. Neoliberal subjects emerge at one extreme as hypermobile cosmopolitans imbued with all the privilege and access that new civic virtues of entrepreneurship and investment can accord. Other kinds of travelers who respond in different ways to the same neoliberal imperatives are rendered "illegal" and therefore amenable to extreme forms of exploitation.

Chapters 3, 4, and 5 expand on these general themes from the perspective of three different contexts. In chapter 3, the focus turns to Australia. Australia has experienced comparatively small volumes of irregular migration, yet its treatment of asylum seekers in recent years has been highly restrictive and punitive. Why has so much effort gone into border policing in this context? In this chapter, I argue that policing

Australia's borders has served to reinvigorate a particular notion of citizenship and national identity made vulnerable amidst anxieties about Australia's neoliberal trajectory. Border policing creates for domestic consumption an image of a state in control: a state with the power and will to defend its sovereign borders in spite of its integration with global governance regimes that defend the right to asylum. This image is precisely the opposite of the one generated by decades of neoliberal reform. In the latter case, painful structural adjustments have been justified as being the result of integration with global governance structures against whose liberalizing drive there is no rational defense. Thus, even where irregular migrants are not employed as a source of essential labor, border policing remains implicated in strategies to contain opposition to the advance of global capital.

The Australian case also reveals an additional layer of complexity in the spatial framing that shapes irregular migrants' experiences. Through the transnational marketization of border policing and various forms of extraterritorial policing, state authorities are engaged in sovereign practices that subvert the territorial clarity that border policing aims to enhance. Through the use of specific technologies such as excision and offshoring, Australia has led the way in this respect. Such practices are extraterritorial in the sense of being exercised beyond territorial borderlines, but also and more crucially in the sense of disrupting conventional spatial frames. As objects of policing, asylum seekers are caught at this intersection of territorial and extraterritorial space. Defined territorially, by virtue of a border crossing, asylum seekers are nevertheless in constant confrontation with a neoliberal rationality of governance that enacts a very different kind of space. As I show in chapter 3 and subsequent chapters, this confrontation has implications both for the forms that policing takes and for the modes of resistance that irregular migrants deploy.

Contestations of citizenship by irregular migrants are the subject of chapter 4. Here I begin by establishing a theoretical distinction between different types of contestations. The distinctions are important because they provide an analytical basis from which to assess the implications of diverse empirical examples. I distinguish among contestations that seek the extension of citizenship as it stands to approved outsiders, that challenge the meanings embodied in citizenship, and that question the legitimacy of citizenship—no matter how transformed—as a measure of political belonging. The third kind of contestation is hard to perceive through a scholarly and political lens that is itself embedded in a discourse and practice of citizenship. It is even harder to articulate what kinds of subjectivities—beyond "citizens" and "aliens"—that such acts of contestation may engender. But it seems to me that a critical approach to the transformation of citizenship must at least remain open to the possibility of political claims that defy the limits of existing conceptual grids.

This discussion foregrounds an examination of the growing political activism of the Sans-Papiers of France in chapter 4. In recent decades, France has emerged as an immigration state with substantial populations from Muslim and North African backgrounds. Controversial legal cases, such as the famous "head scarf affair," have focused public attention on claims to cultural and religious difference within the French republican project. Fierce debate has ensued over the nature of French citizenship and the hierarchies that distinguish citizens on account of their cultural backgrounds. Against this backdrop, the Sans-Papiers seek recognition and regularization. They base their arguments on a history of colonization that has shaped their paths of migration and on their contributions as workers to the French labor market. Claiming to be part of the past, present, and future of what it means to be French, the Sans-Papiers are challenging the reach of citizenship in spatial and temporal terms. They are also faced with dilemmas around the terms in which they stake their claims. Their case is linked to broader opposition to a global neoliberal hegemony, yet by leveraging their value as workers to support their demands, the Sans-Papiers risk weakening other claims to citizenship and legal residence made in nonmarket terms.

Chapter 5 extends the discussion of contestations into the United States. In 2006, hundreds of thousands of irregular migrants took to the streets of cities across the country demanding pathways to citizenship and an end to the brutal consequences of hard-line border policing. Enormous resources are devoted to policing the U.S.–Mexico border, but few genuine attempts are made to stem the demand for irregular migrant labor. The tensions within the globalizing state are especially clear in this case. The sheer volume of irregular migrants in the United States and their structural integration into the economy as workers and consumers create a different kind of "common sense" about who belongs, who participates, and who does what citizens do. Ambiguous forms of status are an outcome of gaps between federal immigration legislation and local communities and municipalities that confront the realities of a migrant underclass in their midst. In chapter 5, I investigate the quasi-forms of political recognition implied in this context, including the growing phenomenon of city sanctuaries for irregular migrants. I examine the terms of reference in which mass demonstrations are staged and discuss the prospects of a movement for migrant rights to genuinely subvert the forms of citizenship according to which the U.S. border is currently policed.

A brief conclusion further reflects on the spatial logics at work in irregular migrants' acts of contestation. If the space of political belonging is produced by sovereign practice, then acts of contestation are also productive in this sense. What, then, can be said about the spatial techniques deployed by irregular migrants as they contest prevailing forms of citizenship and struggle to enact alternatives? What implications can be drawn for the spaces of citizenship to come?

This book investigates citizenship from the perspective of those who are transnationally mobile. Hence, it is subject to at least one significant limitation. Although it attempts to broaden its focus away from more blinkered views of those who cross borders with ease and speed—whether in business-class carriers or with more modest legal sanction—it cannot account for the experiences of those for whom border crossings of any kind remain an impossible prospect. Pheng Cheah justifiably criticizes cosmopolitan theories that generalize about transformative identities based on hypermobility yet "leave . . . out the subaltern subjects in decolonized space who have no access to globality and who view coerced economic migration as a plus."[3] We can question Cheah's assumption that lack of mobility implies disconnection from globality. Surely the extension of capitalism and state-centric modes of governance are globalizing forces that act on the subaltern, even if he or she cannot participate in determining what shape the ensuing globality might take. Nevertheless, the point is well taken that a view of citizenship from those places to which certain migrants are drawn is necessarily partial. Many of those places in the existing and aspiring global North may help to shape new expressions of citizenship that have a broader impact beyond those places in which they first emerge. Although lines of connection thus make trends in those places highly relevant elsewhere, stark differences also shape the contours of the political in unique and nongeneralizable ways.

One further qualification remains. The terms in which citizenship is constructed and policed are far more diverse than I can hope to capture in this single volume. Familiar axes of race and gender, for example, cut across relations between insiders and outsiders to political communities and help to justify arbitrary divisions as "natural." In this respect, the late-twentieth-century feminization of migration plays into the exploitation of many irregular migrants as both workers and women. Differential treatment of men, women, mothers, and fathers in immigration detention fuels distinctions between deserving and undeserving detainees that obscure the illiberal nature of border control in general. Racial identities help to construct would-be migrants as people who are "not like us," thus helping to legitimize the border policing that serves to keep "them" out.[4] Some of these patterns are acknowledged in particular examples that dot the pages of this book. Yet this cursory treatment cannot do justice to the systematic ways in which race, gender, and other hierarchical categories are integrated into the processes of neoliberal globalization with which citizens and irregular migrants contend. This study therefore remains self-consciously partial and invites further scrutiny from a range of different critical perspectives on the transformation of citizenship.

This book nevertheless begins its analysis from the premise that irregular migrants are makers and shapers of citizenship. In doing so, it brings a crucial critical edge to studies of migration, political community, and global social relations in which irregular migrants are largely neglected, except perhaps as victims. The processes through which migrants are made into irregular subjects are a key focus of this study because they illuminate the changing forms that sovereign power takes and alert us to the spatial techniques deployed to obscure its operation. But equally important *and transformative* are the ways in which irregular migrants reconstitute themselves as equal subjects of justice. Such acts of contestation have much to reveal about new lines of social cleavage that punctuate local and global terrains. They also engender new social and spatial terms of reference for emerging political solidarities.

1 / IRREGULAR MIGRANTS AND NEW FRONTIERS
OF THE POLITICAL

This chapter begins with a story about the limits of the possible in a journey toward political belonging. Imagine a Palestinian refugee living in Kuwait in the years after the first Gulf War. Palestinian leader Yasser Arafat has publicly supported Saddam Hussein's 1990 invasion of Kuwait. Palestinians in Kuwait have thus attained a kind of enemy status. Many are forced to leave Kuwait, some are interned, and those who remain are subject to assault and humiliation. A young man of twenty, called Asif, is forced into hiding and manages to get by working as a mechanic. One day Asif is stopped by Kuwaiti police, who ask after his nationality. He hesitates, fearing the worst, and is detained without charge for three weeks. The next time Asif is arrested, he is beaten, stabbed in the arm, and told he will be killed if he doesn't leave Kuwait. Having worked for a few years, Asif is able to purchase a flight out of the country. He is limited in his choice of destination to those countries that will issue a visa to him and those where he is able to apply for asylum. He flies to Indonesia, goes directly to the offices of the United Nations High Commissioner for Refugees (UNHCR), and lodges a claim for refugee status.

Asif spends the next twelve months sleeping on the streets of Jakarta. A number of staff rotations at the UNHCR mean that his application gets put on hold, lost, processed, sent to Geneva, reviewed, and put on hold again. He tries to bring attention to his plight by sleeping outside the office doors, but after a year of bureaucratic inertia he gives up. He makes his way east, traveling on foot through the jungles of West Papua and on to Papua New Guinea. He is arrested there, charged with illegal entry, beaten, and imprisoned before he makes another claim for asylum. Asif spends another ten months awaiting the decision on his application, only to be told that Papua New Guinea does not accept refugees from terrorist countries.

Asif moves again. A network of people smugglers is operating from Indonesian and Papuan islands, ferrying people in cramped and rickety fishing vessels to Australian territories. There, the smugglers claim, a new life is possible. Asif pays for a passage to Saibai Island in the Torres Strait, where he is promptly arrested by Australian police. He again explains his predicament. Four days later he is taken to a custom-built detention center on Manus Island in Papua New Guinea. The center has been established as part of Australia's Pacific Solution to its "asylum seeker problem." Asylum seekers who arrive in Australia without proper clearance are to be taken to offshore processing facilities, where their claims will be filtered through United Nations systems. Immigration officials relate to Asif that he has *not* claimed asylum in Australia because he failed to lodge the appropriate form while in Australian territories. Because he is now in Papua New Guinea, they explain, he should direct his claims to the government of that state.

Asif is trapped by borders that determine his identity and limit his mobility. Born in Kuwait, he is the son of a Palestinian man and an Egyptian woman. He holds Egyptian travel documents that mark him as a Palestinian refugee but provide no right of entry to Egypt. Israel's no-right-of-return policy denies him access to the Occupied Palestinian Territories despite his nationality. And now he is unable to return to Kuwait, which prevents nonnationals who have been outside the country for more than six months from reentering. He is detained on Manus Island for the next seventeen months while the legal obligations as to which state should hear his asylum claim are disputed.

Advocates for asylum seekers hear of Asif's case and begin to publicize his story. Sympathetic lawyers embark on extensive litigation to try and secure his release. Finally, they are successful. Asif arrives in Melbourne with a visa that provides him with temporary protection. Under the terms of the visa, he cannot leave Australia, and he cannot sponsor his family to join him. His father, now in Egypt, finds it hard to understand why he cannot be reunited with his son after such a long ordeal. New Australian laws aimed at deterring asylum seekers like Asif mean that he is prevented from applying for permanent protection.

When his visa expires in five years time, he will have to make his case for refugee status all over again. The most he can hope for, under these laws, is a series of rolling temporary visas. How can he start to rebuild his life when the prospect of removal from the country is an ongoing possibility?

Sometime later Asif visits a different detention center on the Australian mainland. He hopes he can at least momentarily suspend the boredom, if not the madness, of other asylum seekers waiting inside. There he meets a long-term resident, Jacob, whose citizenship is also indeterminate. Asif discovers that he and Jacob have embarked on similar journeys. Around the time that Asif fled from Kuwait, Jacob had arrived by boat on an Australian island in the Torres Strait. Jacob is from a village close to the line of control in Kashmir. His father has disappeared, presumably killed by Indian security forces, and his own opposition to Indian policies saw him detained and tortured some years ago. After five years in hiding, Jacob fled his village and country, traveled through Singapore, and spent fourteen months surviving as best he could in Papua New Guinea without any legal status. Australian immigration officials accepted his story as genuine but ultimately concluded that Jacob did not face a "well-founded fear of being persecuted," the definition crucial to obtaining refugee status.[1] They prepared at that stage to deport him to Kashmir. Jacob had no electoral registration in India, and no one in his village, where security forces were active, was prepared to admit that they knew him. Without proof of identity, Indian authorities refused to accept that Jacob was a citizen for whom they bore responsibility. They refused to issue travel documents or to allow his deportation.

Thus continued Jacob's long ordeal. He spent stretches in three of Australia's more remote detention facilities, where a series of riots, fires, hunger strikes, and suicide attempts took place, alongside the slow mental deterioration of detainees. After escaping for a day, he spent three months in prison in Perth. He spent four months being intermittently hospitalized for severe depression. As Asif hears this story, Jacob is beginning his seventh year in detention. Asif finds Jacob indefinitely detained at ministerial discretion and, like himself, caught in a kind of no-man's land, without rights to belong anywhere and with no clear prospect for any change in his status. Jacob is eventually released with a bridging visa pending removal from the country. By this time, however, he has been admitted to a psychiatric hospital in Adelaide, where his condition is described as suicidal. Psychiatrists are uncertain whether Jacob will ever regain his full mental health.

These stories are disturbing not only in terms of the personal hardships they portray, but also in terms of the political scenarios involved. Asif and Jacob lack the formal status to secure a future anywhere. Their situations disturb an account of political membership that neatly divides the peoples of the world into citizens of nation-states. Their stories, moreover, are drawn from those of two men caught, in recent years, in the legal technicalities of Australia's immigration system.[2] Some of the worst aspects of asylum policies affecting these men, including offshore detention and temporary protection visas, were revoked after 2007 by an incoming Labor government. Asif was finally granted a permanent visa and Australian citizenship in 2009. However, the overall effort to prevent people such as Asif and Jacob from entering Australian territory remains. Their stories are indicative of a growing global trend in hardline border policing against unwanted migrants.

This kind of border policing derives its legitimacy from a series of apparently clear-cut distinctions. In order to conduct this kind of policing, we need to distinguish the territory of one state from that of another; we need to identify whose presence in that territory is legitimate and whose is not; and we base the latter distinction on various kinds of citizen, noncitizen, and immigration status. Yet Asif and Jacob's stories challenge such clear-cut distinctions between citizens and aliens and between genuine refugees and illegitimate intruders. They show us that these identities are far from fixed and that they change in relation to the territory in which a person's status is determined. They prompt us, therefore, to problematize a range of assumptions about citizenship and territory according to which people and places are ordered and policed.

Membership of political communities has never been a matter free of controversy. The histories of cities, states, and empires are as much about struggles over boundaries of belonging as they are about life within them. In the present context, people such as Asif and Jacob (and there are many who are experiencing versions of their stories) push and are pushed against the interstices of borders at a personal cost that is difficult to fathom. Their identities slide between citizenship and statelessness, between asylum seeker and refugee; they move from one jurisdiction to another where the meaning of those identities differs enormously. These transitions tell us something about the ambiguities that structure our present global condition. Asif and Jacob's journeys tell a story about the limits of concepts that cannot account for the range of scenarios and identities that are possible. I show in this book how the journeys of people like Asif and Jacob are integrally related to contemporary dynamics of citizenship. The resources devoted to keeping these men on the wrong side of citizenship says as much about citizenship's vulnerability to new kinds of contestation as it does about heightened determination to defend sovereign borders against unwanted outsiders. This book accordingly examines how citizenship is ordered and challenged in relation to irregular migration.

CITIZENSHIP AND POLITICAL BELONGING

In order to discuss the transformation of citizenship, it is helpful to locate citizenship within the broader conceptual framework of political belonging. Political belonging can be thought of as a dynamic ordering principle that structures different kinds of political communities across time and space. Particular modes of political belonging become deeply embedded in our spatial, temporal, and embodied ontologies. They contribute, in other words, to our conception of who we are. In addition, they contribute to how we perceive the context in which we act politically and the authority we have for doing so. To say one "is" a citizen—as opposed to a feudal subject, a tribal elder, or a jihadi warrior—is to invoke very different relations to space, time, and bodies as implicit justifications for the legitimacy of certain political voices and acts over others. It is to express an identity that is both prescribed and subjectively felt and thus to be engaged with a range of processes and disciplinary effects that give that identity coherence and authority in certain contexts. It is also to invoke a community of citizens, subjects, kinsfolk, warriors, and others alongside the limits of that community—the boundaries of identity and the realm of not belonging, as conceived in particular ways. It is well beyond the scope of this chapter to investigate the diversity of forms that political belonging might take or to identify its dominant modes in historical terms. The key point for present purposes is to conceptualize citizenship as one mode of political belonging among many—albeit one that is currently hegemonic. This broader perspective denies citizenship a natural or essential status and opens a conceptual avenue from which to approach it as a dynamic and contestable identity.

In its conventional form, citizenship is tied to the system of sovereign states that emerged from the European Treaty of Westphalia more than 360 years ago. Since then, this system has expanded through processes of colonization and decolonization to be global in scope. On this basis, political community, identity, and practice have been linked conceptually to a relatively fixed relationship between state, citizen, and territory. There are clearly other contenders in today's world for bases of political belonging. Tribal societies and pan-religious identities are obvious alternatives and are often overlayed with citizenship in complex social structures. Yet a great deal of political practice continues to be shaped by the state/citizen/territory constellation. This is why, for instance, self-determination is commonly associated with claims to independent statehood and designated territory rather than with alternative forms of political organization. It is also the reason why statelessness remains "a condition of infinite danger"[3] that can prompt impossible binds for people like Asif and Jacob.

Asif and Jacob's predicaments show that citizenship comes at the cost of the outsiders it creates. The articulation of citizenship, as of any identity, requires the marking of its exterior, a constitutive outside that is always implicit within the identity itself. Citizens, that is, come into being only alongside noncitizens. This relation of identity and difference precludes the possibility of universal inclusion in a community of citizens because that community lacks substance without a constituent measure of alterity. Thus, any reference to the citizen assumes the existence of the noncitizen, and any consequences flowing from citizenship (rights, opportunities, and so on) are enjoyed in the context of the denial of the same to noncitizens. In reality, of course, there are gradations of citizenship (some citizens belong more than others) and a range of identities (some friendlier and some more hostile) that constitute citizenship's outsiders. Identity and difference are thus established along a spectrum of status categories (foreign enemy; illegal alien; first-, second-, third-generation migrant; legal resident; model citizen; and so on) rather than in crude two-dimensional terms. The naturalization of citizenship as the "commonsense" mode of political belonging depends on the denial of this relational constitution. Cast as constant, universal, and self-evident, citizen identities mask the processes of exclusion that condition their possibility.

This constitutive dynamic between insider and outsider in relation to citizenship is the subject of Engin Isin's book *Being Political*. Isin rejects conventional histories of citizenship that depict its gradual and linear evolution from the ancient Greek polis as an ever more inclusive basis for political practice.[4] For Isin, this dominant account omits those aspects of citizenship that are based on the necessary exclusion of noncitizens. He contends that the story of citizenship that begins with Greek men of high-ranking birth and extends over the centuries to include former slaves, the propertyless, the working classes, colonial subjects, women, and indigenous peoples shields from view the processes by which shifts in the constitution of political membership brought with them, at different times, new and unique forms of exclusion. This story fails to account for those immanent others inside the polity whose relative denial of status helped to create the particular kind of privilege accorded to full citizens. It omits, in addition, the construction of the polity's outside—those distant alien others whose incivility, backwardness, and political immaturity mark, by contrast, the progress of citizenship's evolution in occidental cities. For Isin, the citizen and its others are mutually constitutive. The insider identity is possible only via the parallel marking of the outsider, a marking that will change in space and time as the shape and character of the polity takes different forms. These insider/outsider dynamics are, in Isin's account, an enduring feature of political communities, not only those characterized by citizens and citizenship in the conventional sense, but all those communities engaged in the political organization of affairs and the marking of identities. The attempt to represent citizenship in its present form as a historically continuous identity is not accidental, argues Isin. Rather, this representation is itself a strategy that serves to naturalize citizenship of a particular kind. In this way, he contends, the citizenship enjoyed by the ancients has been appropriated as an ideal type for the purposes of legitimizing more recent hierarchies of membership.[5]

Isin's analysis provides a way of seeing the identities of irregular migrants such as Asif and Jacob as part of a more general history of producing insiders and outsiders to political communities, of simultaneously constructing those who do and do not belong and policing the boundary between them. From this perspective, the stories of Asif and Jacob become integral and necessary to the constitution of contemporary insider status. Although Isin insists on the continuity of this insider/outsider process, he also reveals its susceptibility to particular kinds of challenge. In this respect, his broader purpose is to tell the stories of those who have contested their outsider status, those who have struggled and sometimes succeeded in transforming the boundaries of political belonging through which their exclusion was maintained. In his book, Isin recovers the particular struggles of slaves, women, plebeians, Jews, craftsmen, tradesmen, prostitutes, vagabonds, working classes, aborigines, and others cast as strangers and outsiders in different settings. The unique characteristics of these struggles distinguish the terrain of insider/outsider relations in the Greek polis from that of the Roman civitas, the early Christian empire, the early-modern state, and so on. Isin thus reveals the fractured nature of citizenship and a history of contestation that lies beneath its hegemonic status.

Isin's approach prompts a number of questions about the transformation and contestation of citizenship today. What particular identities shape the contemporary content of citizenship? What strategies and technologies are employed to order and police those identities? What processes and dynamics are producing cleavages where the boundaries of citizenship are in question? Which actors are located on these fault lines? What strategies do they employ to contest their status and toward what ends? This study approaches these questions from a very specific perspective. It concentrates on the fault line of belonging inhabited by irregular migrants.

IRREGULAR MIGRANTS AND CONTEMPORARY DYNAMICS OF CITIZENSHIP

Irregular migrants are noncitizens who have crossed state borders or remain in state territory without the host state's explicit and ongoing sanction. As a consequence, they do not possess the status that fully legitimizes their presence or that makes certain rights associated with citizenship or legal residence available to them. Irregular migrants may be labor migrants who have entered a state illegally or overstayed their visa, or they may be children of such migrants. They may be stateless persons or asylum seekers whose refugee status is not yet formally established. The term *irregular migrant* is not intended to be a rigid category because individuals may slip from one kind of immigration status to another depending on their movements and on legislative and policy changes. An irregular labor migrant, for example, may return to the state where he or she is formally defined as a citizen; an asylum seeker may "become" a refugee; and in some places "being" a refugee allows for access to citizenship and resettlement assistance, whereas in others it denotes a temporary and vulnerable status without any guarantees of full political inclusion. In addition, some people who migrate *within* their state of origin experience a denial of status similar to others who have crossed international borders. Internally displaced persons and some internal labor migrants can thus be included within the scope of the term *irregular migrant*.

Some detail on terminology is warranted here to explain my preference for *irregular migration* as the term that best allows us to talk about hierarchies of mobility. An alternative term, *nonstatus migrant*, is increasingly used in the Canadian context as a shortened expression for those who have less than full immigration status. It is intended to capture the diversity of people involved in irregular migration of one kind or another and successfully communicates the key point at stake—that is, vulnerability to sovereign power on account of lacking secure, unambiguous, long-term status relative to that of citizens. The term *nonstatus migrant* nevertheless implies an evacuation of any kind of status, which seems to work against the recovery of status among irregular migrants that is the concern of the progressive movements from which the term emerged. The more commonly used label *undocumented migrant* has less of the pejorative baggage attached to other terms. It avoids in particular the sweeping and inaccurate depiction of all those attempting to cross state borders without prior approval as "illegal." Yet it does not adequately capture the spectrum of migration experiences that are the focus of this book. The kinds of internal migrants I mentioned earlier are not, for example, "undocumented" in the conventional sense.

In addition, a range of documents often accompany irregular migrants, from refugee identity cards to asylum seekers' passports and identity cards issued by sending states that facilitate the flow of labor migrants' remittances. In some cases, such documents generate ambiguous forms of status. Many irregular migrants in the United States, for instance, are eligible to apply for a driver's license, which may then be used as identification for other administrative purposes.[6] Insisting on documents as the defining measure of status tends to overlook the subtleties of such arrangements and therefore the specific ways in which many "documented" migrants enjoy far less than comparable status with citizens and legal residents.

The term *irregular migrant* remains an awkward one, not least on account of the specter of abnormality attached to not being "regular." This problem of terminology reflects the conceptual underdevelopment of modes of political belonging beyond state-centric ones. Regular versus irregular migration is a distinction that rests on state agents' authority to approve or deny a border crossing. We do not yet have a broadly meaningful vocabulary to articulate the ambiguous status of many irregular migrants in a way that does not immediately imply outsider status. Yet, as I show in subsequent chapters, the question of their status remains controversial and far from resolved. Thus, although I employ the term *irregular* here as the best of a bad bunch, it is with every expectation that irregular migrants will increasingly deploy other terms that express alternative identities.

At present, the status of irregular migrants is deeply implicated in an account of political belonging in which the state/citizen/territory constellation is axiomatic. It is only with reference to the positive status of citizens that the irregular status of certain kinds of migrants is brought into being. Likewise, without reference to the state as bounded and territorialized, the notion of irregular migration would cease to be meaningful. (What would irregular migration look like if there were no borders, as such, to cross?) The migrant as a border crosser is a concept embedded in administrative technologies acquired by the modern state that have allowed it to measure and define populations across a certain territory, abstracted from more local relations that had long shaped political status. Before the late nineteenth century, a "foreigner" was as likely to be from a neighboring village as from a distant land, and measures of rank, lineage, and occupation were far more likely to determine privilege than questions of citizenship.[7] The spatial form of sovereign power is thus central to the parameters we draw around political belonging and the identities that mark "us" in relation to "them." If the spatial basis of political belonging were to be constructed and naturalized in terms other than territorial ones, then our understanding of citizens and aliens, irregular migrants among them, would necessarily be cast in different terms as well. I return to the spatial framing of citizenship later in this chapter. For now, it is enough to recognize that the integral relation between territory and irregular migration makes the study of the latter especially apt for coming to terms with contemporary transformations that place the relation between citizenship and territory in question.

Precisely this question of territorial sovereignty in an age of globalization prompts enormous anxiety over irregular migration in governments and publics alike. In the late twentieth century, migration became an increasingly prominent security issue. The liberalization of exit options from former Soviet states posed a new order of scale to the potential for flows of irregular migrants. At the same time, the rise of neoliberalism radically transformed the social and economic fabrics of highly indebted countries when debt relief was tied to cutbacks in public expenditure and the liberalization of trade. Economic restructuring in South America, Asia, and Africa displaced many people from traditional lands and forms of employment. Rural-to-urban migration in these contexts threatened to spill over into migration paths toward the more affluent global North, where shrinking welfare states and structural unemployment had exacerbated hostilities toward migrants. Commentators warned that unprecedented floods of migrants from the South and from the East threatened to overwhelm receiving states' labor markets and to upset their social stability in general.[8] Spurred by the rise of anti-immigrant national populism across the industrialized world, governments linked border policing against unwanted migration to the discursive and administrative apparatus of broader security functions, tightened restrictions on certain licit forms of migration (including avenues for seeking asylum), and dramatically upscaled their border policing efforts.[9]

For many people who are marginalized by the geopolitical upheavals associated with the end of the Cold War, uneven development within and between states, the destruction of environments, and the effects of neoliberal restructuring on a global scale, there are powerful incentives to seek a better life abroad, regardless of the dangers involved in border transgressions. For many who are endangered by new kinds of civil conflicts and ongoing processes of decolonization, migration is an urgent necessity. For others, living and working abroad is part of a long-established and sometimes state-sponsored means of supporting families and communities at home.[10] For obvious reasons, it is difficult to calculate the extent of irregular migration around the globe. In regions such as Asia and the Persian Gulf states, there are few reliable estimates but wide recognition of significant populations of migrants. More reliable sources estimate that eleven million irregular migrants (excluding asylum seekers) reside in the United States, three to four million in Russia, and two to four million in Europe.[11] Other estimates can be gleaned from figures concerning outbound irregular migration. Government agencies in the Ukraine, for example, estimate that between two and seven million of their citizens are working abroad without regularized status, whereas other estimates make the figure as high as ten million.[12] At the end of 2008, some 827,000 people around the world were awaiting decisions on applications for asylum.[13] Yet this number reflects only those who managed to cross borders and to detail their journeys in ways that prima facie met strict definitions of refugee status. At the same time, more than eight million people recognized as refugees were living in camps, unable to be repatriated, and had been there for ten years or more. Yet official resettlement places were available for only 86,460 people over the course of the same year.[14] Under these conditions, there are few signs that irregular migration is abating, and every indication of increasingly compelling motivations to migrate.

Given these trends, the securitization of irregular migration can be interpreted as a rational (realist) response to changed external conditions with the potential to challenge destination state's cohesion, prosperity, and sovereignty. However, several factors suggest the need for a far more complex reading. Intergovernmental reports on irregular migration increasingly acknowledge the "pull" factors that draw irregular migrants into informal sectors of economies with high demand for low-paid, flexible labor that native workers are unwilling to do.[15] The notion of "demand-driven" irregular migration is thus far from controversial. Yet even this perspective fails to capture a more fundamental driver of irregular flows. Here I want to emphasize the regulatory and discursive work that *makes* migration irregular. Growth in irregular migration should be read alongside an increasingly restrictive immigration environment from the 1980s onward. Circumscribed avenues for licit migration mean that many migrants who in previous eras might have traveled as guest workers now cross borders without official sanction to fill similar jobs. Stricter border policing and the dangers of illicit border crossings mean that many who might otherwise have been seasonal workers, returning to their homelands regularly, now stay on indefinitely because they cannot guarantee subsequent reentry. Douglas Massey has shown how this counterproductive aspect of border policing has characterized the recent experience of the United States in particular.[16]

Tightening criteria for refugee status has had a similar effect. Governments defending such moves hold that migrants increasingly make specious asylum claims in order to circumvent mainstream migration procedures. Rising numbers of rejected asylum seekers accordingly support the notion that the majority are disingenuous and justify ever tighter restrictions.[17] Critics of this viewpoint hold, however, that the proportion of claims rejected is more indicative of unrealistically high burdens of proof resting with the claimant and that many people suffering from genuine political persecution no longer have access to a fair asylum procedure. As a consequence, some prefer to risk an illicit border crossing or to overstay short-term visas rather than return to the places from which they have fled.[18] In an effort to avoid the administrative hurdles attached to deciphering "mixed flows" of "political" and "economic" migrants, policing against unwanted migrants is increasingly conducted well before they reach the border in question. Italy and Spain, for example, work with Moroccan and Libyan authorities to intercept would-be migrants from other parts of Africa as they move toward European destinations. In 2003, British prime minister Tony Blair suggested to the European Council that "transit processing centers" be established outside European territory for irregular migrants seeking entry to Europe. Otto Schily, German minister of the interior,

advanced variations on this idea in 2005.[19] Although these proposals
remain controversial as official policy options, they reflect the growing
phenomenon of informal camps and European-funded detention centers in states such as Morocco, Libya, and the Ukraine, where irregular
migrants congregate en route to Europe and to which they are deported
if they are intercepted.[20] When the European border is externalized in
this way, irregular migrants are prevented from entering territories
where states are obliged under international law to examine claims to
asylum. In states that are not party to the United Nations Convention
Relating to the Status of Refugees (Libya, for example), status categories
such as "asylum seeker" and "refugee" have few means of being realized.
Authorities simply distinguish between "legal" and "illegal" migrants,
and those without a valid visa become "illegal" by default. The effect, in
other words, is to reduce the status categories available to irregular migrants and to generate a generic class of "illegal" bodies whose exclusion from destination states appears a matter of common sense. This
kind of policing is exacerbated by the post–September 11, 2001, security environment. If not directly linked to the threat of terrorism, irregular migrants are invoked as part of a general state of insecurity that
requires a hard-line response.[21] Thus, in 2009 Italy affirmed "illegal
immigration" as a new criminal (rather than administrative) offense,
authorized detention of "illegal" immigrants for up to eighteen months,
and sanctioned the use of citizen patrols to assist the police in identifying criminal migrant targets.

The more general result of this ever more restrictive environment is
a process of *illegalization* of both the means of transit available to people
on the move and of irregular migrants themselves. The securitization
of migration thus involves a circular process of responding to threats
that are generated and exacerbated by the criminal framework applied.
Migration becomes an issue of law and order—at worst of societal
breakdown—rather than prompting political questions of just distribution in an age of globalization. For Nicholas De Genova, this situation
necessitates that the study of illegality become the focus of scholarly
attention rather than "illegal" (or irregular) migrants per se. This shift,
he contends, is essential if studies are to avoid reproducing the very
same discursive tools and administrative categories through which
people's movements and entitlements are unjustly constrained.[22]

Acknowledging this process of illegalization is not to dismiss the very real dilemmas that arise for states on the question of migration in general. There are no easy ways of balancing the rights of political communities to regulate entry and limit group membership with the many compelling reasons for seeking through migration a safer, more decent, and prosperous life beyond what is offered in that place to which one is tied by an accident of birth.[23] The point is not to minimize these complex and enduring questions, but to move beyond the scapegoating and crisis mentality that shape much of the discourse and practice of border control.

Although sharing De Genova's concern to problematize prevailing status categories, this study shifts the spotlight from illegality to citizenship. It asks how citizenship is constructed and contested in relation to irregular migration. It asks, in the first instance, how irregular migrants come into being and how that process is fundamentally connected to the coming-into-being of the citizen. What role do these dynamics play in reinforcing the authority of the Westphalian state system as the lens through which the possibilities for political belonging are conferred? How does this lens filter more creative responses to the apparent impasse between equally valid arguments for open and closed borders? How, moreover, can we reconcile the regulation of borders with forms of citizenship that are emerging alongside globalizing states? At present, irregular migrants are brought into being at a conceptual and political crossroad, where the territorial borders that define them push out against a range of transborder practices that challenge the very substance of those borders. How does the irregular subject reflect these seemingly contradictory trends?

This study of citizenship necessitates an emphasis on border policing. By this, I mean not only the surveillance, interdiction, and expulsion of bodies at the border, but more generally the legal and symbolic ordering of citizen and alien as hierarchical categories. Border policing is carried out, most obviously, by agents of the state at the edges of state territory. But it is also a deeply discursive practice and one that occurs in places well away from the map-drawn border as such. When young white Australians mobilized in 2005 in Sydney's beachside suburb of Cronulla, they, too, were engaged in a kind of border policing against undesirable others. Their slogans, directed at Lebanese Australians, proudly declared: "We grew here, you flew here." The slogan and the violence that accompanied it attribute to certain citizens, although born and bred in Australia, a nonbelonging that depends on the notion of a border. You are not one of us, the slogan implies, and therefore *you cannot be from this place*. The slogan generates a border crossing that did not in fact take place. It is indicative of the centrality of territorial framing to our means of distinguishing belonging from not belonging and, in turn, to our capacity to articulate gradations of citizenship. Understood in this sense, border policing involves much more than sovereign control over territory, though this is a crucial element. Border policing can be understood as a range of social practices (interdiction and deportation of irregular migrants, but also citizenship tests and other far less formal means of establishing who is one of "us") in a range of different places (inside, outside, on the border, and in shifting border zones). Contestations of citizenship likewise involve much more than seeking formal citizenship status. They are also about the struggle to define what being a citizen means.

In the chapters that follow, I take seriously the prospect that contemporary border policing is producing new kinds of subjects—from neoliberal citizens to illegalized outsiders. I take equally seriously the prospect that irregular migrants are finding new ways of contesting their outsider status and, indeed, of contesting the binaries through which hierarchies of status are established. A range of examples exist in which irregular migrants both seek recognition as citizens through regularization and contest the very basis of citizenship itself as the prevailing measure of political belonging. The Sans-Papiers demand their right to stay in France based on the integration of their labor into the French economy and a history of colonial oppression that has shaped their migration paths. They have won some small victories, generating support within the French community and compelling the French administration to regularize their status in some cases. In other cases, irregular migrants seem to act like citizens, fighting for and winning political rights regardless of legal status. In July 1997, a coalition of immigrant workers, many of whom were irregular, initiated and successfully campaigned to pass the Unpaid Wages Prohibition Act in New York.[24] The act provided a legal avenue for workers to have their wage payments enforced regardless of their legal status. Irregular migrants across the

United States have more recently joined in mass demonstrations demanding legalization. Some have been active campaigners for political candidates sympathetic to progressive immigration reform.[25] Chapters 4 and 5 address in greater detail how irregular migrants are mobilizing to insist on the legitimacy of their presence in the places in which they live and work. I suggest that their actions produce new subjectivities—residents who are neither "illegal aliens" nor citizens, but something else within a spectrum of political belonging that challenges the authority of citizenship as we know it.

TRANSNATIONAL/POSTNATIONAL CITIZENSHIP: WHERE ARE IRREGULAR MIGRANTS?

The transformation of citizenship is the focus of much debate in transnational, postnational, and cosmopolitan literatures.[26] Scholars within these fields ask what citizenship might look like in the context of proliferating transnational networks and diverse nodes of power across local and global space. Their insights have made important advances in terms of imagining political communities beyond narrow national and state-centric terms that cannot capture the multiple dimensions of contemporary political identities. Concepts such as "translocality" and "transversality" express new relations to space that inhere in particular in the migrant experience of political belonging. Michael Peter Smith has done important work, for example, on the central role of cities and networks of cities in forging translocal urban subjectivities that resist subordination to territorial norms.[27] Nevzat Soguk likewise theorizes the sociospatial relations of diasporic communities in terms of transversal "trails" that defy representation by fixed (spatial or temporal) geographic coordinates.[28] As I argue later in this chapter, this new vocabulary steers a crucial path toward more spatially heterogeneous accounts of citizenship and political belonging.

Dynamics of citizenship are, however, too often investigated from the perspective of those who have citizenship in more or less substantive forms rather than from the perspective of those who do not. In some cases, this bias produces accounts of the globe-trotting experience of the relatively elite, many of whom enjoy a kind of hypermobility and

flexibility of citizenship (deciding which passport to use for which purpose in which place).[29] Other scholars emphasize the hybrid identities
of more modest but still legally sanctioned travelers.[30] These studies
reveal important dimensions of contemporary citizenship dynamics,
asking how migrants navigate a range of affiliations across transnational space. Yet they fail to theorize sufficiently the vast discrepancies
between different kinds of migrants or to problematize the criteria according to which different "types" appear. Smith, for example, far too
casually groups together "transnational migrants, exiles, diasporas, and
refugees" as the archetypal subjects of a "deterritorialized" transnational
experience.[31] Although irregular migrants thus surface in his otherwise
nuanced study, he tends to overlook the specificity of their circumstances and its significance for a broader view of the transnational.

More troubling still is the relative absence of irregular migrants from
prominent postnational scholarship. In her much cited book *Limits of
Citizenship*, for example, Yasemin Soysal heralds the arrival of a new
form of postnational citizenship. She argues that the integration of
guest workers into the political life of a variety of European polities in
the post–World War Two era is the clearest example of this change.
More than merely present in large numbers, guest workers

> participate in the educational system, welfare schemes, and labor mar-
> kets. They join trade unions, take part in politics through collective
> bargaining and associational activity, and sometimes vote in local elec-
> tions. They exercise rights and duties with respect to the host polity and
> the state. Guestworkers are thus empirical anomalies with regard to pre-
> dominant narratives of citizenship. . . . [G]uestworkers, who are formally
> and empirically constituted as aliens within the national collectivity,
> are nonetheless granted rights and protection by, and thus membership
> in, a state that is not "their own."[32]

What this participation represents for Soysal is a shift in political membership from a basis in the territorial, cultural, and ethnic constitution
of nations to a more universal framework based on "deterritorialized
notions of persons' rights."[33] The legitimating source of these rights is
no longer the nation-state, but a transnational ideology promulgated

through international norms, conventions, and laws. The result is a re-versal of long-held assumptions about the order of rights acquisition: civil and political first, then economic and social. In contrast to this pattern, Soysal points to numerous examples where migrants achieve the latter without attaining the former. Her extensive empirical re-search indicates, she argues, the triumph of human over national rights and of postnational membership over national citizenship.

Soysal attempts to conceptualize and document a novel form of citi-zenship that moves beyond state centrism. However, she exaggerates the extent to which transnational norms undermine state authorities' capacity to inscribe bounded political communities. For example, as others have shown, European citizenship continues to be derived from initial allocations of membership at the nation-state level and thus to be determined by criteria that are far from uniform.[34] A major short-coming in Soysal's work—part of the reason that she overstates the evi-dence for universal norms of membership—is her conflation of all types of noncitizen migrants (legal residents, refugees, former colonial citizens, nonnational European citizens, and undocumented migrants) under the rubric *guest worker*.[35] In fact, her analysis is heavily skewed toward nonnationals who reside in Europe with official state sanction. She fails to incorporate the specific circumstances of irregular migrants whose growing number and hardship appear increasingly determined by the very territorial distinctions that Soysal claims are in demise. She does not comment on European states' systematic efforts to avoid hu-man rights obligations with respect to asylum seekers by narrowing criteria for refugee status and foreclosing access to judicial appeal. Nor does she address the complicity of transnational norms around refugee status in the denial of rights to many irregular migrants whose jour-neys are compelled by factors that exceed stringent definitions of po-litical persecution. Soysal's claims are thus flawed in two respects: first, in terms of her generalized account of migrant membership within the European interior, which simply ignores the growing presence of an ir-regular migrant underclass; and, second, in terms of the deterritoriali-zation of membership itself. Though the European border may repre-sent a new demarcation of territorial limits from national to regional levels, it remains deeply territorial. Policing of the border continues to identify a line between "here" and "there" that determines who belongs automatically and those whose chance to belong remains at the state's discretion.

Soysal's book appeared some fifteen years ago in advance of a range of ever more restrictive immigration and asylum policies. With the benefit of hindsight, it is difficult not to attribute overoptimism to her analysis. States today appear as willing and able as ever to exercise powers of exclusion that exploit and endanger many individuals trapped in cycles of forced migration. Yet Soysal is right to identify new types of membership that are open to particular kinds of migrants. Many states now allocate membership rights on the basis of criteria other than nationality: occupation or labor-market value, the capacity for self-finance, family connections to existing citizens, and so forth. However, Soysal is unable to account for the simultaneous loosening *and* tightening of national and territorial boundaries that are shaping the fortunes of different people in dramatically different ways.

A decade after Soysal's book was published, Seyla Benhabib offered a more subtle and less universalizing case for postnational citizenship, one more closely attuned to the apparent contradictions of neoliberal globalization—the push for more open borders in the economic arena amidst populist calls for national and territorial closure—that had characterized the intervening years: "We are at a point in political evolution when the unitary model of citizenship, which bundled together residency upon a single territory with the subjection to a single administration of a people perceived to be a more or less cohesive entity, is at an end. The end of this model does not mean that its hold upon our political imagination and its normative force in guiding our institutions are obsolete. It does mean that we must be ready to imagine forms of political agency and subjectivity which anticipate new modalities of political citizenship."[36] Like Soysal, Benhabib contends that nonnationals enjoy many of the entitlements that were once the sole preserve of citizens. But unlike Soysal, she insists that such new modalities of membership are starkly disaggregated according to both location and residency status. Benhabib points out that the newfound rights enjoyed by some run parallel with the curtailment of rights for others—notably those rights applying to asylum seekers and refugees. The more general case of irregular migrants nevertheless remains insufficiently theorized. Although

Benhabib occasionally refers to undocumented migrants, her normative claims are focused more narrowly on asylum seekers and refugees—
that is, on those for whom the right to cross borders is already established in law, even if their presence is unwelcome and punished in
practice. She makes clear moral injunctions to extend human rights to
members of this group, who "still find themselves in quasi-criminal
status."[37] Yet she fails to engage the more difficult question of the obligations owed to other irregular migrants in the European context. This
omission is surprising, given that elsewhere Benhabib acknowledges
that citizenship has often been built upon the exploitation of immanent outsiders. Although she notes, for example, "the presence of those
foreigners whose cheap labor in part subsidized the glories of the British welfare state,"[38] she is curiously silent on the claims to citizenship
that might be made by today's irregular migrants on the basis of their
informal labor and its structural integration in societies from which
they are excluded.

Benhabib's accordingly partial view extends to her discussion of "ju-
risgenerative politics"—that is, "contestation around rights and legal
institutions which themselves pave the way for *new* modes of political
agency and interaction." She limits her terms of reference, however, to
"iterative acts through which a democratic people that considers itself
bound by certain guiding norms and principles reappropriates and re-
interprets these, thus showing itself to be not only the *subject* but also
the *author of the laws*."[39] Based in the normative standpoint of delibera-
tive democratic approaches, her analysis is limited by the already established parameters of political community, and her examples accordingly relate to contestations by those with formal, if not always
substantive, citizenship status.

I contend, by contrast, that the mobilizations of irregular migrants
are important but largely neglected sites for thinking through the transformation of citizenship. I contend, in addition, that the spatial moves
made by theorists such as Smith and Soguk are crucial elements of a
critical approach to political belonging from the perspective of irregular migrants. The terms in which irregular migrants make political
claims help us understand how citizenship is shaped from the outside
in as much as from the inside out. They challenge us, moreover, to re-
consider how an inside/outside or territorial framework limits our ability

to recognize claims that operate according to a different spatial logic. In order to overcome the illegitimacy ascribed to their status, irregular migrants are precisely those migrants who are likely to make the most radical contestations of the mode of political belonging through which their marginalization is enforced. The radical dimension is, in part, spatial. When irregular migrants act politically, they disrupt received assumptions about who has the power to do what citizens do and where the work of citizenship gets done. This book thus contributes to a burgeoning field of interdisciplinary inquiry that engages with the prospect of irregular migrants as players in and shapers of contemporary citizenship dynamics.[40] It does so by working with the concept of the political and by using a critical spatial lens. The next section discusses this approach in more detail.

THE SPATIAL DIMENSION OF THE POLITICAL

Political activism by irregular migrants can be understood as a new frontier of the political. This interpretation draws on the radical democratic theory of Ernesto Laclau and Chantal Mouffe, whose pathbreaking work of the mid-1980s developed an account of the political as the defining characteristic of social relations. For Laclau and Mouffe, the social (that sense of who "we" are in relation to others) is "conceived as a discursive space."[41] In my reading, this conception is not to understate the significance of lived and embodied relations in constituting the social. Rather, it is to acknowledge the interplay of more or less concrete and more or less abstract social relations. Whether understood as a racial, gendered, class-based, national, or other kind of grouping, the social is an articulation of who "we" are that claims to be self-evident. It is more accurately the outcome of discourses and practices that flow from particular power relations and ideological projects. The social is in this sense always deeply political. The convergence of power attending the process by which one account of the social achieves a naturalized status is designated by the term *hegemony*. A hegemonic relation renders invisible the political nature of its construction. For Laclau and Mouffe, the field of the political begins with the recognition of hegemony and its contingent nature. It begins, in other words, with the recognition that power and social antagonism lie at the heart of any us/them distinction.

The point, so Laclau and Mouffe contend, is not to attempt to eradicate power from the constitution of the social. Power relations, they argue, are central to the human condition, and any claim to have resolved the question of who "we" are and where "we" are headed on the basis of true consensus masks the political nature of what remains a hegemonic articulation. The point is rather to live more reflexively with the political content of the social and to moderate the worst excesses of power.[42] Their radical democratic project accordingly seeks to articulate alternatives to the hegemonic relations that currently prevail and ones that are more in keeping with principles of liberty and equality. From this perspective, the nature of the social cannot be taken for granted. Politics cannot be limited to determining the interests of preconstituted identities (citizens and noncitizens, for example) but must also engage with the constitution of those identities themselves. If citizens are the subjects of democracy, then radical democracy, for Laclau and Mouffe, is open to a reformulation of what it means to be a citizen or indeed open to challenges to the legitimacy of citizenship itself. When those who are denied substantive citizenship status assert their identity as equal subjects of justice, this act is the stuff of the political.

In the mid-1980s, this approach helped to account for the rise of identity politics evident in new social movements across the industrialized world. It explained how Fordist welfare states in the post–World War Two era could produce a level of economic security never before experienced by so wide a cross-section of society yet also provide the context for a series of new fronts of social conflict (feminist, ecological, civil rights, and sexuality movements). An apparent consensus in support of redistributive welfare states had also entailed the bureaucratization, commodification, and homogenization of social relations in ways that created barriers to full and equal citizenship and brought existing barriers into sharper relief.[43] In this context, the frontiers of the political expanded from concern with questions of resource distribution to questions (in more recent terminology) of cultural recognition and environmental sustainability.

A decade later, once Keynesian orthodoxy was well and truly displaced, Mouffe argued for "the return of the political" on account of the hegemonic rise of neoliberal market values.[44] She highlighted the shrinking distance between the philosophies of mainstream political parties and the absence of genuine alternatives to neoliberal frameworks for determining political futures. This new "consensus," she contended, left few political options open to those adversely affected by a neoliberal agenda and to those who objected to the constellation of power it represented. It therefore created a dangerous opening for the growth of extreme right forces and fundamentalist identity politics. Under these conditions, migrants were vulnerable to populist scapegoating campaigns that were designed to buffer anxiety over the changes associated with the opening of borders to global market forces.

In the twenty-first century, the struggle to define the limits of the social remains profoundly shaped by neoliberal ideology and in particular by this ideology's impact on an emerging global imaginary.[45] *Globalization* remains a widely contested term in spite of its casual deployment by politicians, scholars, executives, and activists alike. The best scholars of the phenomenon attempt to provide conceptual shape to an open-ended process with complex historical origins, diverse manifestations, and unpredictable outcomes. However, much of the discourse on globalization limits the concept more narrowly to the post-Keynesian era and to the steady demise of barriers to global market integration. Neoliberal ideologues prefer this story of globalization—a story told and retold in ways that obscure less prescriptive interpretations of global social relations.

For neoliberal pundits, "the global" exists as a field of market opportunity, no longer constrained by the tyranny of distance, but rather accessible and synchronized through everyday technologies and common consumer desires. Globalization accordingly implies an inevitable unfolding of interconnectedness across social, economic, and political domains that supersede national and other localized distinctions. Less-connected places, so the story goes, will soon become connected and driven unstoppably toward already envisaged outcomes.[46] This account of globalization leaves little room to imagine a space that remains *unconnected*, as it were, or places in which growing consciousness of a global social condition is not directed toward universalizing teleologies. What is at stake in this or any other take on globalization is the definition of who we are as local and global communities, how we are changing, and what our futures hold. Whether we are skeptical of the novelty of globalization from the late twentieth century onward or of the adequacy of contending definitions, it is hard to deny that *discourses* of globalization have been powerful shapers of contemporary identities. This relationship, of course, has profound implications for citizenship as we navigate the contours of civic orientation across transnational space. Globalization compels us to consider whether territorial limits to citizenship can hold out against transnational markets and production chains, digitally networked cultural and professional diasporas, global social movements, and pan-religious affiliations, to name just a few examples. Now more than ever, it seems apparent that the frontiers of the political have a changing spatial horizon. The question of the political thus cannot be focused on the "who" of politics without considering the "where."

In recent years, geographers and urban theorists have been at the forefront of efforts to develop analytical tools with which to assess the "where" of the political in relation to globalization. Studies of the spatial reach of contemporary sovereign power and the global social movements that resist it are dotted with a familiar vocabulary that includes terms such as *place, scale, networks, positionality,* and *mobility.*[47] These terms provide useful ways of thinking about the different dimensions of space that play into our social experience, our subjectivities, and deeply political questions of justice: the symbolic marking of meanings and ownership in place; scalar registers from local to global that shape the jurisdictions and logistical reach of institutions, governance, and communities; the networks that criss-cross territorial expanses and jump scale from the local to the global; the relative experience of place and globality depending on social positioning; and mobility rather than settlement as a social relation. Studies of this kind challenge us to see the operation of power and resistance through different spatial lenses and thus to gain a more complex picture of multilayered sociospatial relations. However, much of this work has a tendency toward closure around definitive levels of analysis—the unspoken claim, in other words, that the latest analytical jargon provides the last word on how to recognize and theorize space. It seems to me that this kind of scholarship fails to engage with space from a substantively ontological perspective and thus remains constrained by a preexisting framework for *being in* space that always already limits the terms of reference. Launching a similar critique of a leading scholarly work that falls into this trap, Michael Shapiro gets to the heart of the matter. His concern is with the failure to specify the contextual conjuncture to which certain levels of analysis (territory, place, scale, and network) are appropriate. Through a series of historical analogies, he points to the serious consequences of failing to reflect on contextual limitations. Following Paul Carter, Shapiro reminds us that

> European settlers in Australia operated with a spatial idiom that articulated their particular, proprietary way of lending value to land. Coming into a domain that was unintelligible within their practices of cultural geography, they inscribed the land with names and boundaries, while effectively erasing Aboriginal practices of space from the map. . . . There, as elsewhere in the contemporary geopolitical world of states, the dominant discourses on space reflect the acts of settlement that imposed the spatial problematics of a colonizing people while dismissing rather than negotiating a bicultural practice of space that would heed the alternative cultural geographies of indigenous peoples.[48]

The lesson from this familiar tale is to "recognize that the 'social' component of socio-spatial relations contains faultlines [*sic*] based on (among other things) the alternative historical trajectories of arrival into social space"—for instance, as colonizers or subjects of colonization.[49] Relating Shapiro's critique to the case directly at hand, we might ask what traces of alternative ontologies "arrive" with irregular migrants whose varied trajectories (via histories of colonization) position them differently in the places to which they aspire. My intention in raising this point is not to object to the spatial terms *place*, *network*, and so on as tools for critical inquiry. As noted earlier, there is much to be gained by reading space in this way. Nor am I suggesting that the encounter between irregular migrants and citizens is necessarily one of ontological difference. Rather, my concern is simply to retain a reflexive standpoint toward the ontologically situated representation of space and to stay theoretically open to the widest potential for spatial contestation as a dimension of the political.

For critical geographer Doreen Massey, coming to terms with "the global" means being open to variation across world space as much as seeing commonalities. She describes the existence of plural ontologies with respect to space in terms of *spatialities* and argues for a reading of globalization as the intersection of multiple spatialities and the corresponding reconstitution of socially produced spaces.[50] Importantly, for Massey, this reconstitution should not be understood as modern or postmodern spatialities replacing "outmoded" alternatives. Such interpretations are at work in descriptions of people and places as "advanced" or "backward," "developed" or "underdeveloped," "primitive" or "civilized" and have the effect of erasing spatial diversity in the service of a singular "developmental" and neoliberal model of globalization. Rather, different ways of *being in* space coexist and overlay each other in the same temporal plane. Massey contends that the recognition of heterogeneous spatialities allows for the possibility of political futures other than those mapped out for us by hegemonic renderings of space. She provides a way of talking about space that acknowledges its fundamentally political nature. Far from a neutral background to politics, space is political in itself.

Throughout this book and following Massey, I employ this sense of spatiality as a conceptual starting point that is open to the diversity and dynamism of space. I refer to spatial frames as particular ways of conceiving, categorizing, demarcating, and experiencing space that are profoundly linked to our ontological selves, our epistemological insights, and thus our sense of what is politically possible. I am especially concerned with the modern territorial frame that has come to shape assumptions about political belonging in terms of the modern state and its citizens. A critical spatial lens compels us to ask why certain people belong within territorial limits, but others are excluded. What is the basis of this territorial distinction, and why does it seem so natural that the question of its origin hardly seems worth asking? By problematizing the spatial frame attached to territorial borders, we also problematize the privileged status of the citizen in relation to a range of noncitizen identities. We open thinking space for alternative social relations.

Framing of different kinds occurs concurrently, and we do not have to settle on the essential preeminence of one frame over another. A city, for example, might be envisaged at once as a territorially defined location, a place shaped through ritualized markings, and a node in more nebulous circuits of global capital. We likewise might conceive of the global as an expanse of territorial space and a field of instantaneous virtual interaction in which bounded territory plays little part. We can hold these different interpretations together analytically even though they may imply practical political tensions. The usefulness of one frame over another for articulating sociospatial relations depends on epistemological starting points. In other words, it depends on what ontologies inform our knowledge-building practices and on the purposes for which we seek that knowledge. The balance between different frames will help to determine what we perceive as workable and thinkable in terms of political practice, and this determination will shift over time. Our institutions, maps, and passports, for example, may not endure in their current forms if social relations are increasingly constituted in deterritorialized forms. In this book, therefore, I consider how the balance between different spatial frames is changing and how this transformation is connected to dynamics of citizenship.

Finally, I refer to "places" as particular sites or spaces conceived within particular or multiple spatial frames. There can be no absolute distinction between places and spatial frames because the latter already determines the parameters of the former. A territorial frame is already at work, for example, in the notion of a place as a site that is distinct and discernable from others. However, this does not mean that the places in question (cities, suburbs, worksites, and so on) are somehow fictive or less than concrete. I want to avoid, as Edward Soja puts it, the reduction of space "to a mental construct alone, a way of thinking, an ideational process in which the 'image' of reality takes epistemological precedence over the tangible substance and appearance of the real world."[51] Instead, I want to emphasize the very material realities of social relations that are the stuff of space to begin with. This means maintaining an analytical tension between everything that is real and embodied about places and everything that is abstractly constituted. It means recognizing that social relations are "both space-forming and space contingent, a producer and a product of spatiality."[52]

In the chapters that follow, this spatial lens on the political implies asking how irregular migrants are situated in places where the ambiguities and tensions surrounding different spatial frames are manifest. Irregular migrants are working in global cities and special economic zones (chapter 2); they are subject to border policing in offshore locations and ambiguous jurisdictions (chapter 3); they are moving from decolonized spaces to the centers of former empires (chapter 4); and they are drawn to city sanctuaries that provide certain safeguards from the whims of sovereign power (chapter 5). How are these contentious spaces related to the emergence of new citizen subjectivities? What spatial frames do irregular migrants deploy in order to contest prevailing registers of political belonging? Antagonism over the boundaries of the social is the enduring theme of the political. Negotiating antagonism across global space is the complex political task of our age.

2 / THE GLOBALIZING STATE

Remaking Sovereignty and Citizenship

As states open their borders to global market forces, they also open their borders to flows of migrant labor. Young Indian information technology (IT) workers, for example, are increasingly on the move. For some highly trained software engineers, a shortage of skilled professionals in the United States, Germany, and elsewhere provide them with a foothold into some of the world's leading financial and high-tech centers. In those places, some will generate the kinds of contacts and income that feed wider aspirations for a self-made transnational lifestyle that the "knowledge industry" affords. Many other aspiring workers are recruited by South Asian firms for a less glamorous transnational experience working at more basic programming tasks or on electronic assembly lines. These workers have often paid considerable sums both for training and for the connections that place them with employers abroad. Yet on arrival they are sometimes subject to highly exploitative forms of debt-bonded labor more common among irregular migrants who have paid smugglers for their passage into the country. In such cases, recruiting agents remain in control of passports, housing, and work placements and threaten to jettison opportunities for the crucial prize of residency status if objections are raised or authorities informed.[1]

What can these mobile workers tell us about citizenship in the context of contemporary globalization? What has the restructuring of economies from the late twentieth century onward meant for the relationship between states, citizens, and migrants? What ideals of citizenship emerge in this context, and what are the spatial frames through which they are constructed? What kinds of sovereign practices generate those ideals, and what do they imply for conventional accounts of citizenship that remain firmly connected to a sense of bounded state territory?

This chapter considers these questions in relation to neoliberalism—a set of ideas and a culture of practice that gained global ascendancy in the late twentieth century and harnessed broader processes of globalization toward particular ideological ends. Neoliberalism can be understood both as an ideology driving certain kinds of policy practice and, in Foucauldian terms, as a rationality of governance that inhabits the logic of government and the conduct of the self. In each of these respects, neoliberalism has shaped the terms in which states conduct their sovereign business and the terms in which they have engaged with the possibilities of a globalizing age. Neoliberalism has also shaped the terms in which citizens orient themselves to civic projects and self-understanding. In what follows, I show how sovereignty and citizenship are being remade in globalizing states with respect to neoliberalism. I show, in addition, how this process involves a new terrain of sovereign practice. This new terrain manifests in offshore markets, special economic zones (SEZs), and networked global cities where irregular migrants, among others, operate within new global hierarchies of mobility, labor, and status. In this context, new techniques of marginalization and modes of resistance arise—none of which necessarily reflects a conventional citizen/noncitizen divide.

The example of mobile Indian IT workers speaks to the kind of transnational entrepreneurialism that is increasingly attached to what might be called neoliberal citizenship—a civic ideal that coheres with market values. Like IT professionals, irregular migrants also respond to growing global demand for flexible, mobile workers. Yet their movements are heavily policed. For many citizens of the conventional kind, border policing against irregular migrants represents a reassuring cap on freer flows of commercial traffic. It serves, that is, to reinstate the function of the border as a meaningful divider between inside and out and a regulating mechanism for access to privilege. In this way, efforts to expedite flows of business-class professionals are entirely connected to the restricted movements of what some scholars identify as growing "kinetic underclasses"[2] or "abject cosmopolitans."[3] Although irregular migrants are undoubtedly exploited in this division of labor and identity, they are also finding ways to leverage their market value toward rights and recognition. By drawing attention to this shifting ground of political belonging, this chapter speaks to many points of intersection between different kinds of migrants, citizens, and mobile workers. It shows how their lives and labor are linked to the transformation of the state and to new citizen subjectivities.

NEOLIBERALISM AND THE GLOBALIZING STATE

In the early 1990s, the term *globalization* rose to prominence across academe, politics, and business as a buzzword for an accelerated process of global interconnection. As scholars attempted to come to terms with the extent and implications of what many considered a new social condition, some argued that the nation-state was in decline. From this perspective, the state confronted a range of transnational forces (most prominently an increasingly integrated global market) that challenged its logistical capacity to operate as an independent sovereign power. Proponents and critics differed on whether this challenge represented a desirable or disastrous prospect, but they both agreed that the state was in retreat as the central authority of global political life.[4] Scholars have more recently emphasized the role that governments and state agencies play in generating laws, regulations, and policies that foster integration with a global economy and transnational institutions. The state is accordingly understood as a driver of globalization as much as being driven by external pressures, with the obvious qualification that some states are more in control than others. Historical approaches have also shed light on a false opposition between state sovereignty and globalization. Thus, the modern state system is itself revealed as the outcome of a longer history of global integration, and globalization in turn appears as a process that works in tandem with the *proliferation* of sovereign borders, though not necessarily in spatially consistent forms. Such work adds a more complex layer of analysis to the causal factors associated with the current phase of globalization. It also establishes a distinct account of the contemporary globalizing state that is not so much in decline as reconfiguring the forms and scope of its sovereignty in ways that subvert long-standing territorial norms.[5]

The changes associated with the contemporary phase of globalization are closely connected with the rise of neoliberalism. Neoliberal ideas began to gain currency in the early 1970s as Keynesian state managers floundered in response to "stagflation"—the unpredicted appearance of both high unemployment and high inflation in industrialized economies. Drawing on the theories of reformers such as Friedrich von Hayek, Milton Friedman, and the Chicago school, the Reagan and Thatcher governments in the United States and Britain instituted a radical shift in economic policy. Widespread programs of reform were introduced to reduce public-sector spending, to privatize government-owned industries, and to liberalize and deregulate the economy. Other Organization for Economic Cooperation and Development (OECD) governments were heavily influenced by the example of the Anglo states, and the integration of neoliberal ideas into the programs of powerful intergovernmental organizations such as the International Monetary Fund provided more compelling reasons to follow the new orthodoxy. The bailouts of indebted states facing crises in the 1980s were in part conditional on neoliberal structural adjustment, and all states became increasingly dependent on these key institutions' positive assessment as a draw card for investors. A circular effect ensued, and neoliberal axioms assumed the status of objective market conditions. The liberalization of state borders appeared to be inevitable, whereas resistance to this process appeared irresponsible, if not futile.

Recent commentators have been right to point out the diversity of approaches that neoliberal policymakers have adopted over the past three decades and the tendency for critics to generalize in terms of the most excessive examples.[6] It is certainly the case that states have been selective in applying neoliberal principles to policy practice, despite often vociferous rhetoric about the need for comprehensive compliance. It is also the case that some of the most prominent neoliberal advocates were prompted to reassess the extremes of their reform programs following the Asian and Latin American financial crises, the failure to generate growth in Africa, and more modest setbacks in the North American context.[7] These reformulations notwithstanding, it is possible to identify key assumptions that shaped neoliberal agendas into the twenty-first century and set them apart from their predecessors in welfare, developmental, and socialist states of the post–World War Two era. These assumptions include a belief in the market as the most effective mechanism for generating growth and prosperity; the prioritization of growth over equity, whether in absolute or temporal terms; and the individualization of responsibility for market success and failure. To the extent that these core ideas became axiomatic to policy frameworks, we can speak of neoliberalism as an ideology. We can also speak of neoliberal globalization as both a particular policy practice and a particular discourse based on the interpretation of globalization through the prism of neoliberalism. Viewed through this prism, globalization represents the inevitable and efficient drive of market forces toward a single global economic order. It brings a series of advantages, including an unprecedented capacity for the generation of wealth and a constraint on conflict between interdependent states. This discourse strips political content from the economic choices associated with globalization and defers causal responsibility to an autonomous market realm. Globalization is thus represented as a singular and predetermined trajectory and as the natural and desirable outcome of a growth and development path to which there is no alternative.[8]

Neoliberalism can also be understood as a rationality of governance. By this, I refer not only to the direct implementation of neoliberal policies, but also to the incorporation of market ideology into the logic of government itself. Thus, for example, neoliberal ideas serve as a rationale for education based entirely on "human capital" rather than on other considerations such as intergenerational equity. Neoliberal ideas also penetrate the terms in which citizenship is constructed and allocated (a process to which I return in more detail in the final section of this chapter). Although some governing agencies may well be driven partly or wholly by other rationalities (more focused, for instance, on concerns for social justice than on imperatives for growth), we can speak of the neoliberal state as a whole to the extent that a neoliberal rationality is overwhelmingly dominant. There is no sense, however, in which the neoliberal state is an uncontested administrative power or necessarily consistent in its policy application. Different neoliberal states do not share a uniform basis for policy rationale or implementation. Instead, neoliberalism is articulated and practiced through distinct cultural codes. Asian governments, for example, have relied on discourses of Chinese triumphalism and of a renaissance of Islamic and Asian values projected transnationally in order to present domestically appealing accounts of neoliberal development that differ considerably from North American and European models.[9] The generality of the term *neoliberal state* is not intended to minimize the significance of this diversity, nor should the term be taken to suggest that the state is the only vehicle for the transfer of market ideology. This transfer also occurs via the private sector and in institutions of global governance, including those concerned with the management of global migration.[10] The term nevertheless provides a useful way of capturing crucial aspects of ideological convergence.

The neoliberal state is an important reference point for a discussion of contemporary sovereign practices. Sovereign practices can be understood in two key senses. First, they can be understood in the more conventional sense as the practices carried out by the state under the authority of the sovereign people in whose name it acts. Second, they refer to the constant reinforcement of the state's very raison d'être. Sovereign practices in this sense have the effect of constituting and reconstituting the identity of the state, including its spatial boundaries, and the identity of the people it represents. Sovereign practices have traditionally established the state's raison d'être in terms of a nexus with territory and citizenship. Hence, the state's legitimacy rests on the perception that it is an entity bound to the interests of citizens who are defined by territorial borders. The neoliberal state in many ways disrupts this neat constellation. As Edward Cohen argues, the shift to a neoliberal rationality entails a reformulation of the state's constituency and primary purpose, away from "the security and protection of . . . citizens from the forces of economic competition and risk" and toward "the promotion of economic globalization itself as a defining purpose of policy choice." Cohen goes on to suggest that "in a globalizing world states will tend to manage the persons and activities in their territories to maximize their attractiveness to global economic, technological, and social concerns and interests, rather than the reverse relationship to which we have become accustomed."[11] This reformulation of purpose involves a significant shift in the spatial terms of reference that have shaped conventional notions of state and citizen.

Because sovereignty and citizenship are typically imagined with reference to a national-territorial frame, we struggle to imagine how they might be realized across an alternative terrain (hence, the "decline of state" thesis). Yet so much of our shared social, political, and economic lives now takes place in ways that territorial frames cannot capture. We are still in the process of developing a conceptual vocabulary for the spaces associated with globalization. The terms *global, translocal, transversal,* and *virtual* are never precise in their meanings but seem to articulate something about increasingly common perceptions and experiences of space that differ from the terms *national* and *territorial.* As digital technologies accelerate our capacity for rapid transit and instantaneous communication, particular places are experienced as local and global simultaneously. The place in which one stands is subject to all manner of market, governance, and cultural forces that traverse state boundaries. Yet each particular place accommodates these forces with its own specificity (geographic, cultural, religious, and so on), which in turn is projected outward toward the globe. Sovereign states increasingly engage with these dynamics as they harness the process of globalization toward their own ends. Yet states also remain constrained by territorial norms that continue to foreground sovereign identity and legitimacy. As states weigh up imperatives that shape and are shaped by different spatial frames, they engage a new terrain of sovereign practice. In the next section, I attempt to give material shape to this terrain by considering three examples—offshore markets, SEZs, and global cities— that reflect the specific historical conjuncture marked by hegemonic neoliberalism.

A NEW TERRAIN OF SOVEREIGN PRACTICE

In the 1960s, Great Britain embarked on a program to make London the world's financial center. The government invited the concentration of Euro-dollar markets there and modeled its regulatory environment along the lines of other offshore centers whereby dollar deposits made by nonresidents were exempt from standard state taxes. Beginning in 1979, the City of London operated as a site of exception to the general regulatory and taxation environment governing transactions elsewhere in Britain. Dollars began to roll into banks, which loaned the funds onward as if they had never passed through U.K. territory. Shortly afterward, in 1981, Wall Street in New York was given a similar status. The same logic driving offshore tax havens in smaller states such as Luxembourg, Andorra, Liechtenstein, and Monaco was apparent in London and New York: fees were small enough to attract large volumes of financial traffic and, in light of this volume, significant enough to generate a sizable income for the city. Although parking funds in offshore centers had long been regarded with suspicion on account of connections with money laundering and moral injunctions against tax avoidance, the practice became legitimized in key financial centers as a "natural" function of the mobility of global capital.[12] Smaller states increasingly emulated leading offshore centers, and by the turn of the twenty-first century some five to eight trillion U.S. dollars in deposits and investment funds were housed in offshore centers, with some half of the world's stock of money estimated to reside in or flow through them. By 2005, assets worth more than eleven trillion U.S. dollars were estimated to be held offshore.[13]

Offshore financial markets appear to compromise the juridical and territorial integrity of the nation-state. Here is a designated part of national territory in which laws applying generally are suspended *as if* that territory were offshore. That the term *offshore* is used to describe what is clearly an "onshore" location is indicative of the extent to which a sense of uniform bounded territory shapes the conventional concept of the state and continues to play powerfully into modes of state legitimation. It somehow helps us to make sense of (and accept) these arrangements by visualizing the City of London operating somewhere in the middle of the Atlantic. Despite the territorial disaggregation that offshore centers imply, their rationale flows from the generation of *national* income, increasingly recognized in aggregate terms (rather than by distribution) as a means of legitimizing states' economic performance to their own populations. The logic proceeds as follows: if we don't regulate to allow banks to attract offshore investors, then in a globalized environment the banks will simply do business elsewhere. As offshore centers proliferate "here" and abroad, domestic actors also reroute their investments to minimize taxation. The goal for investors is to shift their assets from place to place, delinked from any collective obligations that derive

from "home" territory. The business of offshore centers is thus to generate this kind of "calculated ambiguity"[14] and "identity arbitrage between sovereign jurisdictions."[15] A bizarre twist in spatial framing takes
place in the process. The sovereign practices at work in offshore centers
compromise the uniformity—indeed, the very identity—of territorial
space in the name of a national interest derived from territorial norms.

A similar sense of territorial disaggregation is evident in the emergence of SEZs, which appeared in Taiwan in the mid-1960s and since
then have proliferated under different names in Asia, Latin America,
and the Middle East. SEZs are demarcated spaces within national territories where minimal taxation and specific regulations are shaped to
attract incoming capital investors. They are a factor in what Aihwa Ong
describes as "graduated sovereignty"—the differential treatment of territories and populations under sovereign control.[16] She shows how this
variation is often the result of the outsourcing of sovereign decisions
(on labor conditions and migration control, for instance) to private enterprises in order to maximize competitive advantage. In SEZs, the benefits of a cheap, willing, compliant workforce are actively promoted by
governments, and state apparatus is often deployed to resist union organization and strike action.[17] In a distinct variation of SEZs, Indonesia, Malaysia, Singapore, Thailand, Brunei, and the Philippines, under
different joint agreements, have developed a number of "growth triangles." Like SEZs, these "triangles" are specially regulated zones that exploit proximity to cheap labor and to regional hubs such as Singapore.
In these cases, the zoning extends across multiple state territories, and
coordination involves multiple state actors.[18]

SEZs are facilitated by broader transformations in the global political
economy. They are the concrete places where the work of transnational
production circuits gets done. These circuits involve different sites in
the manufacture and assembly of component parts of any one particular product. The unprecedented scale and complexity of contemporary
transnational production have been enabled through the general process of trade liberalization, through decreasing costs and increasing
speeds of transport and communication, and through state regulations
to reduce import duties on the value-added of component parts manu-
factured or assembled offshore.[19] Thus, states and private enterprises
act in concert to maximize profits in the name of advancing national

development goals. The results include sharply disaggregated "national" geographies, increasingly polarized labor markets, and sometimes mixed results on the aggregate gains made by the states in question.[20]

As Saskia Sassen has argued, the greater the dispersal of the production process, the greater the *centralized* control functions required. Sassen has shown how transnational production has driven demand for a range of specialized business services (banking, accounting, marketing, law, communications, personnel, and so on) that support companies operating in more than one national context. Headquarters of these services have become concentrated in many of the world's major metropolises and to a lesser extent in many other cities across the globe, which operate as "command points in the organization of the world economy." These global cities reveal both the hypermobility of capital, on the one hand, and a striking "place-boundedness" to processes of globalization, on the other.[21] The latter effect is often overlooked in studies emphasizing the homogenizing effects of an integrated global economy. On the contrary, government decisions to promote certain cities as draw cards for global traffic and as drivers of innovation in financial, tourist, and cultural industries generate uneven development within national territories. Neil Brenner has shown in the West European context, for example, how states have abandoned Keynesian goals of balanced growth across national territories in favor of promoting certain localities as the engines of polarized growth. Cities and regions are accordingly compelled to compete for favorable state treatment on the basis of their global competitiveness. The results, argues Brenner, are booming cities, independently networked with global circuits of capital and prioritized in terms of investment in physical, technological, cultural, and human infrastructure, alongside declining peripheries and neglected deindustrialized zones. The result more abstractly is that neoliberal values (competitiveness, entrepreneurialism, and individualized responsibility) have come to define the parameters of urban policy.[22]

These new geographies have serious implications for global financial governance. As Jason Sharman argues, financial innovations pioneered in offshore centers make it possible

> to give diametrically opposed but legally valid answers when responding to the same question from different audiences [and different jurisdictions].

In this manner individuals and firms can perform such sleights of hand as taking on the advantages of ownership while divesting themselves of the liabilities, borrowing without taking on debt, simultaneously reporting high profits [to shareholders] and none at all [to tax authorities], and "round-tripping" domestic capital as foreign investment [in order to be eligible for favorable conditions in SEZs, for example].[23]

Given the volume of assets flowing through offshore centers, this "calculated ambiguity" undermines the credibility of key banking statistics and measures of state income determined with respect to national territory and erodes confidence in the financial system as a whole.[24] Well before the confidence crisis that swept global markets in 2007–2008, there were strong indications that financial governance was in trouble. In 2006, Sassen identified a dangerous privatization of trading norms that were increasingly being developed by financial professionals in networked global cities. She highlighted the rapid innovation of financial instruments over the past two decades and the equally rapid dispersal of technical know-how as financial professionals based in various nodes of the global economy instructed each other in the latest trading schemes.[25] That state regulators failed to keep pace with the speed of change in this sector is now only too obvious. Regulatory schemes that were in place were based to a large extent on companies' internal justifications for risk-management models. Firms were thus involved in producing the standards according to which they were assessed. For Sassen, this relationship represented an increasing privatization of norm generation and, more specifically, a centralized form of power—an "informal global culture of interpretation"—based in private hands across a deterritorialized zone of connection.[26] In this respect, "new state spaces," to use Brenner's terminology, are linked to a culture of practice through which governance becomes increasingly framed as nonideological. Set within the pregiven framework of a neoliberal rationality, problems in the marketplace merely require technical solutions and can be managed more efficiently by being outsourced to those with appropriate levels of expertise. Others have pointed to similar shifts beyond the finance sector: private arbitration firms in place of national legal systems resolving growing proportions of transnational business disputes and a small number of accountancy firms and credit-rating agencies auditing and assessing the reputations of states and corporations alike and feeding into the assessment criteria of International Monetary Fund measures of "good governance."[27]

Growth in private forms of authority in line with market innovations are often invoked as arguments for the relative decline of the state.[28] However, in light of the state's often active role in this process, we can view such arguments critically as contributing to the strategies by which sovereignty is reconfigured in line with neoliberal imperatives. Shifting forms of authority may well suggest declining democratic control over increasingly complex markets, but this is not to say that state authorities are not complicit in this process. The increased volume of legislation and regulation that has characterized the work of neoliberal governments in North America and Europe over the past three decades certainly does not suggest a movement away from control.[29] It more accurately suggests a reconfiguration and delegation of the technologies and agencies involved in the exercise of sovereignty.

Several of the cases of privatized governance mentioned earlier are currently the subject of reassessment in the wake of regulatory collapse. The meeting of the world's twenty largest economies in April 2009 announced new intergovernmental oversight over financial actors such as hedge funds and credit-rating agencies and moved for greater transparency in offshore centers.[30] Despite the accompanying rhetoric (such as French president Nicolas Sarkozy's dramatic declaration, "Le laissez-faire, c'est fini"),[31] there are few indications that these sorts of measures represent substantive challenges to neoliberal ideology. They more likely suggest an uneven process of "neoliberalization" in the sense of moderating the worst excesses of market innovation.[32] The more enduring point remains that sovereign practice over recent decades has established an unprecedented capacity both to extend and to contract across a global terrain and to do so in ways that capitalize on deterritorialized connections between the local and the global. Whether sovereign states modify their trajectories or not in order to mitigate crises, the spatial dimension of sovereignty shows no signs of reversion to exclusively territorial norms. Thus, globalizing states seem set to stay even if not in their most extreme neoliberal forms.

At this stage, some important qualifications need to be made in order to argue that the examples I have given are indeed indicative of a *new* terrain of sovereign practice. First, it is not my intention to present an account of the territorial state that acts as a "straw man" for an argument posing an alternative form of state. The modern territorial state that emerged from the seventeenth-century Treaty of Westphalia has never constituted a universally dominant spatiopolitical identity. Although the territorial state system has expanded through the colonial and postcolonial eras, there are numerous contexts in which territorial imaginations continue to have only a fragmented hold over political communities and identities.[33] However, one does not need to subscribe to the historical accuracy of the Westphalian account of the state in order to recognize the ongoing significance of the *story* of Westphalia. It is precisely in terms of that story that a particular account of sovereignty *as territorially bounded* has been conveyed as the *only* form that sovereignty can take. The novelty with which we are here concerned is the recognition of sovereignty via alternative spatial frames. This broadened account of the spatial dimensions in which sovereign practice is possible challenges the power of the Westphalian tradition to shape the parameters of political belonging.

Second, the emphasis on a *new* terrain should not be taken to imply an absence of precedents. Seventeenth-, eighteenth-, and nineteenth-century colonial concessions in Asia and Africa, devoted to development for export and administered by private companies, were surely forerunners of SEZs and of contemporary arrangements to outsource certain forms of sovereign authority. The levels of financial traffic so crucial to the characterization of global cities are likewise regularly compared with those of a nineteenth-century stage of capitalist expansion.[34] These important precedents doubtless reveal capacities and drives long present within the state. However, recent technological developments have enabled those capacities and drives to accelerate in scope, volume, speed, and complexity. Thus, the contemporary terrain of sovereign practice not only differs from that apparent in Keynesian, authoritarian, and developmental states that directly preceded the era of neoliberal globalization, but also emerges in a rapidly transforming technological environment that distinguishes the here and now from earlier phases of laissez-faire and expansionist state practice.

Third, it is not the case that new terrains render territorial norms obsolete. The most cursory survey of current state practices in terms of border policing leaves us with the opposite impression. Territorial borders are tightening against certain kinds of people precisely on account of their loosening for others. In this respect, sovereign practice navigates a shifting ground in which borders and territories remain symbolically resonant and materially consequential but inconsistently invoked. This shifting ground has important implications for the nexus between sovereignty and citizenship. Each sovereign practice that ventures outside territorial norms presents a legitimacy problem for states whose raison d'être is based in the protection and privilege of a territorially bounded community of citizens. The next section reflects on what is at stake politically as globalizing states and irregular migrants straddle the tensions between new sovereign terrains and territorial imperatives.

IRREGULAR MIGRANTS, SHIFTING GROUNDS

Neoliberal restructuring over the past three decades has exacerbated both supply and demand factors with respect to irregular migration, including the displacement of workers from traditional areas of employment in places of origin and the drive toward flexible forms of labor in destination states.[35] In many cases, irregular migrants offer the most flexible labor available. With less working options available to them, irregular migrants are highly mobile, seemingly impervious to wage regulations, and easily expendable according to market fluctuations. As a consequence, they are highly attractive to employers competing for market share in the new spaces of the global political economy. Transnational production circuits, for example, are characterized by dense webs of subcontracted employment chains linking multinational enterprises with factory workers, home-based workers, site managers, recruitment agents, and distributors across the globe. Complex vertical and horizontal chains obscure a transnational informal economy operating in tandem with the formal sector and increasingly blur distinctions between the two. These supply chains allow legitimate businesses whose brand names attach to end products to exploit irregular labor without direct culpability. Lax labor laws in SEZs further facilitate this process. In China, for example, SEZs have attracted millions of rural-to-urban migrants. Though workers who migrate domestically without official permission are Chinese citizens, they are denied rights administered through local authorities—such as legal employment, education for children, and access to various subsidies. They are effectively treated like foreigners and their status reflects that of irregular migrants elsewhere.[36]

Irregular migration in all its forms has since the 1970s become a characteristic feature of many of the world's fastest-growing economies. The oil-rich states of the Persian Gulf region attracted vast numbers of North Asian, South Asian, and Pacific labor migrants in the 1970s. By the 1980s, half the active workforce of Saudi Arabia, Kuwait, Oman, Qatar, and United Arab Emirates were foreigners. Indonesians, Bangladeshis, Filipinos, and Burmese work on plantations and in construction and domestic service in Malaysia; Latin Americans, Thais, and Romanians fill the places of Palestinian laborers in Israel; central Asians work on construction sites in Russia.[37] In all of these cases, irregular migrants meet an unknown but notable portion of demand for labor. The International Labour Organisation suggests that in many countries where the will or capacity to police borders is low, most migration may well be irregular. The organization estimates that in the late 1990s some 65 percent of all nonagricultural employment in Asia, 48 percent in North Africa, 72 percent in sub-Saharan Africa, and 51 percent in Latin America were within the informal sector and thus open to irregular migrants. Informal economies are also growing in most OECD states, especially in major cities.[38]

Sassen argues that the growth of the business-services economy within global cities is too often viewed in isolation from the increased demand for low-skilled and poorly paid work that it generates. She argues that two-tiered economies in global cities disrupt conceptions of a geographical North/South or center/periphery divide. Conditions of both center and periphery are increasingly present in close proximity in the major cities of "northern" states. Sassen shows how the growth of high-income urban centers corresponds with growth in low-wage, part-time, and informal jobs, both those directly related to the maintenance of business-service infrastructure and those related to the consumption needs of service workers with high disposable incomes.[39]

Others have documented the commonplace employment of irregular migrants in order to meet this demand for low-skilled, low-status jobs (small-scale assembly work, domestic service, cleaning, and so on) that native workers are disinclined to do.[40] Increased numbers of low-paid workers have in turn generated an alternative rung of consumer demand catered to by small, culturally specific, family businesses producing low-cost goods and services and running on cheap, informal, and sometimes unpaid labor recruited through well-established transnational networks. Uneven development and the growth of middle classes in industrializing and transition states have resulted in similar labor-market dynamics, with increasing demand for domestic and construction workers in particular. Growing numbers of irregular migrants fill these positions, and a number of industries in diverse countries have now been characterized as structurally dependent on their labor.[41]

In the case of domestic service, irregular migrants are filling gaps that emerge on account of structural adjustments that shift responsibility for social services from the state to private households and, at the same time, require greater workforce participation from all adult household members. In his study of these trends in Singapore, Pheng Cheah notes that foreign maids have come to be regarded as among the necessities of middle-class working households. "In uneven development," he argues, "it is the transitory migrant worker, especially the migrant domestic worker, who sustains the advancement and entrepreneurial spirit of her more privileged fellow southeast Asian sister [and brother]."[42] He shows how the Singaporean government approaches contracts with domestic workers as a private matter between employer and employee that is rightly bound by market forces rather than by state intervention. As a consequence, many domestic workers fare much worse in wages and conditions than, for example, construction workers, whose labor is subject to more stringent regulations. For Cheah, the state exploits the hidden, gendered nature of domestic service in its race to market Singapore as a playground for a global elite. The growth of a migrant underclass is tolerated and even facilitated because it underwrites Singapore's official image as a center of global finance, research, and high-tech industry.[43]

Thus, government authorities pursuing neoliberal trajectories are heavily implicated in the generation of migration flows to which restrictive border policing subsequently responds. Much of the debate on irregular migration fails to explicitly acknowledge this link; however, more critical literature emphasizes states' tacit acceptance of irregular migrant labor as an element of broader economic adjustments.[44] This situation raises the obvious question as to why states have not pursued liberalized borders for labor as they have done for goods and services. There is certainly no shortage of credible advocates for more consistent neoliberal policies in this respect.[45] The reason relates in part to the competitive advantage that informal migrant labor provides. From this point of view, keeping borders closed to certain kinds of workers is not so much an exception to the neoliberal rule, but a more efficient strategy to maintain labor in a vulnerable and flexible position vis-à-vis capital. Inconsistent levels of arrest and deportation maintain the threat of sanction should irregular migrants reveal their identity through complaint or mobilization without necessarily impacting on the overall demand and supply of irregular labor. It is thus entirely plausible to interpret the intermittent policing of irregular migrants as a strategy of neoliberal governance that works in tandem with restricted access to licit forms of migration *to produce* irregular subjects. Nicholas De Genova argues, for example, that border policing against Mexican migrants in the United States is designed to control rather than to eliminate the flow of irregular labor, "like a faucet."[46] Bayram Unal likewise contends that the Turkish government systematically encourages flows of irregular migration. Under pressure to seal its borders into Europe, Turkey takes steps to prohibit this kind of "transit" migration through its territory, but it makes no genuine effort to combat irregular entry into Turkey, visa overstaying, or informal hiring. For Unal, this silent encouragement amounts to a deliberate trap for would-be migrants to Europe that acts to drive wages down.[47]

Neoliberal excesses are nevertheless constrained by a range of competing factors. One factor that operates in complex ways is the culture of securitization that intensified in the post–September 11 environment. Securitization offers new techniques for neoliberal governance. When border control is encompassed within the ambit of state security, irregular migrants become targets for policing on several different fronts, including as potential enemy agents. Migrants can be rendered ever more exploitable by raising the stakes of exposure. In this respect, irregular migrants are increasingly subject to criminal rather than administrative sanction and are targeted by a discourse and policy practice that equates illicit border crossings with national-security risks and the ever-present threat of terrorism.

However, such strategies can also backfire with increased domestic anxiety about *failed* border control as a security vulnerability. This increased anxiety accounts, in part, for the recent resurgence of temporary migration schemes in policy circles.[48] Schemes that carefully monitor the temporary flow of migrants to specific labor-market sectors for limited periods of time balance demand for labor with security concerns about underground status. They also generally tie migrants to specific employers with the threat of visa cancellations should that employment cease. Temporary schemes thus build in disincentives to object to exploitative conditions. Pathways to residence, citizenship, and family reunion, moreover, are often tied to consecutive periods spent "in country" even though temporary migrants may be required to depart at regular intervals. Thus, many workers remain trapped in cycles of seasonal and indentured labor with little prospect of gaining rights attached to permanent residence. If illegalization is one strategy of neoliberal governance, then sustained temporary status is another.

The competitive advantage that irregular migrants provide for globalizing states is only part of the story when it comes to explaining the logic of border policing. The other part relates to an enduring territorial state identity—linked to the notion of security—and to sovereign practices designed to bear that out. This performative dimension of border policing is not a new phenomenon, despite its more recent intensification. In the late nineteenth and early twentieth centuries, the development of effective technologies of border control—passports, surveillance, and so on—corresponded with the consolidation of European state identities over the ruins of former empires. In this context, border control became a key sovereign practice designed to give substance and legitimacy to the centralization of power over nation-state citizens within newly drawn territorial borders. It became, in Adam McKeown's words, "a pre-condition rather than a result of sovereignty and self-rule."[49] As McKeown explains in his account of the globalization of borders,

> The diffusion of migration laws [in the early twentieth century] was not merely a response to growing numbers of migrants. Many countries

established restrictive laws well before the arrival of any significant migration. Their adoption had much to do with a perception of how a civilized country should define its social and political borders. Indeed, laws and techniques were repeatedly adopted as state-of-the-art methods with little evidence of their effectiveness and often with evidence to the contrary. Failed enforcement was rarely interpreted as a call to question the efficacy of the methods, and certainly not to question the basic need of border control. Rather it was interpreted as evidence of the inadequacy of the state or institution that implemented the law, or of the moral deficiency of the migrants who evaded it.[50]

As a consequence, he argues, the enforcement of migration laws through border controls that in earlier forms rested on explicitly racialized criteria for entry and exit cannot be explained as a spontaneous response to changed external conditions. Rather, they "must be understood as part of the spread of institutions and ideologies of population management that were necessary for international recognition as a modern nation state."[51]

In the contemporary phase of globalization, border control acts not so much to *establish* the legitimacy of the territorial state as to *restore* legitimacy to globalizing states in territorial terms. Irregular migration takes on a heightened symbolic value amidst a proliferation of sovereign acts that undermine territorial norms. This chapter has provided a number of examples where the significance and function of territorial borders and territorial state identity is decidedly unclear. Although the effects of these acts are real enough on the ground (not least in global financial crisis), it is difficult to maintain direct association between the rapid transformation at hand and highly abstract processes that are less recognizable as factors driving change. For example, the value of derivatives traded in global financial markets dwarfs the value of goods and services by an astounding and accelerating factor.[52] Yet the complexity of these financial instruments makes this enormously significant element of globalization virtually opaque to all but the most highly trained experts. Is it any wonder that anxieties about the pace and nature of change coalesce around more tangible and embodied symbols of territorial transgression in the form of irregular migrants or that globalizing states cultivate this association as a means of masking their complicity in territorially uneven growth and development strategies?

The apparent lack of efficacy associated with contemporary border policing should therefore be seen not only as a means of supplying cheap labor, but also in the context of its parallel function as a performance of territorial sovereignty. Each act of interdiction, arrest, incarceration, and deportation helps to reestablish the meaningfulness of territory in spite of a globalizing age and to reinforce the naturalness of the citizen–state–territory constellation. The buildup of migration-enforcement budgets, staffing, and technology to police the U.S.–Mexican border over the 1990s, for example, was spectacularly unsuccessful in preventing the flow of irregular migrants from Mexico. Yet it achieved the important sovereign function of projecting an image of control in a decade that was characterized by the uncertain forces of globalization, the introduction of the North American Free Trade Agreement (NAFTA), and myriad anxieties about a range of threatening external intrusions.[53] Restrictive policies elsewhere also appear to feed a largely symbolic need to appear tough on immigration and to maintain the impression of territorial control. Xavier Ferrer-Gallardo, for example, draws attention to the militarization of the Spanish–Moroccan border and its mixed results in terms of policing both people and contraband goods. Against the backdrop of a globalizing Europe, he interprets border policing in the Spanish enclave towns of Cueta and Melilla "as a symbolic performance for domestic [European] consumption, attempting to mark the limits (and hence shape the identity) of the European Union."[54] In this context, as in others, a commitment to border policing provides explicit recognition of the continued significance of sovereign territorial borders and the priority (and possibility) of defining and protecting the community of citizens they contain.

In chapter 3, I undertake a more detailed case study of this performative dimension of border policing in relation to Australia. I also show how sovereign practices are increasingly undertaken across a mobile border zone. I suggest, therefore, that territorial norms are no longer consistently produced, even in those demonstrative acts that purport to uphold and defend them. For now, it is enough to acknowledge that the terrain of sovereign practice is unstable. By this, I do not mean to suggest that the places in which the border is policed, in which markets converge or workers labor, is anything less than real. Nor am I suggesting a wholesale shift from one type of administrative space to another—from map-drawn territories to some kind of abstract system of circuits and nodes, for example. Such suggestions are precisely the kind of exaggerated claim that prompts the rationale for reactionary displays of border policing. The instability to which I refer rests rather with our frames for perceiving the spaces in which sovereignty gains its meaning. We must learn to exchange narrow territorial lenses for a multidimensional perspective that is capable of registering simultaneous and overlayed fields of sovereign practice. This same perspective enables us to grasp more clearly the spatial terrain that informs neoliberal modes of citizenship.

NEOLIBERAL CITIZENS

In a classic text from the 1980s, Jean Bethke Elshtain traced the emergence of the warrior as the citizen ideal of the modern territorial nation-state.[55] She showed how citizenship had been cultivated around the preparedness to fight and die for one's country (or, in the case of women, preparedness to raise citizen-warriors) and how the allocation of rights and privileges associated with citizenship flowed from the expression of this ideal. The citizen-warrior supports the imperatives of a state overtly concerned with defense of the territorial realm and with the territorial conquest of others. For the neoliberal state, by contrast, security is linked to material prosperity and to the civilizing effect of global market forces and economic interdependency. Under these conditions, entrepreneurialism becomes a central ethic of the citizen ideal, and the market emerges as the appropriate arena for civic duty via production and consumption. This is not to say, of course, that the citizen-warrior is an obsolete ideal. The commemoration of sacrifice in battle found in narratives, monuments, and national holidays remains very much a part of many civic cultures.[56] The point more broadly is that citizen subjectivities, like sovereign practices, are dynamic and multilayered and extend across a new terrain.

A growing body of scholarship engages with a form of citizenship that gels with the market orientation and transnational openness of the neoliberal state.[57] It emphasizes, in other words, the subjective dimensions of neoliberal rationalities. As Aihwa Ong reminds us, "neoliberal reasoning is based on both economic (efficiency) and ethical (self-responsibility) claims."[58] Under neoliberalism, individuals and populations are encouraged to self-govern—that is, to view their sociopolitical encounters through the prism of market relations and to take responsibility for their place within the market. Social and political relations are conceived less in terms of common civic endeavors and more in terms of contractual relations on the basis of market exchange. Structural causes of social problems are erased by a discourse of moral culpability (delinquency, irresponsibility, laziness, parasitism) that manifests at the individual level. As a consequence, neoliberal citizens are those who can best orient their self-understanding, behaviors, and capacities to maximize their market value. Ensuing hierarchies do not necessarily tally with a more conventional citizen/noncitizen divide.

Ong draws attention to those who are well positioned within this schema. She refers to "flexible citizenship" as the "strategies of mobile managers, technocrats and professionals seeking to both circumvent *and* benefit from different nation-state regimes by selecting different sites for investments, work and family relocation."[59] Here there are obvious parallels with the "constructed ambiguity" that operates in offshore centers. Indeed, as Bill Maurer shows, promotional material seeking investors for offshore centers encourages a sense of fluid or nomad citizenship and detachment from fixed territory such that "all governments consider . . . [the investor] a tourist—a person who is just 'passing through.'"[60] Those individuals and family units able to position themselves in multiple locations with a versatile range of wealth-generating projects can take advantage of conditions in diversely regulated zones. In other words, they can competitively exploit the new geographies of the global political economy in an environment that favors a high degree of mobility and transnational connectivity. In the process, new subjectivities shape and are shaped by new sovereign terrains.

Ong points to other examples of the Chinese diaspora throughout the economies of the Asia-Pacific and to ethnically Chinese managers of manufacturing contractors in Silicon Valley. These flexible citizens, she suggests, are ideally positioned to use their transnational networks and intercultural literacy to take advantage of the demands of the production process in these contexts and in some cases are offered special incentives by the host state to do so (foreign entrepreneurs who invest more than one million dollars in specific industry areas and employ a certain number of people are eligible for U.S. green cards, for example).[61] The entire process is facilitated by trends in immigration policies to replace exclusionary clauses based on race and family connections with point systems based on skill set and investment capacity. In such cases, new citizenship norms go beyond the symbolic dimension to allocate legal status according to entrepreneurial performance. Without a hint of irony, the *New York Times* refers to "refugee entrepreneurs" who "flee" their own states in search of more business-friendly environments.[62] The implication here is that a business start-up culture is part of the rights of neoliberal citizenship.

Many migrant workers tap into this culture of flexible or neoliberal citizenship without necessarily reaping the benefits that their investor counterparts enjoy. For many young workers, global aspirations are driven by the prospect of rewards abroad and valorization at home. Indian governments, for example, promoting the export of technological competence, praise the service to country of mobile IT workers whose stories appeared earlier in this chapter. Success stories help to promote the idea of an India that has left the "third world" behind and is now a competitive and innovative player in the global economy.[63] Relevant government agencies cultivate an image of overseas workers as national heroes, transforming local economies into entrepreneurial engines of global growth. There are significant incentives for driving these kinds of discourses. From the perspective of sending states, flexible citizens are valued sources of income. States such as Mexico, Morocco, Indonesia, and the Philippines actively promote labor export in view of remittances returned. In many cases, remittances account for greater volumes of national income than foreign direct investment and act as collateral for loans in capital markets. Yet few of the states concerned have made more than token efforts to protect the rights of their workers abroad, despite high-profile cases of exploitation and abuse. In these cases, states accept the payoff from a transnational labor market while deferring associated risks to individual workers.[64] In light of these trends, Nicola Phillips interprets the promotion of migration within sending states as a distinctly neoliberal development strategy. She shows how state programs to fund public infrastructure in proportion to contributions derived from migrant remittances fill gaps in the national tax base by drawing on the incomes of the poorest families and communities. Such development strategies, she argues, "can be understood . . . as . . . exploiting an additional opportunity for a form of proxy taxation of the poor and appropriation of migrants' labor, in countries in which formal tax systems remain inadequate, already skewed heavily in favor of business and rich elites, and central to the structures of persistent and massive social inequality."[65]

How are irregular migrants positioned in this mix? In many ways, they demonstrate precisely the kind of mobility and initiative that is valorized as the neoliberal citizen ideal. It is important to acknowledge that irregular migrants are sometimes positioned advantageously, despite their vulnerability to exploitation and criminalization. For many, the earnings from their labor will support a family or community in their place of origin to an extent that may not have been otherwise possible. For some, their transnational experience will present a range of flow-on economic opportunities and eventually result in regularized status. Precisely for these reasons, sending states incorporate irregular migrants into labor-export strategies. The Mexican government, for instance, issues expatriates with formal identity documents (*matrículas consulares*) and promotes their acceptance in a range of institutions throughout the United States. This form of ID is deliberately designed to facilitate the flow of remittances from parties who would otherwise struggle to open a bank account and be forced to divert their earnings into high fees for transnational money transfers. In one of the more counterintuitive examples of sending states' support for irregular migrants, El Salvador provided free legal assistance to citizens fleeing their own regime in view of the volume of remittances expected should they remain as refugees in the United States.[66] These examples demonstrate the instrumental approach that states often take to their citizens abroad and the multiple factors that contribute to the production of irregular subjects.

Although irregular migration is never an easy option, too sharp an emphasis on irregular migrants as victims of the global economy obscures the moments of agency enabled via their paths. It also creates an oversimplified binary between citizens and noncitizens, which in turn obscures what in many cases is the relative disadvantage of formal citizens in neoliberal and globalizing states. The point to be emphasized is that neoliberal modes of citizenship now overlay the territorial version to which we have become accustomed. A national citizen is privileged in certain regards with respect to nonnationals, but in a different register of status he or she may be disadvantaged as a failed entrepreneur of the self. In a neoliberal era, those who cannot adapt to a flexible labor market are seen to suffer the consequences of their own individual choices. As a consequence, the substantive benefits of citizenship begin to shift from "unproductive" nationals to better market performers. Similarly caught between different status registers, irregular migrant workers on the one hand may be valorized as flexible citizens by sending states' governments, but on the other lack the protection of formal status in the places where they live and work. Heightened attention to security adds an additional layer to justifications and techniques of irregular status allocation—and not only for migrants. Peter Nyers employs the term *irregular citizenship* to highlight the ways in which certain "risky" citizens have had their citizenship effectively revoked in the name of security measures in the "war on terror."[67] Such examples highlight the multidimensional hierarchies of status, mobility, and labor that now produce irregular subjects alongside new modes of citizenship, none of which necessarily conforms to territorial norms.

For those who conform to neither nation-state nor neoliberal modes of citizenship, the situation looks grim. Yet new terrains of sovereign practice are also sites of innovation for those who are marginalized by any or all contemporary measures of status. In North America, for instance, labor movements have recognized that their interests are no longer served by a national frame of reference that pits the interests of low-wage citizens against those of irregular migrants. Unions contend that such an opposition cannot effectively combat the specific forms of exploitation that have emerged under conditions of neoliberal globalization.[68] There are some indications that a similar logic is beginning to surface among unions in Australia with respect to the increasing number of temporary migrants in low-skilled occupations. However, in that context, as in others, new kinds of precarious subjects that cross conventional class lines between students, professionals, migrants, and low-wage workers present new challenges for labor organizing whereby those being exploited may not identify as "workers."[69] This kind of novelty indicates that new strategies are needed that can adapt to the contemporary realities of low-paid work shaped by service-dominated economies, subcontracted employment arrangements, multiple worksites, and the availability of informal and temporary migrant labor sourced from a variety of class backgrounds in countries of origin. Union membership drives are increasingly targeted to those whose work may be short term, indentured, informal, or transferred between different industries, regions, and employers—conditions that are typical of low-wage work in neoliberal environments yet that militate against traditional forms of union organizing. Such strategies provide pathways to mobilization in which the interests of both citizens and irregular and temporary migrants are reframed in common terms.

These strategies are gaining increasing influence within and beyond the United States in regions and industries with significant proportions of irregular migrant workers. The approach of the much cited Justice for Janitors campaign has been taken up by unions and community organizations in Europe, Australia, and New Zealand.[70] Justice for Janitors spread from Los Angeles in the late 1980s with an explicit commitment to representing workers regardless of immigration status. It directly inspired a campaign to organize cleaners working in the City of London that engaged more creatively with the specific geographies of low-paid work emerging in global cities and more specifically with London's migrant division of labor.[71] The campaign was initiated by unions and community networks. It took advantage of the dense concentration of a prestige market for cleaning services in London's financial districts. Organizing according to geographic area (rather than by worksite and employer) not only ensured that the most vulnerable workers (often irregular migrants) were included in the campaign, but also maximized the leverage with which campaign leaders could negotiate with employers in the area. That a small number of transnational corporations now dominate the business of subcontracting cleaning services in London's financial districts also created opportunities to "name and shame" in domestic and transnational forums and circumvented the competition between smaller subcontractors farther down the complex labor supply chain. Such campaigns have secured better pay and conditions for cleaners and other workers and have helped to generate new norms of entitlement and solidarity that cross the conventional citizen/noncitizen divide.

Others elsewhere are attempting to map the spaces of the global economy in order to inform the activist strategies of low-wage migrant workers who are linked through a global production process to workers in other countries and to concerned citizen-consumers. Women Working Worldwide is an organization based in the United Kingdom that networks transnationally with a range of women workers' organizations and with women's projects in trade unions.[72] In 2002, Women Working Worldwide began a research project in conjunction with ten partner organizations in nine countries to map the global production chains of the garment industry in which the women they assisted were working.[73] The research was prompted when the organizations discovered that the links between immediate employers and the companies where contracts originated were not obvious or easily traceable. Neither workers constructing the garments nor companies placing orders for construction were able to identify the full extent of the production process nor the range of actors engaged in that production.

As a consequence, codes of conduct adopted under public pressure by multinational companies offered no leverage whatsoever for workers who could not establish a connection to the company at hand. It was also impossible for ethical trading initiatives to monitor the implementation of the same codes.[74] It soon became obvious that those workers at the farthest and most vulnerable extreme of the production process, working informally in SEZs where unions were effectively banned or in isolated home-based environments, were those least able to benefit from consumer-driven campaigns for their protection. Hence, those campaigns were limited by a spatial imagination that could not conceive of the particular ways in which the exploitation of workers was occurring and that therefore could not contribute to effective strategies for resistance. At the core of this research and at the core of progressive union strategies elsewhere is a call to abandon an exclusively territorial frame for thinking through the space and practice of solidarity.

There are, of course, problematic implications of generating new solidarities based on worker status, regardless of how creative their spatial reach may be. For one, there are gendered implications for those whose work in caring roles is not sufficiently recognized within the scope of the formal economy or is not so thoroughly integrated into existing labor collectives. At the very least, new solidarities would need to encompass less conventional notions of work, including work done in the reproductive economy. But what of those people implicated in new hierarchies of status who through age or infirmity are unable to work at all? It is not clear, moreover, that asylum seekers with comparatively little leverage as essential sources of labor stand to benefit from transnational solidarities based on worker identity. On the contrary, such a strategic move might have the effect of further tightening borders against an even more demonized class of irregular migrant in order to counteract the increased mobility of suitable labor.

I return to these strategic tensions in chapters 4 and 5. For now, it is sufficient to have made the point that new terrains of sovereign practice invite new strategies of contestation. In chapters 4 and 5, I speak to this creative milieu with respect to the strategies that irregular migrants are employing in France and the United States to assert the legitimacy of their presence in political communities from which they are formally excluded. In these examples, multiple spatial frames shape both the experience of "being" irregular and corresponding acts of resistance. From the vantage point afforded by these two cases, we can see in greater detail the contemporary remaking of sovereignty and citizenship.

3 / POLICING AUSTRALIA'S BORDERS
New Terrains of Sovereign Practice

After time I realized these fences around are not to prevent us from escaping—never.

No, these fences have been set to prevent you, the Australians, from approaching us.

It's pretty clear.[1]

Aamer Sultan, an Iraqi doctor and asylum seeker, made this statement from Sydney's Villawood Immigration Detention Centre in 2001. At that time, Sultan was one of hundreds of asylum seekers detained in cities and remote locations, behind barbed-wire fences and security screening processes designed to hinder public access. Sultan's statement captures a dimension of border policing against asylum seekers and others that is not always readily acknowledged. Border policing can be understood, at the most obvious level, as controlling access to territory. However, it also entails the legal and symbolic ordering of citizens and aliens. This aspect of border policing identifies who is one of "us" and what being one of "us" implies by comparison with a spectrum of outsiders. This designation is important because it serves to legitimize the sovereign acts conducted in "our" name. Sultan was prepared for conventional border defenses that he encountered on his journey to Australia. It took him longer to recognize that his incarceration was designed to establish both a physical boundary and a world of ontological difference between himself and Australian citizens. In this respect, the border was enacted each time visitors to Villawood passed through a series of security zones before they could meet with detainees. As a performative gesture, this ritual confirmed that the person being visited was different and suspect—not one of "us," potentially threatening to "us," and appropriately removed from public space.

Australia's recent history of border policing has been subjected to a substantial volume of critique.[2] The analysis in this chapter differs from existing approaches in two key respects. First, border policing is conceptualized in both the concrete and symbolic dimensions highlighted in the previous paragraph and as a crucial legitimizing practice of the neoliberal state. This interpretation differs from those that highlight a paradox in contemporary state policies on irregular migration— that is, movement toward greater transnational openness in the economic arena but growing pressure for domestic and territorial political closure.[3] Here I suggest that these movements are not so much contradictory phenomena as related arms of a common rationality of governance. In chapter 2, I argued that neoliberal imperatives toward ever more flexible transnational labor provide incentives to sustain irregular migrants in a vulnerable, exploitable position inside "national" economies through random acts of policing. In the case of Australia, however, informal labor has not played a key role in economic growth, nor has it been a prominent feature of debate over border policing, which remains largely focused on those who are seeking asylum rather than work. Policing against asylum seekers nevertheless serves a performative function that is crucially tied to Australia's neoliberal trajectory. It was right at the moment when borders were increasingly opened to trade and financial and cultural flows and when new government priorities challenged long-held assumptions about the territorial limits of the nation that border-policing initiatives played into the intensified reification of a territorially contained state and citizen. In this chapter, I show how policing directed at asylum seekers offset this identity crisis and served to legitimize a culture of state practice that was otherwise generating widespread feelings of anxiety and resentment. As such, I contend that border policing is aligned with neoliberal imperatives even when the question of migrant labor is of less direct significance.[4]

Second, I reflect on the limited spatial frames that have been used to interpret and justify neoliberal governance, including border policing. In policy rhetoric, the economic sphere is governed by the realm of "the global," which implies an irresistible set of deterritorialized forces to which the state must adapt. Irregular migration, by contrast, has

been approached from the perspective of "the national." Border policing against asylum seekers demonstrates the capacity to preserve nation-
state sovereignty in territorial terms. This framing has several important
implications. For one thing, it obscures our vision of the intersections
between border policing and global market forces. I examine this intersection via the marketization of border security in the post–September
11 context and the privatization of immigration detention in particular. For another, it obscures a shifting space of the border—a sharply
disaggregated gray zone in which the state works creatively with geography, identity, and jurisdiction in ways that defy conventional territorial logics in the very act of their defense. This shifting ground, I
contend, is indicative of a new terrain of sovereign practice, identified in chapter 2 and at work as much in border policing as in offshore
financial markets. Finally, the spatial frames in question limit our capacity to imagine alternative responses to asylum seekers, financial
markets, and other border traffic in terms that reject either/or choices
between open and closed borders. A concluding section of the chapter
argues for a more complex reading of space in order to move beyond
this impasse.

BETWEEN NEOLIBERAL AND TERRITORIAL IMPERATIVES

In recent decades, Australia has undergone a radical program of neoliberal economic reform. As a global economic downturn ensued in the
1970s, Australia confronted a declining export market and the twin
perils of high inflation and high unemployment. In order to understand
and resolve the crisis, policymakers adopted the logic of neoliberalism—
or economic rationalism, as it became known in Australia. From 1983
to 1996, under the governments of prime ministers Bob Hawke and Paul
Keating, the Australian Labor Party advanced an agenda of privatization, trade and financial liberalization, reduced business taxation, central bank independence, productivity-based wage rises, and later a shift
from centralized wage determination to workplace bargaining. This
policy direction was supported by the opposition, creating a bipartisan
consensus that was sustained over a change in government in 1996 and
continued into the twenty-first century.

What occurred over this period was substantially more than a shift in policy direction. What occurred entailed the transformation of governance itself. Critics argued in the early 1990s that senior levels of the federal public service were stacked with a new generation of elite administrators who shared a neoclassical economic education. Others observed a decade later that neoliberal orthodoxy had stymied debate and reflection in the central and most powerful government departments, had infiltrated recruitment and promotion strategies within them, and was driving patterns of self-censorship in departments and agencies reporting to them.[5] In this way, the rule of the market, as a rationality of governance, was adopted across the broadest range of government activity. It was government, in general, *as* economic policy—and economic policy of a very particular kind.

The simple necessity of a singular and radical path of economic reform was emphasized in rhetoric employed by Australian governments of both party persuasions. The unstoppable drive of the global economy was used to justify the painful effects of structural adjustment, to explain in the early 1990s, for example, "the recession we had to have," and to legitimize a new role for the state as market facilitator.[6] In this respect, the Australian context reflected an increasingly dominant transnational discourse of globalization as the inevitable encroachment of the market on a hapless political sphere faced with the limited option of either adaptation or oblivion. Those convinced of the endless benefits of adaptation in neoliberal terms praised Australia's trajectory as an overwhelming success, with a compelling record of growth into the late 2000s amply compensating for short-term pressures.[7] Commentators expressed a profound degree of confidence in the ideological consensus driving the nation's fortunes. In 2001, one prominent enthusiast and former prime ministerial advisor suggested that political debate now needed to develop a "new language of success" and to focus on issues such as how to approach a political spectrum in which economic consensus has removed the need for the old distinctions between left and right.[8] This "language of success" was reminiscent of Francis Fukuyama's assertion in 1989 that "the end of history" had arrived and that liberalism had won an "unabashed victory" in the struggle over ideas.[9] Against the demise of the socialist alternative, Fukuyama heralded a new postideological age. Others spoke of the peace dividend that would follow from the spread of laissez-faire liberal democracy in the post–Cold War world.[10] Everywhere, it seemed, the path to peace and prosperity had been found.

That such commentators failed to recognize the diversity of ideological objections to the expansionary neoliberal project and to predict the reversal of fortunes awaiting the global economy is now only too clear. The global credit crisis that became apparent in late 2007 prompted leaders around the globe to reign in their enthusiasm for the unfettered rule of the market. Australia's new prime minister, Kevin Rudd, now acknowledged the darker side of "free-market fundamentalism, extreme capitalism and excessive greed which became the economic orthodoxy of our time."[11] In this sobering climate, both the rise of fundamentalisms railing against Western liberal decadence and the many voices of a global social justice movement insisting that "another world is possible" appeared as more obvious reminders of the political nature of pretensions toward consensus. Yet even as the boom years continued in Australia, signs of a darker side to aggregate prosperity were already emerging: a large current-account deficit, casualization, underemployment, and increasing inequality in private incomes.[12] The "language of success" obscured insecurities evident in the Australian population on account of these trends. In this context, the future promoted by neoliberals prompted social tensions as those most marginalized by the changes at hand sought compensation for their pain.

In the late 1990s, many Australians were increasingly resentful of the changes wrought by economic reform. In June 2000, *The Australian*, a national newspaper, reported on changes to family incomes from 1982 to 1997. The findings highlighted that although average real incomes had risen, the distribution of income and wealth was polarizing.[13] Survey data suggest that Australians were aware of increasing inequalities and that changes to the structure of the Australian economy had generated widespread feelings of economic insecurity.[14] Anxiety was concentrated among those with lower incomes and those hardest hit by economic reform. On the one hand, resentment was focused against politicians and an elite rung of unspecified "big-business" interests perceived to have imposed harsher working conditions on the middle and poorest sectors without returning the promised benefits of economic restructuring to those who had made the sacrifices. On the

other hand, it was focused on anyone perceived to be unfairly benefit-
ing from the changed arrangements, from multinational companies to
welfare recipients. Commentators have more recently suggested that
this sense of resentment has more to do with the politics of envy than
with any sense of genuine material need. Others have emphasized the
success of government transfers in compensating those most vulnerable to market-based inequalities under both Labor and Conservative
Coalition governments.[15] What is most important for this discussion,
however, is the *perception* of unfairness and *feelings* of anxiety about
rapid economic and social change. Whether defensible or not, these
perceptions and feelings were important in terms of the context in
which border policing subsequently became a focus of public debate.

A context dominated by increased feelings of economic vulnerability helps to explain the success with which the economically and socially conservative One Nation Party swept onto the regional and federal electoral stage in the late 1990s. One Nation invoked specifically
Australian national myths about a time before the onset of globalization when a simpler, more honest, hard-working people shared a common Anglo culture and forged possession of the land on which they
toiled. The party's leader, Pauline Hanson, rallied on a platform of socio-
economic populism aimed at rural workers, primary producers, and
small-business people and drew support from groups most affected by
the reform process of the 1980s and 1990s. She advocated policies in favor of national economic protection, implicitly rejecting the inevitabil-
ity of neoliberal globalization; she promoted a vision of a self-sufficient,
ethnically homogenous Australia; she argued that special interests (i.e.,
migrants and Indigenous Australians) were receiving unfair advantages
over others and that debate in general was dominated by a "politically
correct" elite out of step with the views of "ordinary" Australians. The
party's views on immigration and Indigenous affairs were shared by
many voters and were a primary factor in mobilizing support. However, these issue areas were always engaged against the background of
economic insecurity.[16]

One Nation's platform was a manifestation of wider trends across
Australasia, Europe, and North America, where right-wing national
populism was on the rise. Like France's Jean Marie Le Pen, Austria's
Jörg Haider, and America's Patrick Buchanan, Pauline Hanson utilized

rhetoric that resonated with genuine anxiety over the pace and nature of change and extended recognition to those who identified as globalization's losers. In the Australian context, she tapped into what sociologist Katherine Betts had earlier described as a "great divide" between a highly educated urban elite and a parochial rural and outer suburban population.[17] The former, Betts argued, was well positioned to benefit from cultural pluralism and was defined by a cosmopolitan worldview. The latter was threatened economically and socially by the transition in values that cosmopolitans represented. In a classic populist move, Hanson interpreted this divide in terms that positioned "real" Australians, whom she claimed to speak for, against a morally suspect elite who betrayed the nation for the sake of their own improvement. Unable to provide an alternative account of cosmopolitan values that could speak to the concerns of those who felt left behind, she instead harked back to a golden era of stable and homogenous nationhood bound by clear territorial lines.

One Nation's success had profound effects on the Australian political landscape. The impact derived not so much from the progress of the party itself, which was short-lived and subsequently mired in controversy over fraudulent electoral practices. The impact was felt, rather, when national–populist tactics entered into the mainstream political game. Hanson's reactionary response to globalization would never be adopted in full by parties and governments that were widening and deepening a neoliberal agenda. But John Howard, as prime minister, would harness her retreat to the nation in a grand deflection of passions and energies away from the drivers of economic insecurity and toward a number of carefully constructed scapegoats—asylum seekers and their advocates among them. This political game would thus combine an embrace of globalization at the level of the economy with a defense of territorial norms at the level of the social.

When in opposition in the early 1990s, the Liberal (conservative) and National parties had also drawn on the notion of "the great divide" to shape their political strategy. Seeking to exploit this divide, Howard argued that Prime Minister Paul Keating had hijacked the national agenda in favor of special interests (a multicultural lobby, an Indigenous lobby, and elite intellectuals). He claimed, by contrast, that "[u]nder us, the view of all particular interests will be assessed against the national interest and the sentiments of mainstream Australia."[18] Following the rise of One Nation, the opposition-turned-government consolidated its efforts to partition the electorate along lines of "us" and "them." Unwilling to compromise on its platform of economic reform, the government attempted to woo the one million voters who had swung to One Nation on the basis of social conservatism. This agenda reinforced traditional ideas about Australian national identity and implicitly defined the terms of territorial political closure. Its rhetoric drew heavily on conservative commentators who berated the views of the "chattering classes"—a university educated inner-city clique whose tastes, values, and education were held to produce an arrogant contempt for the views of the average Australian.[19] From this perspective, at a time of global, regional, and national change, benefits were flowing to an unrepresentative few while the bulk of Australia's honest "Aussie battlers" were "doing it tough." The image of an elite was, of course, crucial to identifying the "mainstream" that Howard purported to defend. The "mainstream" was cultivated around specific themes of an Australian cultural narrative (egalitarianism, anti-intellectualism, racism, and fear of invasion) combined with the virtues of market rationalism. This attack on elites and "special interests" did not, however, extend to the profiteers of "big business" or to the policy and political elites toward whom Hanson had directed her hostilities.[20] By focusing debate on already marginalized groups perceived to be exploiting the community, the Conservative Coalition's strategy succeeded in forging an alliance with many of those voters who were anxious about economic reform, but without challenging the basis of the reform project itself.

It was against this backdrop that increased arrivals of asylum seekers in the late 1990s became so highly politicized. When Hanson first proposed, in 1998, the introduction of temporary protection for refugees until it was possible to return them to safe home states, Philip Ruddock, then minister for immigration, expressed dismay and outrage at the "unconscionable" approach that would bring intolerable uncertainty to the lives of genuine refugees.[21] One year later he would be responsible for implementing a temporary-protection regime and subsequently for other measures originally proposed by Hanson, including the excision of parts of sovereign territory from the Australian migration zone. Border policing against asylum seekers became a platform for assertions about the nature of the Australian community, the limits of its territory, and the expression of its sovereignty. These assertions resonated with an anxious population insecure in the face of an apparently unstoppable globalizing trajectory and in need of reassurance about more familiar forms of territorial control.

BORDER POLICING AS A PERFORMANCE OF TERRITORIAL CLOSURE

Attention to asylum seekers in the late 1990s was focused overwhelmingly on those arriving by boat. "Boat people" first entered the popular imagination when Vietnamese refugees appeared off the coast of northern Australia in 1976. Some fifty thousand Vietnamese were accepted by Australia during the 1970s and early 1980s, though boat arrivals accounted for relatively few of the total.[22] At that time, welcoming refugees from Vietnam was a way of embarrassing Communist governments and provided moral justification for Cold War foreign policies. At the end of the Cold War, acceptance of refugees as a tool in the greater battle against the Soviet threat gradually gave way to the notion of refugees as a threat in themselves. By 1994, the arrival of Chinese nationals by boat was met with newspaper headlines such as "Refugee Crisis" and "Boat People Flood Feared" and with occasional references to "invasion."[23] By 2000, when the numbers of arrivals by boat had increased more than fourfold from the previous year, an official panic ensued. Minister for Immigration Philip Ruddock suggested that a national emergency was at hand, that thousands of "illegal immigrants" were threatening to flood into Australia: "The information that is available to us suggests that whole villages are packing up and there is a pipeline. If it was a national emergency several weeks ago, it's gone up something like ten points on the Richter scale since then."[24] The atmosphere of crisis drew to a climax in August 2001 when the *Tampa*, a Norwegian container ship that had rescued asylum seekers from their distressed vessel northwest of Australia's Christmas Island, was refused entry to Australian waters. When the captain refused to change course on account of passengers in need of medical attention, Special Air Services troops took control of his ship. A diplomatic standoff ensued for days between the Norwegian and Australian governments over who should take responsibility for the asylum seekers on board. In haste, a suite of laws was introduced under the rubric of the Pacific Solution, the implications of which I return to later in this chapter. The laws enhanced the power of Australian authorities to pursue, board, and deter vessels suspected of carrying asylum seekers and effectively to prohibit access to territory in which Australian protection laws applied.[25] In the case of the *Tampa* and other boats intercepted by the Australian navy in the following months, passengers were forcibly removed to Pacific Island states to be processed by the UNHCR. The fate of some four hundred asylum seekers crowded onto a vessel that had left Indonesia in October 2001 received far less media attention than the *Tampa*. Australian authorities had received intelligence advising of the vessel's unseaworthiness, but, for reasons unexplained, no Australian ship was sent to meet this "Suspected Illegal Entry Vessel–X" (SIEV-X), and at least 353 people drowned when their boat sank south of Sumatra.[26]

Between the *Tampa* incident and the tragic fate of the SIEV-X's passengers, the politics of asylum were transformed by the events of September 11, 2001. Asylum seekers now became unwittingly implicated in a broader battle between a coalition of nation-states (Australia included) and a terrorist network that had succeeded in shattering the territorial security of the United States and its allies. Defense priorities rapidly shifted to focus on new kinds of nonstate actors and their modes of operation. Terrorists were organized in networked cells across cyberspace in a decentered structure that appeared to defy conventional territorial defenses. According to official rhetoric, the security environment was best understood as a new terrain of struggle between good and evil. The moment was at hand to draw on what bound us together as a people, a nation, and a civilization in defense against a new kind of enemy and a new kind of existential threat. The prospect of terrorism formed a continuum with economic anxieties because both were framed by the uncertain shape of a deterritorialized world. Against this background, displays of territorial integrity provided moments of reassurance. They gave the impression of a leadership committed to defending a defined territorial zone of safety and stability from an outside realm of danger and immorality. Australia's treatment of asylum seekers was replete with this kind of rhetorical justification, and border policing became rapidly invested with a sense of strategic and moral urgency. In the immediate aftermath of the attacks in New York, Defense Minister Peter Reith reinforced the necessity of employing the defense forces to deter "illegal arrivals" from entering Australian territory. "[O]therwise," he argued, "it can be a pipeline for terrorists to come in and use your country as a staging post for terrorist activities. . . . [I]f you can't control who comes into your country then that is a security issue."[27] Prime Minister Howard similarly observed: "You have to be able to say that there is a possibility that some people having links with organizations that we don't want in this country, might use the path of an asylum seeker to get here."[28]

In this panic-stricken climate, the religion and nationalities of asylum seekers arriving by boat became significant. The vast majority were Muslims from Iraq, Afghanistan, and Iran. Those fleeing the dictatorships that Australia and its allies were shortly to engage in a "war on terror" were paradoxically viewed with suspicion.[29] The threat posed by asylum seekers was systematically linked to the broader challenges of the new security environment and cultivated to resonate with longer-standing anxieties that had shaped traditional Australian security discourse.[30] Despite relatively low numbers by international standards, boat arrivals conjured latent fears of a desperate horde descending on a white island outpost in an alien Asian region. This exaggerated threat enabled a demonstration of strong, uncompromising leadership and a return to the territorial frame that was under siege elsewhere. Thus, Prime Minister Howard expressed the rationale behind his government's hard-line stance on border policing in terms of territorial integrity: "we are not going to be a soft touch, we are going to continue to defend as every country has the right to defend the integrity of its borders, and we are also going to assert the right as every country has the right to assert and that is to decide who comes to this country and the circumstances in which they come."[31]

The government's approach entailed not only repelling asylum seekers from the edges of sovereign territory, but cultivating a border between "them" and "us" at the level of identity. This task had two dimensions: to invoke that particular measure of the Australian "mainstream" to which sovereign power was loyal and to position asylum seekers as alien to the ties that bound "us" together. Official discourse is indicative in this regard. Asylum seekers were no longer referred to as "boat people," an idea suggesting homelessness and genuine need. Instead, they were increasingly described as "illegal immigrants," "queue jumpers," and "forum shoppers."[32] As "illegal immigrants," asylum seekers were by definition deliberately attempting to flout Australian law and exploit the international refugee-protection regime. The language downplayed the right to seek asylum regardless of whether a person holds valid documentation at the time he or she crosses an international border. As "queue jumpers," asylum seekers selfishly took the places of offshore refugees waiting in refugee camps for UNHCR processing and official resettlement places. The language obscured recognition of the minimal odds of being resettled in this way[33] and implied that asylum seekers were anathema to the Australian tradition of "a fair go" or egalitarian opportunity. As "forum shoppers," they rejected existing opportunities for protection in other countries en route to Australia. The government held that most "illegal immigrants" had come from a third country where they could have sought effective protection but had instead engaged people smugglers to bring them to Australia as their preferred place of settlement. This representation rejected evidence of any number of legitimate reasons for secondary movement.[34] At work in this discourse was a complete disavowal of the complexity that characterizes forced displacement and asylum seekers' transit from one territorial zone to another. Instead, the image mobilized was one of cynically motivated and morally suspect intruders who were culturally incompatible with Australian values and society.

There are numerous examples of the repetitive positioning of asylum seekers in this way. In January 2002, three months after the beginning of post–September 11 allied operations in Afghanistan, 259 detainees were involved in a hunger strike at the Woomera Immigration Detention Centre in South Australia. They hoped to bring attention to the indefinite suspension of Afghans' claims for protection while hostilities in Afghanistan continued. Facing the prospect of indefinite detention, 70 people sewed their lips together in protest. Immigration Minister Ruddock interpreted the act as a cynical attempt to blackmail the Australian public into compromising its sovereign rights. Moreover, he implied that the specific mode of action employed by the asylum seekers was indicative of the cultural gulf that divided them from Australians. "Lip sewing," he argued, "is a practice unknown in our culture. . . .

It is something that offends the sensitivities of Australians."[35] Acts of self-harm, so Ruddock argued, were not acts of desperation or legitimate political protests, but the hallmark of a nasty set of cultural values, at once brutal and infantile:

> There are some people who do not accept the umpire's decision [on refugee status determination], and believe that inappropriate behaviour will influence people like you and me, who have certain values, who have certain views about human rights, who do believe in the sanctity of life, and are concerned when people say, "If you don't give me what I want, I'm going to cut my wrists." I'm saying that there are some people who believe that they will influence decisions by behaving that way. The difficult question for me is, "How do I respond?" Because I think if I respond by saying "All you've got to do is slit your wrist, even if it's a safety razor," which is what happens in most cases . . . "you'll get what you want." . . . You say it's desperation, I say that in many parts of the world, people believe that they get outcomes by behaving in this way. In part, it's cultural.[36]

Perhaps the most blatant exercise in this kind of demonization occurred in relation to the Children Overboard Affair. In October 2001, the government made claims that asylum seekers on board an intercepted fishing boat heading toward Christmas Island had thrown their children overboard in an attempt to force navy interceptors to bring them ashore to Australian territory. As Prime Minister Howard stated at the time, "I don't want, in Australia, people who would throw their own children into the sea, I don't and I don't think any Australian does. . . . I don't accept that it's a measure of . . . desperation . . . it's a determined attempt to intimidate us."[37] The whole affair was subsequently exposed as having been managed for a preelection audience that had already indicated its support for hard-line border policing.[38] According to an account of the incident by a senior government advisor, asylum seekers escaping from a sinking vessel with their children were knowingly misrepresented as opportunists just days before the federal election.[39] This misrepresentation positioned the government as defender of the nation's territorial and moral boundaries in the face of reprehensible intruders.

In each of these cases, moreover, a clear line was drawn between citizen and "alien" that helped to define the nature of the "us" supposedly threatened by "them." The political will and apparent logistical capacity to maintain territorial integrity against irregular migration appeased a more general unease with increasingly vulnerable borders. In the face of a deterritorialized terrorist threat, official discourse cultivated a "win on terror" by associating border policing against asylum seekers with broader security priorities. In the face of a global marketplace that appeared to eradicate hierarchies based on borders and citizenship, asylum policy practice reified a bounded community that defended its sovereign territory *despite* its integration with transnational legal regimes. Border policing resurrected the possibility of solid boundary demarcations that seemed to be fading from relevance in other fields of practice. As a consequence, it assuaged at least some of the disaffection borne of economic reform and dampened questions of legitimacy around the state's globalizing agenda.

In political terms, the strategy succeeded. The Howard government won an election in November 2001 on the basis of security issues (the combination of September 11 and the politics of asylum) and remained in power until 2007.[40] Over these years, border policing directly extended to immanent outsiders—that is, to a number of citizens and residents who found themselves on the wrong side of the us/them distinction. The government's willingness to craft the borders of the nation in this way was borne out in controversial cases where long-term residents with little if any practical association with their countries of birth were deported on character grounds and in some cases rendered stateless.[41] In other cases, Australian legal residents and citizens were subject to immigration enforcement. In a case that came to media attention in February 2005, Cornelia Rau, a mentally ill resident of Australia, was mistakenly detained by immigration authorities in a Brisbane jail and later in South Australia's Baxter Immigration Detention Centre for a total of ten months. Vivian Alvarez Solon, an Australian citizen, was deported to the Philippines in 2001 on the basis that she was an illegal alien. Steps to remedy her wrongful deportation were undertaken only some four years later when the case was made public despite the mistake being discovered and reported by a number of immigration officers much earlier, in 2003. The Immigration Department subsequently admitted to more than two hundred additional cases of suspected wrongful detention of Australian citizens or legal residents.[42]

An inquiry into the detention of Cornelia Rau identified "not so much incompetent management [on the part of the Immigration Department] but instead an absence of management—not on a single occasion but during 10 months, in two jurisdictions and involving a wide range of practices, procedures and executive conduct that all pertained to the management and care of [immigration] detainees more generally."[43] Although the cases thus reflected administrative negligence more than departmental intent, they nevertheless highlighted a reckless culture of administrative practice that had hardened into the departments and agencies concerned with citizenship and immigration control. This culture was enabled and emboldened by association with broader security imperatives and rendered increasingly arbitrary the fragile line between "us" and "them" and decisions about who belongs where. Extensive media coverage of the Rau and Alvarez Solon affairs brought the dehumanized figure of the "illegal" detainee closer to identification with the vulnerable "us." These cases therefore began to unravel at least part of the rationale for some aspects of asylum policies and to highlight some of the human costs involved. The details of the cases were the subject of sustained media attention and were catalysts for challenges to asylum policy initiated by government backbenchers.[44] When a new Labor government came to power in 2007, it acted quickly to end the Pacific Solution along with the more controversial aspects of border policing such as temporary protection and indefinite detention.

BORDER POLICING AND A NEW TERRAIN OF SOVEREIGN PRACTICE

Reflecting on the practice of border policing in the context of Australia's economic and security priorities, we are confronted, in effect, with two different stories of the place of Australia and the nation-state in the world. One begins from a territorial basis. In this version, the state appears as the willing and able regulator of global flows—especially unwanted migration. It draws its authority from a bounded national community that is concerned with sovereign defense against a range of outside forces that threaten its territorial integrity. The other takes "the global" as its starting point and emphasizes the deterritorialized dimensions of contemporary economy and society. From this perspective, the nation-state cannot hold out against a range of actors, processes, and affiliations that defy territorial boundaries and modes of organization. The logical response is to abandon anachronistic ties to bounded communities and embrace an inevitable progression toward a common sphere of activity and universal goals. Neither of these stories adequately captures the complexity that characterizes the spatial and social phenomena to which they refer, nor, therefore, do they illuminate the full range of options open to political communities as they come to terms with the shifting terrains that globalization implies. On one hand, the rhetoric of global openness obscures the extent to which the globalizing state's purpose and priorities are actively constructed at home rather than imposed from beyond. On the other, the rhetoric of territorial closure fails to engage with the range of flows across trans-local and global space that have long transformed borders and political communities.

A closer reading of sovereign practices in relation to border policing reveals a far more complex environment that sits uncomfortably within both strictly territorial and deterritorialized frames. Two examples from the Australian context illustrate this point. The first concerns a global market in security that manifests via the privatization of border-policing functions. The second concerns the shifting space of the border itself.

Border policing in Australia has been subject to the same neoliberal rationality of governance that has shaped services such as health, education, and housing in recent decades. A range of private companies now compete, for example, to design, produce, install, and maintain sophisticated technologies (biometrics, motion sensors, databases, and so on) employed to prevent unwanted migration. These changes have also affected immigration detention. In 1997, the provision of detention was outsourced in the search for more "efficient" private providers and was carried out from 2003 by Global Solutions Limited (GSL), a significant corporate player in the transnational business of operating prisons, psychiatric facilities, and immigration detention centers. According to the company's corporate profile, asylum seekers are now "consumers" of GSL's services.[45] Detention in centers managed by the company is accordingly recast as market demand for the product supplied by a corrections-industrial complex and as part of the daily transactions that factor into measures of local and global economic growth.

In the increasingly securitized post–September 11 context, immigration detention is a good business investment and is promoted as such by industry leaders. Steve Logan, for example, CEO of Cornell Companies, prominent in managing corrections facilities throughout the United States, described to investors the heightened market opportunities in immigration detention as follows:

> I think it's clear that since September 11 there's a heightened focus on detention. More people are going to get caught. So I would say that's positive. The other thing that you're seeing, and to be honest with you I have no idea how this is going to impact us, but it's not bad, it can only be good, is the focus on people that are illegal and also from Middle Eastern descent. There are over 900,000 undocumented individuals from Middle Eastern descent . . . and that is a population, for lots of reasons, that is being targeted. So I would say the events of 9/11, let me back up: the Federal business is the best business for us. It's the most consistent business for us and the events of September 11 is increasing that level of business.[46]

Logan's comments are shaped by the U.S. context, where the volume of irregular migration far exceeds the volume that reaches Australia. Yet he also taps into a changing discursive, legal, and commercial environment with respect to irregular (or "illegal") migration that is far more global in scope and that shapes the incentives of industry as much in Australia as in the United States or elsewhere. In the aftermath of September 11, the fact that many irregular migrants are from Middle Eastern backgrounds generates a market opportunity for a specialized service that delivers local administrative functions linked to broader security operations. Logan thus reveals that his global industry has strong incentives to support the criminalization of immigration offenses and the performative function of immigration detention and border policing in general. Other industry leaders have noted the market opportunities of this kind of "national imperative" in hard economic times.[47] As pawns in these commercial maneuvers, asylum seekers and other migrants remain constrained by territorial identities that determine where they can and cannot go. Yet their journeys are also commodified in a global security marketplace facilitated by the neoliberal state. In the very act of territorial defense, the state opens its territory to this growing security market.

The entry of market rationality into immigration detention raises other important questions about the influence of private and nonnational actors in shaping the conduct of border policing itself. Audits of Australian government contracts with GSL found no specification as to how the central task of providing "lawful, appropriate, humane and efficient detention" was to be defined or assessed. Audits also brought to attention unclear lines of accountability for subcontracted services such as food provision, maintenance, health, and psychiatric services.[48] According to at least one well-positioned observer, the responsible government department had a history of outsourcing not only service delivery, but also the development of standards of practice within detention centers in order to avoid duty-of-care obligations under international law and to distance itself from public accountability.[49] A global trend toward privatization in immigration detention has elsewhere been identified as part of state strategies to avoid association with the less palatable aspects of border policing and to optimize the effects of border policing on state legitimation.[50] In the Australian case, prominent findings of fundamental flaws in government contracts with detention providers resulted in some improvements in contract administration.[51] Yet the preference for outsourcing survived a change in government in 2007, and in 2009 Serco Pty Ltd., another global player with experience running detention centers in the United Kingdom, and GSL were awarded five-year contracts for detention center management and community-based immigration housing, respectively. Critics continue to raise concerns about transparency and accountability. For instance, standards for detention are contract based with limited public scrutiny and not guaranteed by legislation.[52]

This lack of government oversight resonates with what Saskia Sassen calls "privatised norm-making"—the gradual shift into private hands not only of government functions, but of whole systems of governance.[53] In chapter 2, I raised this issue in relation to the normative influence of transnational accounting and arbitration firms that increasingly set corporate standards of practice and settle business disputes that were once the preserve of national legal systems. The consequences, argues Sassen, are twofold: the transferral of normative authority from public to private hands and the direct inflow of transnational corporate interests into institutions only nominally coded as "national" and "public." Sassen's argument, posed in 2006, rings true in the context of regulatory collapse in 2008 and beyond. Yet her point carries over into other spheres of public-private practice less obviously connected to the excesses of global finance. In this respect, we can draw analogies to the privatization of immigration detention and its implications for a culture of administrative practice that impacts on the distinction drawn between citizen and "alien" and the consequences of being marked as either. Detention, moreover, is outsourced in the context of a broader policy discourse that speaks directly to the "homeland-security marketplace" and attempts to incorporate private security providers into decision making on state security needs (including border policing against "illegal" immigrants). Policy analysts in favor of such an approach consciously advance the shift in emphasis from privatized service delivery to privatized system design. The Australian Strategic Policy Institute, for example, advocates leveraging the expertise of private security industries in precisely these terms. It reports that "some Australian industry providers see themselves offering homeland security capability solutions, *not just delivering a product or service.* Providers suggest that, on balance, they possess a much broader view of market trends and user requirements than the users [predominantly state agencies] themselves."[54]

This presence of "the private" and "the global" inside "the public" and "the national" should caution us against simplistic references to sovereign territorial norms in relation to border policing. There is no sense in which we can logically separate those sovereign acts that defend territorial integrity from those that invite a closer connection with a global marketplace. Instead, we are dealing with a new terrain of sovereign practice and a range of techniques designed to manage the political fallout from this uncertain transition.

Territorial norms run deeper into trouble when we reflect on the space of the border that comes into view through contemporary policing strategies. Far from a solid map-drawn line that demarcates territories and jurisdictions in unambiguous terms, the border is revealed as a shifting ground, dynamic in space and in time and varied in its relevance to different kinds of traffic. The Australian government's decision to excise Christmas, Ashmore, Cartier, and Cocos (Keeling) islands from the Australian migration zone following the *Tampa* incident is one clear case in point. When asylum seekers without a valid visa arrive in excised territories, they are *not* in Australia for the purposes of applying for a visa. They instead arrive in a legal loophole—an offshore site that is onshore. This newly crafted space generates in turn "a new category of person known as an 'offshore entry person.' "[55] With this administrative category, the state's spatial strategies directly shape and disaggregate rights-bearing identities. Deemed to have not fully arrived in Australia, offshore entry persons have no automatic right to claim asylum and only limited access to judicial review. They become deportable, in other words, in ways that depend on "who" and "where" they are said to be in relation to offshore space. In 2003, when fourteen Turkish Kurds landed on Melville Island in the eastern Timor Sea, the island was excised retrospectively, from the midnight *preceding* their arrival. Before the Australian Senate disallowed this excision, the Kurds were removed to international waters. In a press statement given some days after the incident, the foreign affairs and immigration ministers announced the return to Indonesia of the boat in question as part of the government's ongoing success in border protection. The ministers bluntly stated that "[t]he passengers . . . did not claim asylum in Australia."[56] Yet from Indonesia the Kurds claimed they had made their claim to refugee status known to authorities on Melville Island.[57] Any claims to asylum that may or may not have been made had been invalidated *post factum* as legally impossible. In 2005, excision was extended to still more islands; however, a 2010 High Court decision restored some aspects of judicial review to asylum seekers in excised territories.

If excision represents a contraction of the border, other policing strategies extend the border beyond territorial limits. Australia has pioneered growing trends in extraterritorial policing, effectively pushing borders into international waters and embarkation points where unwanted migrants are immobilized during or prior to transit and prevented from accessing territory where human rights obligations apply. In the name of border security, Australian officials work closely with their counterparts in Indonesia, Malaysia, the Philippines, Thailand, Vietnam, and the Pacific to prevent irregular migration, generically cast as "illicit" from the vantage point of spaces that are not bound by the Refugee Convention.[58] Government officials work in transit country airports to assist airline staff and customs agents in profiling "risky" passengers, including former asylum applicants. Transport carriers face significant penalties should passengers attempt to enter Australia without valid documentation. They therefore engage in proxy immigration screenings at the point of departure. Australia's Pacific Solution entailed a more direct deployment of the border to offshore sites when Pacific states were contracted to detain and process potential asylum seekers. In New Zealand, Nauru, and Papua New Guinea, those intercepted en route to Australia were not subject to Australian law, but rather to the protection laws of other states or to international status-determination systems. Australia, moreover, offered no guarantee of a settlement place should asylum seekers be accorded refugee status. Offshoring in this way had serious implications for the consistent rule of law, including the fact that asylum seekers had no access to judicial review. The Commonwealth Ombudsman did not have jurisdiction over offshore detention centers, and the Immigration Department obstructed the Australian Human Rights and Equal Opportunity Commission's attempts to investigate abuses in the centers.[59] This effective outsourcing of protection obligations came at considerable cost: some three hundred million dollars to run detention centers on Nauru and Papua New Guinea between 2001 and 2008. In the case of Nauru, Australia made a sixfold increase in aid to the near-bankrupt state in exchange for its compliance.[60]

These extraterritorial strategies have found broader purchase in regions facing significantly larger flows of irregular migration than Australia. Australian initiatives have directly inspired proposals for offshore "transit processing centers" for irregular migrants seeking entry to Europe; the European border is increasingly externalized via collaboration with authorities in sending, transit, and neighboring states; and "temporary stay and assistance centers" in Italy's island territories have been widely criticized for poor conditions, lack of substantive access to asylum procedures, and mass removals of irregular arrivals to Libya.[61] As recent critics have argued, Europe's common security agencies are increasingly focused on policing a mobile and fragmented space of the border (a *"Grenzraum"*) that defies representation in the form of a demarcated line.[62] Although borders are fewer for European nationals in the space of the union's interior, certain third-country nationals face a growing array of border controls via targeted surveillance and ever more restrictive administrative procedures. These trends suggest that the Australian case is part of a broader phenomenon of border space emerging wherever sovereign agents seek to instigate new hierarchies of mobility and status.

In light of these disaggregated spaces, expansion and contraction are not sufficient metaphors for the bordering processes in question. Borders are activated differently depending on who one is or who one is said to be. Identity, in turn, depends on *where* one is are, and "the where" of political jurisdiction is rendered ambiguous as a matter of government policy. Australian government publications describe its approach as establishing a "border continuum" that works simultaneously to distinguish desired from undesired human traffic and to ease or restrict flows accordingly.[63] This shifting space of the border is not limited to territory's edge but follows its targets as they move through spaces well within and beyond the interior and surfaces in various commercial and administrative practices— in visa classifications, in airline procedures, in the making of security markets, and in the transfer of biometric data through global information systems. Far from disappearing, borders are being reconstituted in ever more ephemeral forms. They are increasingly mapped directly onto suspect bodies whose fingerprints and face scans activate border controls not only at airports, but also at police stations, immigration offices, and conceivably hospitals and schools. These new technologies in no way suggest the declining relevance of borders for the neoliberal state. On the contrary, they reveal the border as a site of intensified governmental activity and a new terrain of sovereign practice.

THE FUTURE OF BORDER POLICING

In the wake of the global financial crisis, Australia's prime minister Kevin Rudd published an essay in which he promoted a social democratic future built on the basis of "a system of open markets, unambiguously regulated by an activist state, and one in which the state intervenes to reduce the greater inequalities that competitive markets will inevitably generate."[64] These ambitions suggested that some of the incentives to demonstrate national credentials and territorial defense through the practice of border policing might be less apparent in the future. It is certainly the case that Rudd's government initially retreated from rhetoric that scapegoated asylum seekers for the ills of an anxious nation. In 2009, however, when the number of asylum seekers arriving by boat again began to spike, the opposition launched a scathing attack on a government that was "soft" on border protection. Unwilling to back away from the performative dimension of border control, Rudd shifted his government's focus from "queue jumpers" and "illegals" to the "people smugglers . . . engaged in the world's most evil trade . . . [who] should all rot in jail because they represent the absolute scum of the earth."[65] Rudd deflected rising anxiety toward a new populist target and added little complexity to the debate on irregular migration. Eventually retreating to legitimation through hard-line border policing, Rudd suspended processing of all asylum claims made by Afghanis and Sri Lankans in 2010 and reopened remote detention centers to accommodate growing numbers of detainees. This move was designed to communicate a message of deterrence to asylum seekers in general and a message of territorial integrity to domestic constituents in the lead up to a federal election. Those asylum seekers affected were returned to the prospect of indefinite detention on the basis that their countries of origin were now so secure as to render their claims for protection obsolete— to be confirmed three to six months into the future when the suspensions would be reviewed. Rudd had reinstated temporal strategies of border policing where borderlines shifted in time as much as in space.

Rudd's new take on "the global" as a field that is open to state-led interventions is not, of course, very new. It was, after all, *the kind* of interventions made under previous governments that generated so much angst around Australia's neoliberal trajectory and that prompted the political need for compensatory tactics in the form of border policing. The important point for this discussion is that Rudd's approach fits comfortably with trends in border policing across a new terrain of sovereign practice. It fits, that is, with extraterritorial strategies to preempt the arrival of asylum seekers, justified as sovereign defense against generically illegal flows and the "scum" that profits from them. Announcing changes to the provision of detention in 2008, Immigration Minister Chris Evans was at pains to insist that the immigration system would continue to "be characterised by strong border security, [and] firm deterrence of unauthorised arrivals."[66] Framing the issue as a matter of national security, Evans placed an emphasis on strategies of prevention aimed at policing "unauthorized" transit well before asylum seekers arrive at the border itself. In this respect, there is continuity with the former government's stated goal to "push . . . the border offshore"[67] and with wider efforts to prevent asylum seekers from access to places where states have responsibilities to process claims for refugee status. That Evans includes excision as an important plank of Australia's border protection only confirms this alignment and the ongoing use of creative jurisdictions and temporal arrangements in the bordering process.

   If this is indeed the future of border policing, and if, more generally, that future is indicative of a new terrain of practice through which globalizing states assert their sovereign power and redraw status hierarchies, then what response is required at the level of political theory? One thing is clear: conventional territorial spatial frames do not illuminate the creative and disaggregated mapping of space as a sovereign technique. One-dimensional readings of a deterritorialized world are similarly unhelpful and clearly implausible because territorial identities continue to figure prominently in the lives of irregular migrants everywhere. These limited frames obscure the interconnections between border policing and global market ideological forces and lock us into unhelpful debates about the wholesale decline or resurgence of territorial sovereignty. A far more multidimensional spatial lens is required— one that recognizes the different modes of being in and moving through space that operate simultaneously across different fields of practice and impact diversely on different kinds of traffic. This kind of perspective allows us to see the reconstitution of borders across a new terrain.

No one as yet has a clear conceptual handle on these spatial dynamics or on how they will play into new subjectivities that emerge on account of the social and political cleavages taking shape. New spatial metaphors are essential but imperfect tools for analysis of contemporary sovereign power and the forces that contest it. Given the ongoing tragedy of deaths at the border, there is an urgent normative imperative to develop new ways of articulating space and to harness this more abstract move toward concrete political change. Our borders, economies, and identities are far more complex than conventional spatial frames allow us to see, and our political response to the movement of people requires a corresponding degree of sophistication. The task of political theory, therefore, is to generate thinking space for alternative expressions of sovereignty and new modes of political belonging that are more dynamic and less life threatening for those who currently find themselves on the wrong side of sovereign terrain.

In the following two chapters, I turn to the ways in which irregular migrants themselves are resisting and challenging the border policing to which they are subject. These contestations, I contend, also entail a new terrain of practice—one that emerges from the edges of citizenship and asserts new modes of political belonging across local and global space.

4 / ACTS OF CONTESTATION
The Sans-Papiers of France

On March 18, 1996, some 324 irregular migrants occupied the Church of Saint-Ambroise in Paris, calling themselves the Sans-Papiers (literally "Without Papers"). Some of the Sans-Papiers were asylum seekers, and some were long-term working residents of France whose status had been made irregular as a result of recent legislative changes. This initial action prompted collectives of Sans-Papiers to organize across the country and was followed by further church occupations, hunger strikes, demonstrations, and petitions. The Sans-Papiers demanded the right to stay in France with regularized status. They rejected the illegality with which they had been charged and insisted on the legitimacy of their presence. On August 26, twenty thousand people marched through the streets of Paris in support of the Sans-Papiers who had earlier been evicted from the Church of Saint-Bernard, where they had gone on a hunger strike. Some subsequently gained temporary papers, but others were detained and eventually deported. Laws passed in 1997 allowed for the regularization of seventy-eight thousand migrants. However, many who applied for regularization did not meet the set criteria and remained without papers, vulnerable to deportation.

More than a decade later, the Sans-Papiers continue to struggle for recognition as rights-bearing claimants upon the French nation-state. In May 2008, the Coordination de Sans-Papiers 75, an autonomous group of irregular migrants with some two thousand members in Paris, occupied the union hall of the General Confederation of Labor. They brought attention to their central role as workers within the French labor market. They objected to the terms in which the confederation had spoken for the Sans-Papiers and demanded to negotiate their own regularizations directly with government authorities. The occupation continued for fourteen months. It was followed by a series of strikes and rolling workplace occupations that brought temp agencies, restaurants, restaurant associations, tramlines, building sites, and construction employers' associations to a temporary standstill. By February 2010, six thousand Sans-Papiers had been involved in the actions that had directly affected some forty worksites across the greater Paris area. Refusing the terms of government offers for limited regularizations and ridiculing immigration officials' authority, irregular migrants inaugurated their own alternative "ministry," the Ministry for the Regularization of All the Sans-Papiers, in 2009. Operating out of a disused government health office, the "ministry" continues to call for a moratorium on immigration raids and deportations and a blanket regularization for all Sans-Papiers.[1]

When ostensibly "illegal" noncitizens draw attention to their presence, insist on their right to residence, and assert themselves as protagonists in public-policy process, how is the substance of citizenship affected? A brief historical analogy may help us to see the potential significance of the Sans-Papiers' struggle. Laurent Dubois reminds us that unlikely contenders for citizenship have been far more important to citizenship's genesis than is generally recognized. He argues, for example, that in the late eighteenth century insurgent slaves in the French Caribbean helped to inform republican ideals emerging concurrently in France. The slaves made a case for freedom by expressing solidarity with the republican project. The slaves' claim to citizenship, though strategically designed to capitalize on divisions between republican administrators and royalist plantation owners, "ultimately expanded—and 'universalized'—the idea of rights." In the 1790s, this was radical indeed. The extension of rights regardless of racial identity "outran the political imagination of the metropole, transforming the possibilities embodied in the idea of citizenship."[2] For Dubois, the slaves' actions represent an important contribution to the transformation of political ideas that is rarely acknowledged. It shows that citizenship is shaped as much by those on its edges as by those at its nominal center. It shows, moreover, that a history of citizenship's diverse origins in time and space has largely been eclipsed by conventional accounts of a one-way journey outward from a European center.

Can the Sans-Papiers also push our thinking on citizenship to new frontiers? Might it be the case that they are engaged in the stuff of the political—that moment of rupture and reconstitution of political belonging? This chapter is an attempt to understand the kinds of contestations of citizenship in which the Sans-Papiers are engaged and to think through what this engagement means for political belonging more generally. What can we learn from the Sans-Papiers about dynamics of citizenship under conditions of neoliberal globalization? How might their political claims challenge the temporal and spatial limits of citizenship as we know it? Before a detailed discussion of the terms in which the Sans-Papiers have staked their claims, I begin by outlining a conceptual approach to acts of contestation. This approach provides some starting points from which to assess the Sans-Papiers' struggle.

THEORIZING ACTS OF CONTESTATION

By focusing on the political activism of irregular migrants in this chapter and the next, I work against the trend in critical refugee studies to interpret both the sovereign acts that constitute irregularity and the potential for acts of resistance (or more frequently the lack thereof) through the work of Georgio Agamben.[3] Agamben rejects an inside/outside territorial logic of citizenship and sovereignty. Instead, he emphasizes zones of indistinction, where persons are no longer recognizable in a political form that allows them some modicum of protection against the exceptional power of the sovereign. Agamben has theorized the figure of the refugee as the exemplary subject of contemporary sovereign power. Contained in camps where the rule of law is abandoned, refugees expose the normalization of the state of exception, when the juridical order that prohibits torture, arbitrary incarceration, and killing is suspended. Following Carl Schmitt, Agamben argues that sovereign order is fundamentally based on the power to enact this exception and not, as liberal theory contends, on a social contract and collective will of the people. Thus, the refugee is only the clearest contemporary example of *every* individual's vulnerability to sovereign whim. The

notion of the camp is likewise a graspable metaphor for a space of law-
lessness to which *all* are potentially subject. From this perspective, irregular migrants' struggles for citizenship are misdirected because citizenship offers no ultimate protection against the exigencies of sovereign
power. Agamben's theory speaks powerfully to the contemporary experiences of many irregular migrants, whether detained in offshore detention centers or surviving in the informal shadows of the economies
and societies in which they live and work. Yet his analysis of the modus
operandi of sovereign power is too often accepted in ways that obscure
or deny the modes of resistance and acts of contestation that irregular
migrants (and citizens) pursue. As William Walters points out, "In these
types of accounts, . . . [irregular migrants] are subjects to whom all manner of things are done, often in arbitrary and violent ways, but rarely
agents in their own right."[4] It seems to me that there are serious political consequences to embracing Agamben's work in this way. Chief among
them is the failure of such accounts to engage in theorizations of transformative politics, despite a critical normative stance that clearly identifies the injustice of the irregular condition and those sovereign acts
that create it.

My intention, by contrast, is to steer a balanced path between the
kind of pessimism inspired by Agamben and an overly prescriptive
transformative agenda associated with the "autonomy of migration," a
standpoint that crosses both academic and activist milieus. This standpoint has been most prominently expressed in the English-speaking
world by Michael Hardt and Antonio Negri.[5] These widely read leftists
call for a new world citizenship, envisaged not so much in a positive
sense of belonging to a global institution, but in a negative sense of
eradicating restrictions on human mobility. For Hardt and Negri, world
citizenship entails a reclaiming and redrawing of space in defiance of
borders that determine where one can and cannot go and where one is
entitled to what. They valorize migrants, whether clandestine or otherwise, as members and makers of a new global "multitude" that comes
into being through concerted resistance to an equally global "Empire."
"Empire" refers to a constellation of power, incorporating but not limited
to certain governments, intergovernmental organizations, and collabo-
rating nongovernmental organizations that sustain the state system and
its sovereign borders as instruments of oppression. This teleological ac-

count of a transnational underclass poised to overcome the strictures of nations and states presents an overgeneralized reading of contemporary social cleavages and a predetermined vision of the path to which existing social movements will lead.

Not all studies that adhere to the "autonomy of migration" ethos necessarily subscribe to Empire as the contemporary locus of power. In the main, however, they share with Hardt and Negri the view that seeking forms of recognition (as nation-state citizens, for instance) buys into the very regimes of control through which migration (and labor and life) is policed. Such studies favor the strategy of preserving an underground status that refuses the administrative categorization through which control is exercised. The "autonomy of migration in action," they hold, "is the imperceptible politics of escaping subjectivities [in general]."[6] There is much to be said for remaining open to forms of politics and subject formation that are inarticulable by conventional means and are thus resistant to co-option and regulation. As I outline later, my own approach to theorizing acts of contestation attempts to capture the potential for acts that cannot be contained or even necessarily imagined by existing conceptual vocabularies. Yet what remains inarticulable may also remain politically impotent precisely because being political means being recognizable in social terms. This is merely to say that theory is wise to engage with a spectrum of resistance strategies and that irregular migrants, in any case, are unlikely to embark on a common preordained struggle. On the contrary, their political activism is likely to reflect the specific geographic, historical, legal, and cultural contexts in which they are placed and thus to engender diverse results and unpredictable trajectories. The "autonomy of migration" literature, however, finds little of value *at all* in conventional acts of contestation that work in the currency of status that is subject to administrative control. It seems to me that this approach places far too high a burden on irregular migrants to abandon (limited) gains that might be won by invoking the language of citizenship and rights and to do so for the sake of a radical politics that may or may not reflect their diverse experience, goals, and desires.

Finally, I want to avoid the kind of analysis that attributes an *inherent* radicality to irregular migrants as if their positioning as outsiders to citizenship were *in and of itself* insurrectional. I have in mind here an

essay by Nevzat Soguk in which he reflects on the ontological challenges to state-centric identity categories (citizen, state, and bounded
territory) posed by irregular migrants' journeys. Soguk implies that irregular migrants are engaged in ontological contestations even as they
die in border crossings:

> Surely, where refugee, illegal migrant and asylum seeker bodies fall, they
> mark borders in their resourceful and rich unfolding temporally and
> spatially. Bodies fallen, drowned, frozen, mangled, and suffocated high-
> light borders' capture of people daring to move unauthorized. On the
> other hand, they also point to the trails through which border-crossing
> people turn insurrectional, capturing borders and harnessing them to
> their movements. In this way, while reflecting the dead certainties, stop-
> pages, and terminations effected by the border, they also point to the
> ambiguities energized through border practices, which manifest pas-
> sages, continuities, and interactions. Even the dead bodies, to recollect
> de Certeau, "mark the stages of advance."[7]

I am sympathetic to the argument that the growing presence of irregular migrants potentially subverts the power of state-centric categories
as exclusive measures of political belonging. This, as I see it, is Soguk's
broader argument, and this chapter is premised on precisely this potential for subversion. I am, however, reluctant to accord an ontologically
subversive status to deaths at the border without an account of how
those deaths effect symbolic or material change in the mode of political belonging that allows them to continue. For me, Soguk tends toward a romanticization of apparently political acts that irregular migrants pursue in their everyday lives (and deaths). His interpretation
belies the extent to which deaths at the border remain *un*remarkable—
untallied and unconnected to broader claims for justice, the unpleas-
ant but predictable comeuppance of "lawbreakers" who fail to adhere
to citizenship's rules. I want to insist, therefore, on a theorization of
contestation that links ontological rupture at the level of ideas to political practices that seek transformation. It is what one does *politically*
with the potential for transformation that determines whether the ontological possibilities, to which Soguk rightly points, make a difference
in people's lives.

Toward this end, a more clearly defined conceptual approach to contestations of citizenship may help us to navigate the Sans-Papiers' struggles. Contestations of citizenship can be understood on at least two levels. The first relates to the formal legal status that citizenship implies and attempts to extend that status to those who lack an automatic entitlement to it. Calls to regularize irregular migrants work at this level of contestation. They deploy an understanding of citizenship as a static possession that is controlled by state authorities with the power to transfer it to approved noncitizens. A second level of contestation engages the representational dimension of citizenship. This dimension generates an unquestioned "common sense" about who belongs to what kind of political community. This common sense tells us who a citizen is and what being a citizen implies. Being a citizen, in its conventional formulation, is linked at an ontological level to being part of a nation-state. It is also linked to racialized and gendered discourses through which citizenship takes on specific embodied meanings. This process raises questions as to whether particular kinds of bodies ever really belong to the nation-state, despite their formal citizenship status. Contestations that operate at the representational level challenge these *meanings* of citizenship and, in their most radical forms, undermine the legitimacy of legal status as a self-evident determinant of political belonging. In these cases, citizenship is engaged as a dynamic and contestable identity. Far from static, it is always "in the process of becoming."[8] As I argue, this second level of contestation is also evident in the political strategies of irregular migrants who sometimes invoke a radical discourse of belonging even while they seek to be included within the boundaries of citizenship as they currently stand.

Engin Isin gets at this sense of radical contestation with what he describes as "acts of citizenship."[9] For Isin, these acts differ from those carried out by substantive citizens, for whom claiming rights, as citizens, is uncontroversial. Acts of citizenship, in Isin's formulation, bring into being new kinds of citizens and rupture existing models of status and institutions. Acts of citizenship generate new modes of recognition of subjects, in Arendt's famous phrase, with the right to have rights.[10] Isin is interested in this creative moment, where citizenship exceeds its definition in law. Thus, noncitizens and, indeed, "illegal" noncitizens may be implicated in acts of citizenship insofar as those acts challenge the very terms in which citizenship and noncitizenship as well as legality and illegality are defined. Formal citizens whose legal status is not *substantively* recognized may make similar kinds of contestations. Recall, for example, riots in the *banlieues* of Paris in 2005. Commentators were quick to point out that the issue at stake in these riots was the denial of *substantive* citizenship to generations of migrants who had been spatially and politically alienated in the outer suburban fringes of France's major cities.[11] Although the riots lacked leadership and did not give rise to an organized social movement, they succeeded in challenging, if only momentarily, the givenness of universal citizenship in France. Such acts prompt reflection on the substance of citizenship and on the justice of its current distribution.

Isin provides a compelling way of thinking through how contemporary migration is challenging the spatial frames and subjectivities that have long given shape to citizenship. By identifying acts of citizenship, we can start to see the potential for alternative configurations of political communities. Yet Isin's approach also contains an inherent limitation. He interprets political acts through the language of citizenship—a language embedded in a specific mode of political belonging that cannot therefore capture *all* ways of being political. One does not have to buy into a Eurocentric reading of the history of citizenship in order to make this claim. The issue is not that citizenship has evolved in a process endogenous to Europe, reflecting an exclusively Eurocentric experience. Dubois's account of the Caribbean slaves, among other examples, suggests a far more complex process of global interconnection at the heart of citizen identities. Nor is the issue that we cannot identify modes of citizenship long present in non-European settings. Indeed, part of Isin's project is to reimagine citizenship as a dynamic process of group constellation in ways that render visible non-European citizenship practices.[12] The issue is rather that citizenship always comes with the baggage of its history—however diversely and multidimensionally it may have been constituted across space and time. Precisely on account of citizenship's current hegemonic trajectory, the language of citizenship retains connections to a reified spatial frame (the modern territorial nation-state), a specific subject (the autonomous citizen), and mode of political practice (claiming rights)—all of which can capture only partial expressions of political belonging. The problem, as Sanjay

Seth contends, is that the language of citizenship is "fully adequate nowhere."[13] How, then, can we ensure that acts of contestation are theorized from a broader field of potential? Because we cannot be confident that the language of citizenship is enough to do justice to the broadest range of ways of being political in the past, present, or future, the language we use to talk about political belonging must at a minimum capture a degree of reflexivity with respect to its own limitations.

On this point, I echo Judith Butler's comments on how we might proceed in coming to terms with new subject formations arising in the context of contemporary social struggles. Thinking through the challenging prospect of strategic transnational alliances between sexual and religious minorities, Butler highlights "the tension between *(a)* expanding the existing normative concepts of citizen, recognition, and rights to accommodate and overcome contemporary impasses [between seemingly disparate minority groups and their struggles for justice] and *(b)* calling for alternative vocabularies grounded in the conviction that the normative discourses derived from liberalism and multiculturalism alike [including the language of citizenship and rights] are inadequate to the task of grasping new formations of the subject and new forms of social and political antagonism."[14] Drawing on this tension, I want to highlight a third way of understanding acts of contestation as acts that rupture the very terms of reference to which our conceptions of political belonging are limited. Such contestations generate new interpretations and articulations of power, agency, community, justice, and all the other elements that currently inhere in diverse meanings of citizenship—as well as something exceeding these concepts that we cannot yet describe. Existing vocabulary is unable to capture the full extent of this challenge, and this not-yet-knowable quality is precisely what makes the prospect of such acts so radical. Yet we do have the theoretical wherewithal at least to remain open to the possibility of more than what our current conceptual limits allow.

None of this suggests that the language of citizenship and rights-based claims offer little to irregular migrants trying to secure their futures. On the contrary, as I show here, the San-Papiers have deployed with success this kind of discursive framing. I emphasize rather that there are limits to claims presented in these terms and, moreover, that these may not be the only terms of reference available. I do not assume, either, that the third kind of contestation is necessarily present in the struggles of irregular migrants—certainly not in all of them. But I also acknowledge the difficulty of "seeing" such acts or understanding their terms of reference from a starting point already embedded in a specific culture of analysis—one, for example, that isolates the political dimension of social struggle from other dimensions of human experience. Although citizenship remains a rich and dynamic reference point for contemporary political struggle, emerging political subjectivities may well exceed the spatial imaginaries and modes of practice that the language of citizenship is capable of conveying and this possibility should factor into critical inquiry. From this starting point, we might be better equipped to recognize the struggles of irregular migrants as steps, however partial and cumbersome, toward alternative modes of political belonging.

THE SANS-PAPIERS OF FRANCE

The Sans-Papiers have become politically active against a backdrop of fierce debate over immigration to France and French national identity. Following industrialization, France fostered immigration from its colonies and from Mediterranean states as a bolster to its national workforce, and in the 1920s and 1930s it rated among the highest per capita immigration countries in the world.[15] In times of prosperity, migration schemes remained largely uncontroversial. However, the notion of France as a land of immigration came as something of a shock to policymakers when in the early 1970s immigration proved harder to stop than it had been to start. The problem was not only new labor-market conditions following global economic downturn, but the volume and type of migrants becoming increasingly visible—black and Muslim migrants from former French colonies in the Maghreb. As the French economy slumped, immigration became the focal point for a sense of national crisis, spurred on by the path of European integration and widespread opposition to the loss of national sovereignty apparent in this process. The opening of borders to European nationals corresponded in France, as elsewhere in Europe, with increased hostility toward immigrants of non-European descent and a "fortress Europe" mentality designed to keep them out. Black and Muslim immigrants, in particular, appeared in racialized discourses as precisely the kind of threat to France's cultural, economic, secular, and political integrity that resonated with a public concerned about the rapid pace of globalization and, after 2001, with fear of radical Muslim terrorism.[16]

The most prominent public face of this discourse was Jean Marie Le Pen. His Front National was a typical expression of the national populism that swept across Europe in the late twentieth century. Bringing together a staunchly nationalist and reactionary antiglobalization agenda, this extreme-right party would go on in the early 2000s to become France's third-largest political force and to challenge for the presidency in 2002 with a level of support that shocked complacent pundits across the mainstream political spectrum. Both the far and moderate right exploited the events of September 11 in the 2002 elections, raising concerns about Muslim immigration and the case of "bogus" asylum seekers.[17] National-security issues thus provided a compelling focus for a longer-standing and highly racialized anti-immigrant platform. From the 1980s onward, restrictive immigration and citizenship policies were specifically targeted to win the support of voters drawn to the Front National cause. As France became increasingly exposed to European and global market forces, border policing against unwanted outsiders enabled a populist performance of sovereign defense of territory. Mainstream parties struggling to distinguish themselves in economic terms increasingly seized on immigration to display their "French" credentials. Criteria for gaining asylum were progressively tightened, as was access to citizenship, and restrictions were placed on family reunion and rights and services available to immigrants. Police powers to detain and deport on immigration grounds were also progressively extended. Of particular significance to the Sans-Papiers were laws introduced in the early 1990s by Minister of the Interior Charles Pasqua that resulted in the abolition of automatically renewable ten-year residency permits. Conditional one-year permits introduced in their place made many long-term foreign residents' situation uncertain, particularly so for those who had lost any claims to citizenship elsewhere. In many cases, migrants became irregular by default rather than by clandestine entrance to the country. Others saw their status suspended in temporal uncertainty, with the potential for irregularity in the immediate future.

Restrictions on the citizenship of children born in France to nonciti-zens led to instances of statelessness in some cases. Combined with a general reduction in avenues for licit migration, the Pasqua laws had the perverse effect of sending immigration underground and increas-ing the numbers of those with irregular status, many of whom were legally undeportable.[18]

Border policing as a performative practice finds its most recent mani-festation in the politics of Nicolas Sarkozy, both as minister of the in-terior and later as president. When campaigning for power, Sarkozy combined a neoliberal agenda to rescue France from its economic mal-aise with a rhetoric of sovereign protection from unwanted effects of globalization—read "immigration." Freely acknowledging his efforts to court the far-right vote, Sarkozy exploited the social crises in the *banli-eues* in order to depict immigration in general as a problem of law and order. Sarkozy determined to clean up the "scum" in the *banlieues* and issued an order to deport any foreigners found to be involved in the riots, regardless of their legal status. In his bid for the presidency and in a classic populist move, he presented himself as a strong "Bonapartist" leader willing to take a stand against criminal elements and to defend the French nation against the moral decay to which "inflicted" immi-gration (*immigration subie*), as he described it, had led.[19] He accordingly closed down previously existing avenues for long-term irregular mi-grants to be considered for regularization and dramatically expanded police powers and incentives to follow through on deportations.

The steady "illegalization" of both regular and irregular migrants is perhaps the most fundamental point of critique raised by the Sans-Papiers. They explicitly reject the language and image of illegality in favor of the language and image of entitlement. Hence, the term *illegal immigrant* (or *clandestin*), denoting illegitimacy by definition, is replaced by the term *sans-papiers*, a new identity that carries an assertion of le-gitimate presence hamstrung only by bureaucratic and procedural for-mality. This identity, precisely because of its association with the falli-bility of documents, highlights the legal construction of irregularity and therefore its potential to be changed. In the wake of the Pasqua laws, the Sans-Papiers acknowledged the irony of their situation: "Most of us entered France legally. We have been arbitrarily thrown into ille-gality both by the hardening of successive laws which enabled the authorities to stop renewing our permit to stay, and by restrictions introduced on the right to asylum which is now given only sparingly."[20]

"French legislation," argued one spokesperson for the first church occupations, "has created the very illegals it was supposed to be removing."[21] Via strategies reminiscent of "outing" in other identity-based politics, the Sans-Papiers challenge their ascribed illegal status by publicly identifying themselves in occupations and demonstrations as legitimately present despite the potential for seizure and sanction. Madjiguène Cissé, delegate for the Sans-Papiers' occupation of the Saint-Bernard Church in Paris in 1996, explains the political effect of this strategy:

> In France up till now our fate as immigrants was: either take part in the Republic's process of integration, or be deported like cattle. At the heart of this approach was the notion that we are "underground," which has a very strong negative charge. A person who is underground is someone who hides, who conceals himself, and if you conceal yourself it must be because after all you have something to hide. . . . We have made ourselves visible to say that we are here, to say that we are not in hiding but we're just human beings. We are here and we have been here a long time. We have been living and working in this country for many years and we pay our taxes. In the files of the Saint-Bernard people you will find wage slips, income tax declarations, old documents giving leave to stay. There are also passports and visas issued by the consulates of our countries of origin.
>
> At the beginning of our struggle, they tried to label us as people who are underground. But they couldn't: the authorities of this country have known us for a long time. Now we feel that we have taken a step forward: even the media no longer talks about people who are underground, but of Sans-Papiers. The fact that we've been seen on TV, that we've been interviewed in the press, I think that that has helped people to understand that we've been here for years, that we haven't killed anyone, and that we are simply demanding the piece of paper which is our right, so that we can live decent lives.[22]

This strategy rests not on a moral plea for special consideration. Such a gesture would reinscribe the authority of state agents to engage the Sans-Papiers as outsiders and to determine which among them is worthy of sovereign benevolence given and withdrawn at will. Rather, the Sans-Papiers demand that preexisting entitlements to reside in France be recognized. The claim that "we are here and have been for years," merely without papers, is a claim to belong in ways that exceed the formal allocation of citizenship and legal residence. It is a claim to the illegitimacy of the laws and discourses that define "illegality" itself.

In what terms do the Sans-Papiers justify the entitlements they claim? From the first church occupations, the Sans-Papiers have presented claims to freedom of movement, asylum, and other forms of legal residence in terms of rights. Calls have been made for the Sans-Papiers' rights to be observed according to obligations stemming from a variety of European and international treaties. In April 2005, for example, the Sans-Papiers occupied the Paris offices of the European Parliament and UNICEF in protest against the detention and deportation of children with irregular status as contraventions of the United Nations Convention on the Rights of the Child.[23] Although such strategies draw on the notion of universal human rights, they also appeal to a specifically French discourse. "We came to France," argue the Sans-Papiers, "because we had been told that France was the 'homeland of the Rights of Man.' "[24] Here they play with the history of France as the birthplace of modern citizenship and a nation forged through the very extension of rights that the Sans-Papiers now claim. They thus work with a tension between national and universal (citizen and human) articulations of rights. They insist accordingly that "the principles of humanity often proclaimed by the government [of France] be implemented."[25]

The Sans-Papiers express a complex relation to the French nation-state and multidimensional contestations of citizenship. On one hand, their claim to the rights that define the nation-state appear to reinforce the nation's boundaries as they stand, merely extended to include newly identified claimants. Yet the Sans-Papiers are also seeking something more transformative. Their claim is to be part of France but in terms that differ from a reified account of what and whom France consists. Tension ensues as the language of inclusion is deployed to reject the assimilatory framework that has heretofore framed the French immigration bargain—foreigners were accepted provided they assimilated to a common national project based on linguistic, secular, and republican principles.[26] The Sans-Papiers' demonstrations, occupations, and other publicity, in contrast, have been marked by a distinct cultural presence that includes foreign-language placards, music, dress, and performance. The Sans-Papiers thus insist on both cultural difference *and* belonging.

In this respect, their claims resonate with broader attempts to reinterpret republican ideals for a society increasingly characterized by cultural and religious diversity. There are clear connections, for example, with the head scarf affair that first came to public attention in 1989 when three Muslim girls were expelled from their school in Creil, to the north of Paris, for refusing to remove their head scarves. The school's head teacher considered the scarves to contravene the laws of *laïcité* that guaranteed the principle of secularism in public institutions. Yet when the case was taken to court, it was not the girls' actions that came into question; rather, the head teacher was accused of discrimination. When Muslim girls later defended their right to religious expression, they did so in public, draped in republican red, white, and blue while playing "The Marseillaise."[27] The initial decision to uphold their right to wear head scarves proved highly controversial. Despite its basis in the republican tradition, it seemed, for many, to capture the vulnerability of French national identity to threatening foreign influences and to resonate with broader anxieties about declining national sovereignty. Capitalizing on these sentiments and keen to be seen to be acting against radical forms of Islam, President Jacques Chirac introduced a ban in 2004 on conspicuous religious symbols in public schools. Although the ban applied to religious symbols of any kind, it clearly targeted the head scarf.[28]

The challenge represented by the head scarf affair, as by the Sans-Papiers, is an insistence that the republican project remain dynamic if it is to adhere to its original ideals. What distinguishes these struggles is the extent of the dynamism sought. In the head scarf affair, the republic is challenged to rectify the gap between formal and substantive citizenship such that formal citizenship necessarily implies substantive political equalities to cultural and religious minorities. In the case of the Sans-Papiers, an alternative subjectivity is mobilized—neither fully citizen nor fully noncitizen, neither fully French nor fully not French. The Sans-Papiers' struggle, in this way, pushes the symbolic parameters of citizenship itself, even though their ultimate ambition may be to acquire citizenship in its current form. This slow tension between change and continuity challenges us to be open to gradual transformations that do not sit easily with existing status categories.

On what basis do the Sans-Papiers claim to be part of the French nation-state? First, they draw on France's colonial history to make their case:

> Where do we come from, we *Sans-Papiers* of Saint-Bernard? It is a question we are often asked, and a pertinent one. We didn't immediately realize ourselves how relevant this question was. But, as soon as we tried to carry out a "site inspection", the answer was very illuminating: we are all from former French colonies. . . . So it's not an accident that we all find ourselves in France: our countries have had a relationship with France for centuries. . . . And of course, as soon as there is any question of leaving our country, most of the time in order to find work, it's natural that we turn to France. It's the country we know, the one whose language we have learned, whose culture we have integrated a little.[29]

Cissé goes on to insist that colonial relationships between France and the Sans-Papiers' countries of origin are integral to the forced migratory flows of the present. She argues that, as such, the Sans-Papiers' migration is part of the history of the French nation-state. Another delegate of the movement explains: "We are not in France by chance. Our background is in ancient colonies and our riches have been plundered by France as well as by other European countries. It is legitimate that we flee our drained countries and come here to look for our subsistence."[30]

Expressing a similar viewpoint, the slogan of thousands of irregular migrant workers striking in 2010 was "Colonised yesterday, exploited today, regularized tomorrow." These sentiments question whether the privilege attending national (French) citizenship can ever be divorced conceptually or materially from the exploitation of the labor, movement, territory, and identity of the state's colonial others. This critique provides an important historical perspective, expressing continuity between the Sans-Papiers and a range of constitutive outsiders who have at different times given shape to French identity while being denied recognition (the Caribbean slaves come to mind). The critique is more than a justification for the Sans-Papiers' presence. It ruptures the notion that the borders of France have *ever* been uncontested. From a theoretical perspective, it resonates implicitly with a radical critique of territorial space as the container of citizenship.[31] From this point of view, a territorial spatial frame narrows conceptions of citizenship to only those acts, identities, and institutions apparent on the inside of the border. Territorial borders, however, obscure the diverse social relations across time and space that are implicated in the privilege of the nation-state's insiders. Citizens and noncitizens, metropole and colony, rights-bearing subject and slave are not identities that emerge in isolation, but together, through political processes. What the Sans-Papiers highlight in their postcolonial critique is accordingly their own and others' thorough imbrication as colonial subjects and migrants in the past, present, and future of what it means to be French.

More specifically in regard to the present context, the Sans-Papiers point to the structural relationship between their labor and the French economy. In France, as in other liberalized economies of Europe and North America, increasingly competitive conditions and the rise of service industries have led to the growth of the informal economy. In some sectors, subcontracted employment arrangements allow the public face of business to be distanced from its dependence on informal labor, much of which is drawn from irregular migrants.[32] Employers' associations have lobbied to prevent effective sanctioning of employers who hire illegally and to shift punitive consequences onto the employee. Commentators suggest that this arrangement amounts to official acquiescence to the informal market because it does not reverse the incentive to hire informally and exacerbates the exploitability of migrant workers.[33] Acknowledging this situation, the Sans-Papiers argue that they are economically integrated into the French community regardless of the absence of formal recognition: "We pay our taxes, our rent, our bills and our social security contributions—when we are allowed regular employment! When we are not unemployed or in casual employment, we work hard in the rag trade, the leather trade, the construction industry, catering, cleaning. . . . We face working conditions employers impose on us which you can refuse more easily than we can, because being without papers makes us without rights. We know this suits plenty of people. We produce wealth, and we enrich France with our diversity."[34]

The choice of venue for a 2005 occupation, the headquarters of the French Federation of Construction, reflects the Sans-Papiers' role in filling labor shortages in key industries as well as the embedded relationship between the formal and informal economies. Since 2008, the Sans-Papiers have undertaken waves of strikes and occupations of their own places of work as well as of agencies that benefit indirectly from their labor, including tax offices and employer associations. In 2010, following the example of undocumented migrants in the United States in 2006, they organized a "day without immigrants." On March 1, Sans-Papiers and immigrants in general were encouraged not to go to work and not to engage in consumption as a show of their market force. Such actions have prompted at least some union officials to rethink the potential for building solidarity between citizen and migrant workers.[35] The Sans-Papiers have long highlighted the connections between their exploitation and that of other French workers. Cissé had spoken a decade earlier of a "shared social fate" in this respect.[36] In a neoliberal environment in which market value increasingly determines the validity of one's social contribution, the Sans-Papiers' claims *as workers* provide a powerful form of leverage and a legitimizing image that directly contradicts the right-wing assault on migrants in general as antisocial lawbreakers. This new image is a problem for an administration that has built much of its success on scapegoating migrants for any number of social upheavals. As commentary in the left-wing *L'Humanite* observed, "The clandestine workers, in coming out of hiding, appear for what they are: wage-earners like any others, who participate in the social and economic life of the country. The Minister [for Immigration and Citizenship] wants to avoid at all costs that recent growing awareness, as that would make the strategy of the foreigner, made the scapegoat of the social sufferings engendered by the policy-making of the right wing majority, seem out of date."[37]

This issue of worker status raises other complex dilemmas for the Sans-Papiers and accounts for what seems an unlikely choice of venue, the General Confederation of Labor, for the occupation mentioned at the beginning of this chapter. In response to the workplace strikes that

corresponded with this occupation, the Paris Prefecture agreed to negotiate regularizations for those Sans-Papiers with current employment
contracts represented by the confederation. The government conceded
more generally that case-by-case regularizations would be considered
for those Sans-Papiers with employment in industries with specified
labor shortages. Thus, the Sans-Papiers' market value is proving to be
an effective path to regularization. However, the Sans-Papiers occupied
the union hall in part because they were not prepared to let the claim
to regularization rest on worker status alone. A statement on their Web
site, devoted to documenting the occupation, explains, "The unions
wanted to treat all of our files within the framework of work, but this is
not applicable for all the occupiers of the Center of the Unions: there
are also . . . [t]hose that do not work, like the housewives, the children,
the old, the sick ones."[38] The Sans-Papiers also object to the government's unwillingness to deal with them directly. Direct communication is of crucial symbolic value to the Sans-Papiers' status. To sit at the
table with the government is to be recognized as having a worthy case
to make—precisely what Cissé earlier intended by her description of
migrants coming out from underground. It is also to keep control over
the terms of negotiation. Precisely because of the union's intermediary
role, negotiations have been fixed around the issue of work. In line
with its raison d'être, the General Confederation of Labor refused to
represent Sans-Papiers who were not workers and members.

The Sans-Papiers are playing out a strategic and normative tension
between the leverage obtained through worker status and the further
reinforcement of the very market values that contribute to their exploitation. As I show in chapter 5, this tension is also increasingly visible
in the strategic options faced by irregular migrants in the United States.
The case in France is complicated by the Sans-Papiers' identification of
their struggle as the extreme end of a more general opposition to "neoliberal capitalism" as the market ideology that manifests in both the
structural adjustment of their countries of origin, prompting migration
flows, and the "pauperization and casualization" of workers in industrialized countries.[39] They are able to frame their case against market ideology within a French national context, in which opposition to neoliberalism has been far stronger than in English-speaking countries. Here again,
the Sans-Papiers field a tension between national and transnational

dimensions of the politicoeconomic cleavages that have shaped their struggle and negotiate the strategic options open to them to meet their urgent need for security of status. By accepting regularization in terms that reflect the neoliberal rationality that governs migration management in general and border policing in particular, the Sans-Papiers become implicated in the reproduction of borders in those very terms and thus in the closure of borders to future Sans-Papiers who cannot demonstrate their labor-market value.

Perhaps on account of this dilemma, some Sans-Papiers are staking their claims as more radical contestations of citizenship framed within an unmistakably transnational milieu. Consider, for example, the text of an open letter, "To Our Sisters and Brothers in Africa: A Common Struggle for the Freedom of Movement and the Right to Stay," published in 2007 in a newsletter distributed by the NoBorders Network, which aims to foster transnational linkages between migrant struggles within and beyond Europe. The letter is endorsed by individual Sans-Papiers based in Italy and France and by migrant organizations in Greece. The first thing to notice in it, in comparison with earlier statements, is a shift in the discursive framing of the impetus for migration:

> When we, migrants, have chosen to leave Africa, we did so as free women and men. Some used to say that we are victims of hunger, wars, poverty, that we were forced to escape. It is often true. But we always decided to move because we had and we have a project, we want a possibility, we want to keep our future in our hands. When we have chosen to migrate we wanted to free ourselves from those who pretend that some are rich and the others poor, some European, the others African, to free ourselves from a system of exploitation which has no borders, while it builds up borders and wars in order to exploit our needs and our projects, in Africa as well as in Europe.[40]

At least in this rhetorical exercise, the Sans-Papiers are not seeking recognition within the scope of existing categories—as asylum seekers or otherwise forced migrants. Nor are they justifying themselves as partners in specific national projects. Rather, their starting point is recognition as active agents in their own political futures, both at the point of

choosing to migrate and within the context of their migration destination. They express a new kind of subjectivity that moves beyond the
message of being "Sans-Papiers" to question the source of authority
provided in the form of papers. These papers are documents that, for
better or worse, continue to determine freedoms through the prism of
bounded national communities. "We do not want to be victims," the
authors declare, "we want to be protagonists, and the space of our freedom, today, is the space of our common struggle!" They assert the right
to move through what they consider to be artificial borders that mark
neither the genuine fault lines of contemporary social antagonisms nor
legitimate boundaries of political belonging. They identify the European border as the common site of struggle and call for a specifically
transnational "movement of migration."[41]

This letter is filled with rhetoric largely aligned with the "autonomy
of migration" ethos championed by Hardt and Negri. Yet it should not
be taken as evidence of a growing global "multitude." This letter represents only its authors' views and is not at all indicative of the future direction of the Sans-Papiers' struggle. I use it to close this section merely
as a reference to the diversity of claims emerging in the context of
contemporary European border policing and to highlight an example
that shifts the discursive terrain. Studies of citizenship that wish to address the farthest frontiers of the political may do well to think through
the implications of these kinds of more radical claims, even if they are
asserted only at the level of rhetoric. It seems to me that the authors of
this letter are somehow engaging with novel forms of subject formation that have the potential to multiply and diversify or to coalesce
into identities that fuel strategic ambitions. Either way, such subjectivities engage a spatial terrain that challenges the boundaries of citizenship. They emerge at the crossroads of a system of borders both increasingly fragile and strong.

EMERGENT POSSIBILITIES FOR POLITICAL BELONGING

The Sans-Papiers' struggle shows no signs of resolution in the short or
medium term. As the informal economy grows and as compelling reasons for migration persist, there is every likelihood that the Sans-Papiers

will continue to raise diverse political claims against French and European political communities. However, border policing against irregular migrants remains a powerful political buffer against the upheavals and anxieties of contemporary France and Europe. Thus, minor wins for the Sans-Papiers are likely to go hand in hand with setbacks and complications both in terms of material security and in terms of developing more radical contestations. This pattern is already evident. The church occupations in the mid-1990s were brought to an end when riot police evicted the Sans-Papiers, using axes to break down the doors. However, televised footage of the evictions proved a public-relations disaster for the border-policing state, contributing to a wave of public sympathy for the plight of the Sans-Papiers and some relaxation of restrictions affecting them in the late 1990s.[42] The regularizations of status that followed were in turn far from the blanket ones that the Sans-Papiers had demanded. On the contrary, the criteria set were seen to heighten the vulnerability and criminalization of some sixty-three thousand migrants whose applications for regularization were rejected. Having revealed their whereabouts to the authorities, they were now confronted with the choice of either being deported or going into hiding.[43]

Sarkozy's rise to power a decade later has again seen the intensification of border policing as a key site of governmental activity. Sarkozy introduced annual quotas for deportation as a measure of border-policing success, and via France's temporary presidency of the European Council in 2008 he pushed a hard-line stance against irregular migration at the European level.[44] He successfully garnered the council's support for the detention of "illegal" noncitizens without charge for up to eighteen months, for instance. Yet these moves remain controversial in public and policy circles. Both the United Nations Human Rights Committee and the European Council human rights commissioner have been critical of the French approach.[45] As Sarkozy proceeds with a populist assault on irregular migrants, thousands of people have formed an informal sanctuary network for those facing deportation, aligning their cause with that of the wartime French resistance that hid Jewish refugees. The Education Without Borders Network works with education union members to mobilize teachers, students, and staff of shipping companies to strike in cases of scheduled deportations of children attending French schools or of their parents.[46] Such alliances have provided crucial support for recent strike action. Yet broader support among the French Left is often fraught with tensions over solidarity, leadership, and strategy—hence, the occupation of the General Confederation of Labor union hall. In the end, the Sans-Papiers were forcibly removed from the hall, and concessions won by the protest action once again fell far short of the goals originally set. The government agreed to reexamine only three hundred of more than one thousand applications for regularization in question.[47]

Different assessments of the Sans-Papiers reflect a greater or lesser emphasis on the transformative power of their claims. On one hand, it seems that their success in achieving limited regularizations has had little disruptive impact on prevailing forms of citizenship. Any concessions won on account of occupations, demonstrations, strikes, and other publicity have not been granted on the basis of existing entitlements, but rather on the basis of the state's discretionary powers to include and exclude according to market criteria. From this perspective, the Sans-Papiers have worked to expand existing boundaries to approved outsiders rather than to present a challenge to the boundaries themselves. Their activism works to contest citizenship in only the most elementary way, and its results have reinforced new neoliberal hierarchies of status and mobility. Thus, for Miriam Ticktin, the reinscription of sovereign authority is the paramount effect of the Sans-Papiers' struggle.[48] This sovereign power is reformulated at the intersection of the territorial state and its neoliberal imperatives, leaving vulnerable those marginalized by both a transnational political economy and a reinvigorated discourse of national citizenship. Far from revealing the decline of the state in the context of globalization, the dynamics of irregular migration reveal instead the strength of its grasp on the levers of cross-border flows of both capital and labor.

For Etienne Balibar, by contrast, there is a transformative quality to the Sans-Papiers' movement. By asserting their legitimate presence and exposing their centrality to the community that excludes them, Balibar contends, the Sans-Papiers remind us that legality and illegality are contestable performances of the state. He points out that the San-Papiers' resistance to official but arbitrary boundary inscriptions strengthens the life of democracy at great personal costs—costs as high as deportation and endangered life. For Balibar, therefore, the wider political community owes the Sans-Papiers a great debt for the reinvigoration of citizenship "in as much as it is not an institution or a statute but a collective practice."[49] This second sense of contestation—questioning the meaning of citizenship through reflection on the nature of political community more generally, is an aim and effect of struggle to expand the republican project and is acknowledged directly by the Sans-Papiers themselves: "We can see the results today. . . . Little by little masses of people have understood that our struggle was raising questions which go beyond the regularization of the *Sans-Papiers*. New questions have gradually emerged: 'Do you agree to live in a France where fundamental human rights are trampled on? Do you agree to live in a France where democratic liberties are not respected?'"[50]

As this statement confirms, so much of the Sans-Papiers' activism is shaped by a discourse that reinvigorates the spatial framing of citizenship within the nation-state. However, I want to suggest that there is also a third sense of contestation at work—one that undermines, in slow, subtle, and incomplete ways, the legitimacy of citizenship itself and raises the possibility that political life might be ordered according to other frames of reference. Balibar brings us closer to this third sense of contestation when he points to the Sans-Papiers' "contribution to the birth of a political 'subjectivity' with respect to globalization."[51] He contends that their struggle goes beyond the right to mobility and the right to residence and into the realm of creating new modes of being in political relation to others with respect to the specific and novel conditions of contemporary global capitalism. That he uses the term *contribution* is significant in that it gives us the sense that this process of subject formation is an unfinished task and one whose scope we cannot predict nor yet fully comprehend. When the Sans-Papiers argue that European laws make certain migrants "illegal" and pit citizen and migrant against each other in competitive labor markets, they acknowledge the arbitrariness of prevailing identity categories.[52] They also challenge us to think outside those categories. Might their actions suggest an alternative "common sense" about moral and political connectedness across space and time that defies—indeed, renders ridiculous—the legitimacy of borders in their present form and even of citizenship itself, at least insofar as it remains attached to a territorial frame?

We do not necessarily have to choose between different acts of contestation, either in attempting to interpret the significance of the Sans-Papiers or in assessing strategic options for their struggle. Such a choice buys into the notion that the possibilities open for political belonging are limited either to citizenship as we know it or to its complete eradication. There are few empirical or theoretical cases to support the likelihood of either option. Rather, this spectrum of contestations reflects the broader transformations apparent in the space through which we perceive our social relations and the consequent overlapping of multiple frames of reference. In this context, the Sans-Papiers, as much as the states that police them, are implicated in the generation of new spaces and subjects of struggle. As we grapple to comprehend emergent possibilities for political belonging, there are advantages to keeping this multidimensional spatial field in mind. This field enables us to acknowledge the transformative potential of the Sans-Papiers' struggle without discounting the powerful reassertion of state sovereignty with respect to irregular migration. It allows us not only to see the ontological shifts emerging in political communities as irregular migrants become increasingly visible within them, but also to remain alert to the systematic ways in which their exclusion from those communities is sustained. In addition, it prevents us from drawing too stark a division between irregular migrants and citizens because the fault lines of political belonging no longer correspond exclusively to this territorialized dichotomy.

5 / FROM CITY TO CITIZEN

Modes of Belonging in the United States

An excerpt from Alan Weisman's *La Frontera* captures a moment on the U.S.–Mexico border some twenty-five years ago:

> Alan Eliason, the tall, ruddy chief of the San Diego sector of the Border Patrol, has spent the morning reading a study just released by the Rand Corporation, which concludes that Mexican immigration does not pose a crisis for California. Rather it states that the influx has "provided strong economic benefits" and that the undocumented immigrants' "use of public services is not generally a problem."
>
> Eliason has heard this before. He has also heard the scholarly theories that most aliens prefer to be in their own country and intend to return there after working a while. He doesn't buy it. He tosses the report on his desk. Resignation and contempt commingling in his voice, he tells . . . the two agents sitting in his office, that "we are no longer determining the composition of U.S. society. It is determined for us by alien smugglers and people in remote villages all over the world."
>
> Eliason has been at this thirty years. . . . His first decade made sense: apprehend aliens, send them back. In 1965, they caught 6,500 in San Diego. It seemed a reasonable figure.
>
> In 1985, they caught 427,000. In twenty years, the problem they were supposed to be controlling was sixty-six times worse. "How long," Eliason asks, "can we let this unmitigated disaster go on? The strength of the United States is a viable middle class. What's developing here is a poor class living outside society, a subculture of illegal status."[1]

As chief of the San Diego Border Patrol, Alan Eliason sat literally on a fault line of political community, attempting to control the flow of migration into California. In the decades since Eliason began his work on the border, irregular migration has remained a prominent and controversial feature of the U.S. political landscape. What seemed to Eliason in 1965 to be a straightforward proposition—that apprehended aliens could be effectively returned to the place where they belonged—had by 1985 become a far more challenging exercise. More than two and a half decades on, the challenges remain as great as ever. According to the Department of Homeland Security, the number of immigrants living in the United States without authorization increased by 27 percent between 2000 and 2009, bringing the total number of irregular migrants close to eleven million.[2] This increase occurred despite the dramatic upscaling of border-policing agencies, budgets, operations, and technologies during the 1990s and over the course of this period. A ten-foot-high steel wall along much (but not all) of the U.S.–Mexico border separates would-be migrants from their desired destination. Congress has mandated 670 miles of secure border fencing, most of which was completed by 2010. Yet this initiative has merely shifted illicit border crossings to ever more remote locations. The result has been not only an increase in the number of border crossers who die in the desert, but also a *reduction* in the probability of apprehension at the point of border crossing.[3] This apparent policy failure in fact reflects parallel dimensions of a neoliberal rationality at the heart of immigration control—a logic that sustains a flexible workforce through techniques of illegalization, securitization and vulnerability to deportation. Thus, irregular migrants are policed in performative but disingenuous displays of sovereign territorial integrity while they are simultaneously integrated into the U.S. and global economy as expendable sources of labor.

Observing border dynamics in the mid-1980s, Eliason recognized that irregular migration was changing the constitution of U.S. society. At that time, he identified an underclass "living outside society" as a threat to the stability of a middle class way of life. Others writing subsequently reinforced this theme and raised the specter of alien cultural enclaves developing in isolation from mainstream America. Thus, Victor Hanson berated the transformation of California into "Mexifornia," and Samuel Huntington warned of the "hispanic challenge" that threatened the very life blood of a civilization built on Anglo-Protestant values.[4] For these commentators, the issue was not only the undesirability of Hispanic ways of life, but the dangers of cultural and linguistic bifurcation. A society divided along Spanish/English lines would be unable, so Huntington contended, to find the common civic ground needed to pursue the causes of a great nation. The problem, for Huntington, however, was not so much that Hispanic migrants were "living outside society," but that they were present at its very core. His anxiety related, implicitly, to shifting grounds of citizenship—the potential for migrants, irregular migrants in particular, to challenge traditional notions of who a citizen is and what a citizen does. At present, irregular migrants constitute a considerable numerical, cultural, and economic presence—some 4 percent of the U.S. population and more than 5 percent of its workforce.[5] They are, in addition, finding ways to participate in the nation's civic life. As a consequence and as Eliason anticipated—albeit with a certain foreboding—a dynamic edge between here and there, us and them, belonging and not belonging is transforming the contours of citizenship. For many, including Huntington, this state of affairs is deeply threatening, calling into question the privileges long regarded as the natural preserve of certain kinds of citizens and rendering unworkable the allocation of resources according to territorial limits. Eliason's concerns thus speak to enduring antagonisms that shape contemporary struggles to defend and contest an ideal of U.S. citizenship and territorial integrity.

In this chapter, I investigate this frontier of the political on the border zones of U.S. citizenship. I reflect, in particular, on the mass mobilization of irregular migrants in 2006 when millions of people took to the streets in cities across the country, seeking recognition for undocumented people and pathways to citizenship. Through an analysis of the rhetoric and performative dimension of this mobilization, the discussion is linked to the theoretical framework for acts of contestation developed in chapter 4. I show how the terms in which irregular migrants stake their claims to belong reflect different levels of contestation, from those that seek to extend to approved outsiders the limits of citizenship as they stand to those that rupture the conceptual vocabulary that shapes our understanding of political belonging in general.

In addition, I reflect on the spatial dimension of the political that emerges in and through the struggles of irregular migrants. I investigate the divergence in policy, policing, and activist milieus across different spatial scales and levels of government. I compare the different approaches of local (city and state) authorities that are increasingly taking the matter of irregular migration into their own hands—whether in punitive or progressive terms. The results, I contend, are shifting grounds of status and expressions of political belonging that depend very much on the specifics of the place in question. An analytical approach that is attentive to this kind of spatial variation offers unique insights into contemporary dynamics of citizenship. I therefore highlight a number of place-specific examples (from labor organizing to student networks) whereby irregular migrants are becoming politically active and claiming certain rights. I suggest that in the process of this activism a mode of belonging is enacted that challenges the limits of citizenship in its conventional territorial form. The chapter as a whole attempts to identify signs of an alternative "common sense" around citizenship and political belonging emerging in the U.S. context.

U.S. BORDER CONTROL AS A FRONTIER OF THE POLITICAL

In public discourse on the current state of U.S. border control, it is not uncommon to hear reference to a "broken immigration system."[6] The "broken" narrative arises on account of the perception that demand for irregular migrant labor works in opposition to border-policing initiatives. In fact, the two complement each other with a certain degree of logic that reflects the current phase of global capitalism and the corresponding strategies of the globalizing state. Hundreds of thousands of people are compelled every year to seek a better life in the United States despite the risks of illicit border crossings and unauthorized residence. The effects of neoliberal restructuring, intensified under NAFTA, have impacted significantly on Mexican migration in particular (Mexicans account for some 62 percent of the total population of irregular migrants in the United States).[7] In Mexico since the 1980s, the privatization of collective farms and the removal of agricultural subsidies have

led to widespread displacement of rural populations and the entrench-
ment of a culture of migrating north as one of the few realistic options
for work. Remittances sent home by Mexicans abroad amounted to more
than twenty-six billion U.S. dollars in 2008 and are a crucial element
in family, community, and government strategies for economic development.[8] Within the United States, there is widespread demand for the
informal labor that irregular migrants provide. Irregular migrants represent 14 percent of construction industry workers, 13 percent of agricultural workers, and 10 percent of the leisure and hospitality sector
(including 23 percent of those in private household employment).[9] Under these conditions, calls for mass deportations are not only logisti-
cally impossible but also economically infeasible for both migrant-
sending and receiving states. Irregular migrants thus remain subject
to all the exploitation and marginalization that goes with informal
labor, but their structural place in the U.S. economy remains formally
unacknowledged.

The place of irregular migrant labor in the everyday working economy is acknowledged in other quarters, however. This kind of recognition is exactly what made an audience laugh at a joke delivered by Paul
Rodriquez in a stand-up routine on the day of the largest migrant demonstrations in 2006: "I'm for building a wall at the border. . . . But I'm
concerned because who's going to build it? The last white guy in construction was in the Village People."[10] The joke is funny precisely because it ridicules efforts to police the border as being out of step with
labor-market demand. As I argued in chapter 2, the promotion of free-
market values under the rubric of globalization has in the United States,
as elsewhere, prompted reactionary calls for territorial closure. In this
context, irregular migrants have become visible symbols of an outside
world encroaching on a vulnerable inside and scapegoats for a range of
anxieties about external forces that appear to defy sovereign control.
Hence, over the same period that the Clinton and George W. Bush administrations advanced a neoliberal agenda to open borders to trade
and financial flows, they also pursued a series of initiatives to demonstrate the political will to close those borders to certain kinds of people.
The past two decades have seen massive injections of funding, infrastructure, and personnel into border policing in all its forms—from the surveillance and militarization of land and sea borders to the development

of sophisticated data-tracking technologies and strategic coordination of immigration enforcement across multiple agencies as well as source and transit countries.[11] Yet the number of irregular migrants continues to grow. Efforts to police their employment have been token at best, despite recent efforts to introduce an e-verification strategy for identifying fraudulent Social Security numbers.[12]

U.S. border policing can thus be understood as a two-pronged strategy of the neoliberal state, designed on one hand to address legitimacy problems that arise on account of global market exposure and on the other to render migrant workers available and amenable to ever more "flexible" conditions. Since the 1970s, the U.S.–Mexico border zone has become the site of heightened governmental activity in terms of both material policing and discursive representation of an "out of control" divide.[13] The characterization of migration flows across the border zone as a weakness in sovereign defense belies the extent to which Mexican labor has long been part of the U.S. nation-building experience, whether in temporary, permanent, official, or informal capacities. The effect of increased border policing is not so much to counter this trend, but to change the status of migrant workers to "illegal immigrants" and to intensify the surveillance to which they are subject. Illegalization has more recently combined with securitization as strategies of neoliberal governance. Since 2003, the agencies responsible for border security and immigration control have been incorporated into the broader apparatus of the U.S. Department of Homeland Security. This shift has helped to justify vast increases in spending on border control and the militarization of the task. Efforts to target dangerous criminal aliens— those who pose violent threats to U.S. citizens—have resulted in the criminalization of irregular migrants in general and a massive diversion of resources toward largely political displays of making the homeland secure.

These patterns are increasingly obvious in the operational strategies of U.S. Immigration and Customs Enforcement (ICE). In 2008, the agency made headlines by raiding a meat-processing plant in Iowa and an electrical equipment factory in Mississippi where irregular migrants worked. In place of administrative violations, irregular employees were now charged with identity theft—a criminal offense that rests on the use of fake Social Security numbers. Despite dubious legal grounds for the charges (later successfully contested before the U.S. Supreme Court), most of those charged were compelled to accept plea bargains and prompt deportations in order to avoid lengthy periods in prison awaiting trial.[14] Since 2005, under Operation Streamline, federal agencies have targeted immigrants in southern states with criminal prosecution for unauthorized entry. Between 2006 and 2007, ICE quadrupled the number of its "Fugitive Operations Teams . . . dedicated to identifying, locating and arresting fugitive aliens."[15] "Fugitive aliens," previously referred to as "absconders" (the change in language is indicative of a culture of securitization), are those who have failed to abide by an order to leave the country or who have failed to report to immigration authorities as required. Fugitive Operations Teams were mandated to target dangerous fugitives. However, a quota system for arrests introduced in 2003 and increased in 2006 has driven agents to "apprehend . . . the easiest targets, not the most dangerous fugitives." As revealed in a damning report on the agency's failure to meet its own goals, some 73 percent of irregular migrants apprehended by the teams had no criminal conviction, and the proportion of those arrested who were not even fugitive, under the agency's definition, rose to 40 percent in 2007.[16] This conflation of administrative offenses with national-security risks allows ICE to represent its misdirected energies as "extraordinary results in its homeland security mission to ensure a safer, more secure America." The agency thus reported "an unparalleled record of success in the . . . fiscal year [2007]," and in this way irregular migrants became implicated in misleading statistical wins in the war on terror.[17]

The move toward criminalization was directly encouraged in 2005 when the House of Representatives passed the Sensenbrenner bill and sought to make it a felony to be, to hire, or to harbor an undocumented noncitizen.[18] The devastating impact that this bill would have had— not only on irregular migrants, but also on their families, employers, and supporting communities—prompted some of the largest demonstrations in U.S. history in the spring of 2006. Between three and five million irregular migrants and their supporters in more than 150 cities throughout the United States mobilized against the passage of the bill and in support of progressive reform. The largest rallies were held in Los Angeles and Chicago, each attracting more than five hundred thousand people, and Dallas, Washington, New York, Phoenix, and San Jose drew crowds of between one hundred thousand and five hundred thousand. Los Angeles saw the largest student strike in U.S. history with some forty thousand students joining the demonstrations.[19]

Unlikely allies have emerged in support of immigration reforms that include a large-scale legalization process. Conservative business lobbies are keen to free up flows of cheap and willing labor via conditional guest-worker schemes; city councils, police foundations, and local employers know that raiding workplaces and arresting workers does little for the local economy, compromises hard-won law enforcement gains achieved through community policing initiatives, and threatens to alienate large sections of the increasingly Latino voting public.[20] The issue has sharply divided conservative politicians. Traditionally tied to highly restrictionist policies, some Republican Congress members have sided with business lobbies, acknowledging the infeasibility of mass deportations, the demand for migrant labor, and the need for guest-worker programs. As a consequence, Republicans have also been key sponsors of more progressive reform bills. In mid-May 2006, President Bush released a comprehensive immigration-reform proposal. The proposal included a substantial reinvestment in border control but also advocated guest-worker programs in areas of labor shortage as well as qualified routes to citizenship for irregular migrants, dependent on time in country, payment of substantial fees and taxes, and English-language acquisition. In late May, the Senate approved a more moderate version of Bush's proposal.[21] However, the legislation that finally passed through both houses of Congress was a purely restrictionist package that abandoned pathways to citizenship altogether and failed to address demand for irregular migrant labor.[22] Following the 2006 demonstrations, ongoing tensions between labor-market imperatives and domestic pressure for border control led to a congressional stalemate on reform. The Obama administration likewise postponed a promised overhaul of the immigration system in its first year of office in view of significant opposition.

The promise of legalization creates an important temporal dimension to neoliberal strategies, dampening dissent by irregular migrants in their workplaces and on the streets by offering a view of future pathways to citizenship that will rest on demonstrations of hard work, remorse, and good character. Recent reform proposals endorsed by Barack

Obama include such provisions, combining conditional legalization for those already present with upscaled border policing against future flows and absconders.[23] The trend is toward easing restrictions on high-skilled professional migrants and limiting access for low-skilled workers to temporary guest-worker schemes that are tied directly to specific labor-market shortages. In the end, for critics of such schemes, low-wage workers remain vulnerable to exploitation on account of the essentially indentured conditions attached to guest-worker programs and the lack of recourse to effective rights protections.[24] For Nicholas De Genova, both illegalization and legalization are equally techniques of migration management designed to facilitate the flow of labor as an object for capital. The choice of strategy depends on the balance between neoliberal imperatives to attract transnational labor and render it ever more flexible, on the one hand, and the performative sovereign practices required to restore the impression of territorial integrity, on the other. "The two phenomena," he explains, "must therefore be understood to be complementary, rather than paradoxically opposed. The more that the figure of the 'illegal alien' can be conjured as the sign of a crisis of national security, so much the more are guestworker proposals promoted. They are presented as a congenial panacea that satisfies U.S. employers' deeply entrenched historical dependency on, and enduring demand for, the abundant availability of legally vulnerable and ever-disposable (deportable) migrant labour, while simultaneously pandering to the pervasive rhetoric of 'securing' borders."[25]

From this perspective, the point of transition from "illegal" to "legal" migrant holds no guarantee of escape from precarious working conditions and an insecure future. Legality and illegality are merely statuses deployed as strategies of governance that mask broader hierarchies of mobility and labor that determine access to many substantive rights. This is not to say that legalization makes no difference. Ease of daily life is profoundly related to the piece of paper that justifies presence in the United States through conventional means. The point is, rather, to recognize the limits of legalization as a critical response to the neoliberal rationality that governs migration control, not least on account of the unresolved issue of future irregular flows and a likely new underclass of hyperillegalized migrant. It is also conversely to highlight the critical potential of mobilizations where irregular migrants generate counternarratives that legitimize their presence *in spite* of their "illegal-ity." Such performative acts that reinvent subject status and assert po-litical belonging destabilize the identity-crafting tools of neoliberal governance.

In this respect, the mobilizations of 2006 were significant as dem-onstrations of irregular migrants and their allies' political force. The marches were organized by coalitions of Latino civil society organiza-tions, worker centers, and church groups and were promoted by an ex-tensive Spanish-speaking media. As such, they obtained credibility as "grassroots" phenomena and, according to commentators at the *Wash-ington Post*, had a "bottom-up, organic quality that often surprised or-ganizers and opponents alike."[26] A national survey conducted among Latinos in the wake of the demonstrations revealed that more than two-thirds considered the events to be the beginning of a new social move-ment that would continue for a long time.[27] Irregular migrants, it seemed, were poised to make their place publicly felt, not only as an economic and cultural presence, but as makers, shapers, and inheritors of a broader civic sphere. Irregular migrants self-identified their cause as a struggle for rights and recognition in the tradition of U.S. democracy, and commen-tators likewise drew comparisons with the American civil rights move-ment.[28] As a crystallization of the frustrations and energies of an emerg-ing social force, this mobilization is important for what it reveals about the spectrum of contestations being made of U.S. citizenship. In the previous chapter, acts of contestation were theorized on three different levels: first, in terms of the extension of formal legal status to approved outsiders; second, in terms of a challenge to the national, racial, gen-dered, or other meanings given to citizenship; and, third, in terms of a rupture to the very conceptual vocabulary that limits our understanding of political belonging more generally. As I show in the next section, all three levels of contestation are present in the U.S. context.

"WE DECIDED NOT TO BE INVISIBLE ANYMORE":
THE 2006 DEMONSTRATIONS

In strategies similar to those employed by the Sans-Papiers of France, irregular migrants in the United States asserted an open display of collective confidence in spring 2006: "Yes, we can!" was the rallying cry. They publicly identified themselves in rallies across the country and counteracted the potential for seizure and sanction through overwhelming strength of numbers. This visceral assertion of legitimate presence challenged the terms of reference through which impressions of irregular migrants are shaped. No longer avoiding scrutiny or pleading their case from a position of little leverage, irregular migrants now *demanded* recognition of their social and economic contribution to the communities in which they live and work. "We decided not to be invisible anymore," read one placard. "We are not criminals. . . . We are workers and we deserve respect," read another.[29] Irregular migrants rejected the criminalization of their status and positioned themselves as parties to debate—as shapers rather than subjects of policy.

The case for reform made by irregular migrants was based overwhelmingly on their integration into the U.S. labor market. Demonstration placards simply posed the question: "Who will pick your fields and build your houses?"[30] Demonstrations on May 1 (International Workers' Day or May Day)) were timed to coincide with a nationwide boycott of business, or Day Without Immigrants. The boycott was intended to demonstrate not only the extent to which U.S. businesses rely on irregular migrant labor but also the collective power of migrants as consumers. Irregular migrants and their supporters were asked to stay home from work and school and not to buy anything on that day. Certain business districts of Los Angeles and other cities were rendered entirely inactive.[31]

In his analysis of the mobilizations, Leo Chavez points out that despite exaggerated claims from opponents about the anarchic nature of the protests, the rallies were generally calm and orderly and based on the good character of irregular migrants as workers.[32] For Chavez, this strategy plays directly into the mutation of citizenship into neoliberal forms. In a context where one's civic value is increasingly determined by entrepreneurial capacity, irregular migrants presented themselves as ideal would-be citizens. Chavez draws on Aihwa Ong's Foucauldian approach to the neoliberal subject as the basis for this interpretation. For Ong, neoliberal subjects internalize market values not only in terms of adapting their labor to fit with market demands, but also and more crucially in terms of cultivating a notion of the self.[33] Entrepreneurialism and self-management accordingly become the driving force of the neoliberal subject in all aspects of social life. The neoliberal subject approaches citizenship less in terms of a reciprocal and collective contract with the state and more in terms of an individualized problem-solving attitude brought to bear on market-induced conditions. Neoliberal citizenship thus has less to do with nation-state membership and more to do with flexibility and adaptability within a global political economy. Hence, Chavez contends that "during the marches, immigrants reassured the public of their internalized self-monitoring and their self-engineering; they emphasized their embodiment of the type of workers required in today's competitive labor market. They presented themselves as neoliberal citizens, asserting their positive economic contribution to society despite a lack of government support and often vociferous anti-immigrant sentiment."[34]

Chavez identifies an important tactic employed in the demonstrations. Irregular migrants were clearly taking advantage of their significant economic leverage in ways that resonate with the virtue and status accorded to the neoliberal citizen. We can see the motivation for this strategy in the rhetoric attached to reform proposals that followed the demonstrations. President Bush justified his proposal via references to the proud tradition of the "melting pot" and a pioneering work ethic.[35] This rhetoric serves both to appease populist critics by reference to traditional American values and to establish the suitability of industrious migrant workers for a role in the flexible U.S. economy. Insofar as irregular migrants are recognized as entrepreneurial workers rather than as persons with broader fundamental rights, the reforms represent the slow and select admission of approved outsiders in line with neoliberal prerogatives. In this respect, Bush's plans for immigrant workers were tellingly tied to reductions in family migration schemes that offered less obvious market value.

Although Chavez highlights an important dimension of contemporary citizenship dynamics at work in the demonstrations, he does not tell the whole story. His account underplays the extent to which irregular migrants' contestations reinforce or modify conventional links between citizen, state, nation, and territory while simultaneously registering new modes of political belonging. To reduce the events of spring 2006 to an expression of neoliberal citizenship fails to acknowledge the complexity and multidimensionality of the claims and contestations being made.

Much of the rhetoric surrounding the demonstrations argued the case for progressive reform in terms that appealed to traditional narratives of nationhood. As one demonstrator observed, invoking the notion of a land of opportunity: "We are here today, because America represents hope. I know you have to control this country but you have to respect people as well. People just want to be free."[36] At the same time, however, these traditional narratives were also disrupted by the prominence of the Spanish language and Latino culture. Demonstrations were marked by placards, songs, and chants in Spanish and the waving of various homeland flags alongside the U.S. flag. These symbols express a powerful message that recognition as full political subjects is not dependent on cultural or linguistic assimilation or on the abandonment of transnational ties. The expression of Latino identities and loyalties *as part* of a claim to belong suggests a challenge to the meaning of belonging itself in the U.S. context—a contestation of citizenship in the second sense established earlier. The claim seeks more than the opening of borders as they stand to approved outsiders—or "entrepreneurial workers." The claim, by contrast, is that citizenship be broadened to encompass others *as they stand* in all their difference. A Latino cultural presence also acted as a tool for building solidarity across a citizen/noncitizen divide. In this respect, shared goals and collective identities counteracted the individualizing effects of neoliberal subjectivities.

The presence and purpose of Latino culture in the context of the demonstrations proved controversial. It is precisely these kinds of cultural assertions that have prompted the reactionary responses outlined earlier in this chapter. For some within the movement, the expression of national ties to Latin American countries undermined the strategic usefulness of irregular migrants' identity as workers, with all the moral authority that comes from this designation in the U.S. context.[37] For other commentators, the very demonstration of a countercultural presence had the most transformative potential and the best chance of resisting the pull toward neoliberal and Anglo-American modes of citizenship.[38] For yet others, cultural presence tied into a far more immediate and pragmatic strategy to mobilize the Latino vote in support of progressive immigration reform. As banners proudly declared, "Today we march, tomorrow we vote."[39] This strategy has strong precedents. In 1994, Latino activism helped to defeat Proposition 187 in California, a proposal to deny education and other social services to children of irregular migrants. The proposition prompted a surge in Latino voter registration that backfired against Republicans and helped to establish the Democrats in longer-term political control of state and city electorates. At all levels of government, politicians are increasingly responsive to this sector of the U.S. electorate. Four out of five irregular migrants come from Latin American countries, and many have family or other close connections to U.S. citizens of Latin American origin. At the federal level, Latinos constitute the only fast-growing group, with the number of voters growing by 23 percent between 2000 and 2004. A relatively high proportion of minors ensures that this growth will continue in years to come.[40]

Contestations of citizenship are thus being made across a range of levels, from pressure for legalization to more fundamental challenges to citizen identity. Perhaps the most radical aspect of irregular migrants' mobilizations lies in the demand for recognition as integral rights-bearing members of the polity *despite* lacking legal status. One clear expression of this radical challenge to citizenship norms (in the third sense I have identified) is a slogan printed on T-shirts worn at the Los Angeles demonstrations: "I'm illegal. So what?" Here is not only a public "outing" of irregular status, but the sentiment that this status *has no bearing* on whether one is deserving of legitimate residence and political equality. The gesture works at once to make migrants visible via the very status that should keep them "underground" and to refuse the implications of assigned subjectivities and administrative categories. In these respects, the slogan represents a direct contestation of the legitimacy of citizenship itself and a challenge to consider how political belonging might be reformulated in terms that render legal status irrelevant. The sense of shared fate evident in the marches as irregular migrants stood alongside citizens and other migrants further undermines citizenship and legality as meaningful markers of social cleavages rent along more intuitive transnational racial and economic lines. More recent mobilizations in 2008, when Indian guest workers in Texas and Mississippi became "illegal" when they walked off exploitative jobs to which their visas were tied suggest that the terms of mobilizations around mobility and labor will increasingly expose "illegalization" as a tactic of neoliberal governance.[41]

We cannot, of course, read too much into T-shirt slogans, neither in terms of their literal message nor in terms of the broader aims around which demonstrators rally. The consequences of "being illegal" clearly remain grave for those who live with the ongoing prospect of arrest and deportation. In turn, the overwhelming goal of the majority of irregular migrants who mobilized in 2006 was not to destabilize the boundaries that constitute their status as irregular, but rather to seek immediate regularization.[42] As at least one movement organizer commented in the wake of the major demonstrations, "I suspect a lot of people will start busying themselves with getting on the path to legal permanent residence, and that could take the political momentum out of . . . [the movement]."[43] His statement reflects the political limits of regularization as the material resolution to a radical critique of citizenship. Irregular migrants retain a highly subversive edge when they are technically "illegal" but obviously integrated into the political, economic, and cultural landscape—an edge that is lost on the pathway to formal citizenship. At the very least, however, the T-shirt slogan represents a moment of playful ridicule with its own discursive power. Like the joke about the Latino workers required to build the wall along the U.S.–Mexico border, the slogan is understandable only because it captures a shared acknowledgment of the ambiguity of irregular migrants' status. The slogan suggests, moreover, that formal citizenship status has been rendered unstable as a means of distinguishing those who belong from those who clearly do not.

We can also look to more formal spheres of politics to witness this instability. The appearance of the term *undocumented citizen* in public discourse is indicative. In one instance, a Florida legislator suggested using this term in preference to *illegal alien*; in the city of Los Angeles, council community workers employ the term *undocumented citizen* self-consciously to reflect the full spectrum of those they consider their constituents; in another case, a journalist posed a question about "un-documented citizens" to the Homeland Security secretary, who failed to correct the terminology.[44] For the secretary of the agency responsible for policing against irregular migrants, this slide into ambiguous language is an extraordinary gaffe, if not a remarkable admission of forms of status that cannot be captured by clear-cut distinctions between citizen and noncitizen, legal and illegal. These discursive slips suggest, at the very least, a sense of confusion over the relevance of legal status to questions of belonging.

FROM CITY TO CITIZEN: THE QUESTION OF SPATIAL FRAME

The 2006 demonstrations represented a dramatic performative moment when irregular migrants claimed public space—and a space in the public—as their own. There are, however, many other small-scale and more subtle ways in which irregular migrants are contesting what it means to belong and, importantly, in which they are *being recognized* as a legitimate presence. The visible long-term presence of irregular migrants, especially in urban settings, where that presence is densely concentrated, creates opportunities for the public playing out of questions of belonging. In such contexts, irregular migrants and other residents negotiate the utility of citizenship with and against other expressions of political belonging. When these negotiations generate divergent results on localized levels, a disjuncture occurs in the spatial framing of federal immigration reform. From the federal perspective, local variation in policy approaches is a problem to be overcome through territorial consistency. From alternative perspectives, spatial diversity and increasingly urban expressions of political belonging reflect contestation over the "what," "who," *and "where"* of citizenship.[45] I suggest, therefore, that local variation with respect to irregular migration can serve as a laboratory for new frontiers of the political.

Anthropologist Nicholas De Genova has theorized some of these place-specific issues with reference to the effects of Mexican migration to Chicago.[46] Mexican migrants provided a source of cheap, compliant, and expendable labor in Chicago for much of the twentieth century and continue to do so today. A demand for this type of worker has been integrated into the city's economy and landscape. For De Genova, this integration has implications for the spatial frames underwriting conventional accounts of nation, state, and citizen. De Genova argues that the ways in which the United States and Latin America are understood as discreet, bounded, and territorialized identities is radically undermined by the presence and practices of Mexican migrants in Chicago. He emphasizes the ambiguous identity of Mexicans as both the measure of the outside of a racialized, homogenized, and imagined United States and as evidence of the fiction that constitutes the state and its nationals around a corresponding ideal of the citizen. Thus, Mexican Chicago serves at once to reproduce *and* undermine this imagined community. De Genova's argument is suggestive of parallel political imaginaries—one that corresponds to conventional national narratives and another that reflects an already active everyday recognition of the house cleaners, builders, child carers, dish washers, and others who make the city run. The latter imaginary challenges the notion that these people are somehow not really there or do not belong in any substantive way. It amounts to an alternative "common sense" of political belonging and an alternative basis, therefore, for the making of political claims.

De Genova provides a good starting point from which to investigate spatial variation with respect to the economies, social networks, civic relations, and policy frameworks in which irregular migrants are positioned. Recent controversies over the use of local government ordinances in relation to day laborers provide a good example. Across the United States, irregular migrants frequently congregate on street corners and in parking lots that operate as informal day-labor markets. These markets often surround home-improvement stores, where employers can source both labor and materials together. A number of cities are attempting to eradicate these markets through the use of antisoliciting and trespassing ordinances.[47] A number of cities have in turn created new ordinances specifically designed to prevent irregular migrants from living or working in city limits. Illegal immigration relief acts incorporate English-only language regulations for municipal services and allow for the suspension of employers' business permits and landlords' rental licenses (as well as other penalties) should irregular migrants be discovered as employees or tenants. The results, so critics argue, include the denial of essential services to non-English speakers, an unconstitutional intervention into areas preempted by federal immigration law, and pressure on employers and landlords to discriminate against anyone who "looks" like an irregular migrant.[48]

Other cities, however, take a very different approach. Los Angeles, for instance, has taken steps to formalize day-labor markets by contracting community organizations to run worker centers on day-labor sites. These organizations provide shade and amenities for workers, organize workers to set minimum wages and working conditions, assist in negotiations between worker and employers, and generally provide a safer and more dignified context for the exchange.[49] In 2008, the city passed an ordinance that compelled new home-improvement stores to negotiate with key stakeholders, including immigrant community organizations, in order to provide services for day laborers before the stores could be granted a permit to operate.[50] The result, in marked contrast to measures elsewhere, is an explicit acknowledgment of the place of irregular immigrants in the local economy and the incorporation of their interests into the city's regulatory practices.

A second example of spatial diversity concerns city-level cooperation with federal immigration authorities. In 1996, the federal Immigration and Nationality Act was amended to allow ICE to deputize local law enforcement officers as proxy immigration authorities. The amendment was designed to encourage collaboration in the arrest of dangerous and criminal aliens. More recently, however, local law enforcement agencies have used this authority to target irregular migrants in general.[51] The issue gained prominence in February 2009 when Maricopa County sheriff Joe Arpaio in Arizona publicly humiliated more than two hundred immigrants by marching them in black-and-white prison stripes from a county jail through the streets of Phoenix to an immigration detainment camp where he was segregating irregular migrants from the general prison population. He had previously initiated neighborhood sweeps to seek out irregular migrants from their workplaces, homes, and vehicles. In a comment to the media, the sheriff contended that "we know how to determine whether these guys are illegal . . . the way the situation looks, how they are dressed, where they are coming from."[52] Yet his sweeps also resulted in the general harassment of legally resident migrants and Latino U.S. citizens. As Arpaio instituted his own racialized register of legitimate presence in the city, he encountered diverse responses from different levels of government. The governor of Arizona, Janet Napolitano (subsequently appointed by President Obama as the secretary of homeland security), blocked state funding to the sheriff's department for immigration enforcement on account of the controversial tactics, and the U.S. Department of Justice investigated Arpaio for civil rights violations. When the State of Arizona introduced laws in 2010 that criminalized "illegal" presence and obliged police to check the status of anyone "reasonably" suspected of being in the state without authorization, other jurisdictions likewise upped the ante. The federal Justice Department challenged the law in the federal court for encroaching into federal jurisdictions. Migrants' rights coalitions called for a boycott of businesses in Arizona because of the racial profiling that the law effectively condoned. The U.S. Conference of Mayors condemned the Arizona law, and several cities placed a moratorium on all official travel to the state.[53]

In the neighboring state of California, the Los Angeles Police Department's approach stands in marked contrast to Sheriff Arpaio's. Since 1979, the department has operated under Special Order 40, which prevents officers from initiating any action for the purpose of eliciting a person's immigration status. This order works, in effect, as a "Don't Ask, Don't Tell" policy and encourages irregular migrants to cooperate with police in maintaining law and order without the threat of apprehension and deportation. More than fifty cities in the United States have instituted versions of this policy across different municipal services (policing, health, education, and so on). In some cases, the policy extends to an official city sanctuary for irregular migrants.[54] Other city-led initiatives bring irregular migrants into the sphere of civic engagement and place-based recognition. San Francisco and New Haven, Connecticut, issue identity cards to municipal residents regardless of legal status and encourage banks, real estate agents, hospitals, and employers to accept the IDs. Some twenty other cities are considering similar schemes. In the case of San Francisco, companies holding contracts with the city are compelled to accept the cards as a legitimate form of identity.[55] Growing numbers of public and private institutions also recognize identity cards issued by the Mexican government to its citizens abroad and designed unofficially for use by irregular migrants residing in the United States. Acceptance of these *matrículas consulares* (literally "consular registrations") is often negotiated directly between the Mexican government and local-level U.S. authorities in recognition of the mutual benefits gained from irregular migrants' labor and remittances in their respective economies. The police encourage acceptance of the document by banks in particular because without such forms of identity irregular migrants are unable to open bank accounts, are thus compelled to keep wages in cash, and become vulnerable to theft. In addition to its helpfulness in banking, the card can also be used to enroll children in school, use local libraries, and apply for birth and marriage certificates.[56] In Takoma Park, Maryland, irregular migrants are able to vote in city elections, and campaigns to allow voting at the local level are active in other places. In Chicago, New York City, and Arlington, Virginia, irregular migrants can vote for the boards of schools that their children attend.[57] In ten states, irregular migrant residents are eligible to apply for "in-state" college tuition and thus able to avoid the fees associated with out-of-state or foreign-residency status. This measure is more than a quietly maintained legal loophole. The Los Angeles City Council, for instance, sponsors high school workshops in order to raise awareness of relevant students' eligibility for tertiary education in California.[58] In each of these cases, there is a remarkable level of government recognition of irregular migrants as partners in community. Irregular migrants are invited to contribute to governance structures and institutions that help to shape and regulate local communities' civic identity and futures.

In many ways, it stands to reason that the local should emerge as a frontier in struggles to belong. Local communities are confronted with the everyday realities and public-policy imperatives that result from the integration of irregular migrants into U.S. society: adapting to growing numbers of "mixed-status" families where the citizen/"alien" distinction divides parents from children and spouse from spouse (in 2008 such families totaled 8.8 million people);[59] maintaining law and order when sectors of the community are too fearful because of their immigration status to report crimes or to act as witnesses; sustaining economies built on businesses where irregular migrants are a large part of the workforce; and avoiding the emergence of an underclass of marginalized immigrant youth. When in response to these imperatives authorities consider the pros and cons of instituting a "Don't Ask, Don't Tell" policy or other related initiatives, they implicitly acknowledge the border policing against irregular migrants that is triggered by a range of administrative functions well within the interior and far from the border as such. They acknowledge their capacity to "open" those borders in ways that compromise the territorial integrity of migration regulation and irregular migrants' taken-for-granted outsider status. The cumulative momentum of these kinds of initiatives bring into being alternative registers of legitimacy based on *presence* in the city rather than on legal status. As one mayor advocating local identity cards for irregular migrants explained, "We want you in our community, and we want you to feel like you belong."[60] As a consequence, the everyday experience of "being illegal" and "feeling like a citizen" may be remarkably different and by no means mutually exclusive depending on the place.

Such measures, of course, are no panacea for irregular migrants. For every initiative that appears to advance their recognition as a legitimate local presence, there are others that loudly pronounce their ongoing illegitimacy. For each local government that tries to improve conditions at day-labor markets, there are others that use the markets' presence as a rallying point for anti-immigrant sentiment. Indeed, Sherriff Arpaio and others are working hard to enforce immigration policing that is *more* restrictive and *more* punitive than federal law requires. Federal authorities are also attempting to reassert control over local policy divergence, seeking, for instance, to standardize forms of identification and prevent irregular migrants from using state-issued licenses and identity cards for purposes such as catching a plane.[61] The nexus between security and migration in the post–September 11 context provides additional means and motivation for federal agencies to pursue these kinds of endeavors. Even in city sanctuaries, as Peter Nyers insists, irregular migrants' access to the city remains premised on the ongoing secrecy of their presence.[62] This status falls far short of equality with citizens. There is every reason, therefore, to be cautious in interpreting the significance of local-level gestures of sanctuary. Given the intersection between border policing and neoliberal governance, it seems reasonable to suggest that quasi forms of recognition for irregular migrants simply exacerbate their exploitability as more available *and* more vulnerable workers. From this perspective, it is no surprise that elected officials and local business leaders come together in opposition to federal immigration workplace raids. For Nicola Phillips, such gestures are part of an unspoken strategy to entrench existing divisions of labor, albeit with minor modifications to wages and working conditions, and to maximize local business profits.[63]

Yet even a cynically driven approach to the local integration of irregular migrants provides enabling conditions for more profound challenges to citizenship norms. Progressive city initiatives, for example, generate an atmosphere of ambiguity in which it is possible to push at the limits of citizenship in new and unpredictable ways. Where the local emerges as a site of contestation, it becomes very clear that state-based territory is not the only or the primary space in which political belonging takes shape. Citizenship in its conventional form and the territorial norms that sustain it begin to coexist *openly* with multiple arrangements and modes of belonging across citizen/noncitizen, official/informal, and local/global divides. From this place-based starting point, the field of the political extends to unknown horizons. Citizenship transforms between the push and pull of public modes of recognition and acts of contestation.

BECOMING CITIZENS: FROM PRACTICE TO SUBJECT FORMATION

New modes of belonging are more than the result of jurisdictional issues, policy divergence, and government initiated action. We can also observe a much more active sense of contestation that emerges from the ground up, as it were, as irregular migrants engage in public acts of struggle. In the very act of speaking out as residents, workers, parents, students, consumers, commuters, and so on, irregular migrants institute a process of civic subject formation. By struggling for certain kinds of rights and recognition, they engage in practices with political effects that go beyond the success or failure of the immediate pragmatic issue of concern (wage claims, for example). Their struggles are simultaneously *reactions* to their marginalized condition and *productive* of new forms of political belonging.

A number of observers of irregular migrants' mobilizations have drawn attention to this sense of transformation. Fran Ansley, for example, describes a coalition that campaigned in Tennessee for the provision of drivers' licenses to irregular migrants. According to Ansley, the success of the campaign resulted in a range of flow-on effects that far exceeded the direct benefits of the licensing arrangements. The most obvious effect was that a license allowed irregular migrants to get to work with some relief from the constant fear of detection behind the wheel, whether for breaches of immigration or for driving regulations. But it also allowed them more ready access to social life in general and the networks established through the mobilization provided bases for further actions. For the broader community, the campaign brought into relief the paradoxes of belonging in Tennessee. It created a platform for migrants "to describe in arresting detail the irrationality and strain of their situation: thoroughly integrated into the mundane workings of the aboveground economy, and at the same time legally excluded, forced to traverse daily an uneven and unpredictable minefield of simultaneous normalcy and criminality."[64] The campaign thus generated an alternative discourse where broader questions of belonging, border policing, and reciprocal relations between citizens and irregular migrants were raised and problematized.

In another example, Monica Varsanyi documents the role irregular migrants have played in campaigning for political candidates in Los Angeles. By attending campaign rallies, endorsing candidates through immigrant-dominated unions, and knocking on doors in (especially Spanish-speaking) business districts and neighborhoods in "Get Out the Vote" drives, irregular migrants effectively act as model active citizens. Whether their campaigning achieves success for their candidates of choice is immaterial to the broader effects of their civic participation. For Varsanyi, this engagement is "in and of itself, an act of legitimacy and belonging, and as such, an important step toward demanding recognition as full members in society."[65]

Jennifer Gordon similarly describes in her book *Suburban Sweatshops: The Fight for Immigrant Rights* how migrants contributed to the campaign for the Unpaid Wages Prohibition Act passed by the New York Legislature in July 1997. The act provided for the enforcement of wage payments to workers regardless of their legal status. The act was the brainchild of a coalition of immigrant workers, many of whom had irregular status, organized under the banner of a local legal clinic and worker center. Although claims were posed in a variety of terms, including those appealing to the protection of wage levels for low-paid citizen workers, the migrant activists nevertheless acted "in ways beyond the boundaries of the law's definition of who was entitled to do the work of citizenship."[66] The very idea of an irregular migrant campaigning (in Spanish) for changes to employment law in the office of a Republican senator dramatically upset the line between legitimacy and illegitimacy. According to Gordon, the sense of ownership that migrants had over all aspects of the campaign, from initiation to strategic planning and direct lobbying, was central to both its sustainability and its public credibility. She contends that such broad participation was made possible through rights-based discussions that crucially "changed not only how . . . [non–English speakers, noncitizens, and irregular migrants] saw themselves but what they were capable of doing" and that ultimately generated a "belief in themselves as legitimate and effective political actors" regardless of their formal status.[67]

There are many other similar examples of small-scale practices that generate new norms of status and belonging. Irregular migrant students attending various campuses of the University of California have organized a network of support and advocacy groups. The students have lobbied at state and federal levels, through media outlets and congressional hearings, in support of legislation that will provide them with conditional permanent resident status for the duration of their studies and a subsequent pathway to citizenship. Their public acts of protest have also involved rallies, mock graduations, and hunger strikes. "I consider myself American," states one participating student who arrived in the United States some eighteen years ago. "My friends, boyfriend, family, hopes, and dreams are in this country. Thus, I work in every way I can, in every movement I can, to be recognized by the nation I have lived in for so long."[68] As parents of children in schools, irregular migrants are also engaging in education programs sponsored by community organizations, where they are learning to navigate the various U.S. education systems in order to advocate better on their children's behalf.[69] Such programs have the potential to create a considerable impact on the direction and composition of school boards, for instance, especially in districts where parents from immigrant communities form a significant majority.

Irregular migrants are also active in numerous labor campaigns via "worker centers" that target services for working people to immigrant communities. Within the broader labor movement, organizing strategies have adapted to the realities of contemporary low-paid work that cut across the citizen/noncitizen divide. New coalitions have formed on this basis among unions, worker centers, community organizations, immigrants' rights groups, faith-based organizations, and schools with which workers, migrants, and their families are associated. These alliances have been central, for example, in establishing campaigns in Los Angeles where janitorial, garment factory, supermarket, restaurant, and car-wash workers have organized against exploitation by employers. Campaigns have involved pickets, protests, and business boycotts as well as lawsuits, speaking tours, and outreach to other industry workers.[70] In June 2007, migrant workers from across the United States formed the National Domestic Worker Alliance in order to campaign for changes to labor laws affecting domestic workers. In 2010, the alliance successfully lobbied state legislators in New York to sign on to a domestic workers' bill of rights. According to observers, the alliance is changing the ways in which "[w]omen from Mexico [and] South and Central America" negotiate their own political futures; "once scared, powerless, and limited in their English language skills, [they] now organize marches, bring speakers who discuss their legal rights, and talk about change."[71] Through these mobilizations, the interests of citizens and all kinds of migrants are reframed as the common interests of workers.

Across this array of activism, new subjectivities are forming in ways that shift what it means to be an irregular migrant away from exclusive association with arduous labor and a preparedness to carry it out.[72] To be sure, much of the activism irregular migrants engage in has been focused on working conditions and identities as workers (who will do the work that natives no longer want to do). Such identities provide leverage for their claims. But in the very act of refusing exploitation, a sense of entitlement emerges as irregular migrants transform assumptions about how it is *possible* to treat them. A "becoming" of the citizen takes place. It is in and through these struggles that this transformation occurs. From microlevel expressions of belonging to local communities as parents, workers, students, and so on, irregular migrants redefine what it means to be equal subjects in a civic life.

For Monica Varsanyi, such gestures of citizenship by irregular migrants negotiate a constant tension between different civic spaces: "In which public can undocumented residents claim membership and rights? The local public? The national public? What happens when the inhabitants are 'illegal,' and not considered appropriate members of the national public according to federal laws, but are simultaneously caught up in struggles over their ability to be present in the public spaces of the city?"[73] Varsanyi emphasizes the constant vulnerability of irregular migrants to the whims of sovereign power when they make themselves public as rights-seizing subjects. This vulnerability, she contends, radically distinguishes irregular migrants' claims to the city from the claims made by other marginalized groups whose formal citizenship status is not in question. This distinction, I suggest, is precisely what positions such struggles in the realm of the political. We are dealing here with the edges of citizenship and its contestation from beyond the point of its limits, both socially and spatially. Varsanyi is right to point to the inherent risks that come with this positioning. We cannot underestimate the hardships of irregular status or the life-and-death stakes involved in deportations and repeated border crossings. Nor, indeed, can we fail to notice the radically different trajectories faced by irregular migrants should they cross metropolitan and regional lines. A bus ride from Los Angeles to Phoenix may well result in a fast-tracked arrest, prison time, and deportation. Yet strategic opportunities for transformation also arise from diverse conditions across different civic spaces.

RADICAL FRONTIERS

It remains unclear what sort of political momentum more radical contestations of citizenship might gain. It will depend on the strategies deployed by irregular migrants and the modes of belonging they invoke in their struggles. It will also depend on the reactions they encounter from citizens increasingly overwhelmed by the fragility of borders and the loss of stable identities. In the face of this crisis of citizenship, governments in the United States and around the world appear ever more willing to assert their sovereign power in demonstrations of territorial control. In this chapter, however, I have chosen to focus on ambiguities of status, gestures of inclusion, and alternative modes of belonging over and above the very real forces that continue to police irregular migrants as undesirable and criminal outsiders. In doing so, to be clear, I am not suggesting a resurgence of the local as evidence for a decline in state-based modes of belonging. There is little about border policing against irregular migrants today, in the United States or elsewhere, that suggests such a decline. On the contrary, the state is alive and well as a marker and enforcer of citizenship. Rather, I have tried to emphasize that *multiple* spatial scales and corresponding levels of government, community, and identity are increasingly part of the dynamics that shape prevailing ideas about who belongs where. These spatial scales are not so much competing for primacy as existing in tension with each other. When irregular migrants act as citizens do in local public spheres, they draw our attention to place-based modes of belonging. When acts are scaled up to other levels, we are moved to consider how modes of belonging diverge, intersect, and transform across different spatial frames.

As irregular migrants assert their presence across these various spaces, their struggle to belong may well take shape in ways that we cannot predict, on scales that will vary in ambition, and with results that will flow into unforeseen strategic possibilities. Political struggles far less ambitious than those asserting an unconditional claim to citizenship may nevertheless destabilize citizenship boundaries in subtle but significant ways. In this regard, the most radical act pursued by irregular migrants may well be to remain "illegal" but not "underground." This act implies drawing attention to a growing vocal and visible presence that generates authority by changing the rules of the game such that illegality no longer equates with illegitimacy. Such a scenario would conceivably enable irregular migrants to undermine state authorities' capacity to deploy legality and illegality as effective tools of control through temporary guest-worker schemes, for example.

Attentiveness to spatial framing enhances our recognition of these new frontiers of the political. The spaces that shape our concept of the citizen do not prefigure the political claims that play out in and through them. Irregular migrants actively *constitute* the spatial dimension of political belonging in the process of their struggles. Our habit of looking to certain kinds of spaces (more often than not the universalized space of nation-state territory) to see enactments of citizenship with which we are familiar limits our view of the acts and actors in play. The task for theorists, therefore, is to look to unexpected places, to the local and particular, to the edges, and to outsiders as makers and shapers of contemporary dynamics of citizenship. The task is to think more creatively about subtle transformations in the "who," "what," and "where" of political belonging that emerge in unlikely sites.

CONCLUSION

Contentious Spaces of Political Belonging

In May 2009, I met a group of women in the northern suburbs of Los Angeles who were members of a business cooperative: Magic Cleaners. The cooperative was a limited liability company formed under California law and an economic development project of a local worker center. The women, all from Mexico, were equal owners in the business, and income earned was split after operating costs had been covered. Members thus avoided paying high commissions for agency placements and could independently negotiate the clients they did business with and the conditions under which they worked. Those involved had previously suffered from repeated exposure to toxic cleaning substances. Using only environmentally friendly products, Magic Cleaners had carved out a lucrative market niche as a green cleaning service.

The remarkable thing about Magic Cleaners was that all of its members were also irregular migrants. Their status prevented them from legal employment, but under a quirk of California law there was nothing to stop them from opening their own business.[1] Clients engaged the business rather than its owners directly, and the exchange took place entirely within the formal economy. This cooperative generates an avenue of social recognition that challenges prevailing assumptions about authorized presence, legitimate business activity, and civic contribution. "Being in the cooperative," Manuela explained, "clients have learned to respect us, because the company is backing us up."[2] In discussion, members expressed pride in their work and in their status as business owners. They felt more secure and could plan with more certainty for the future.

This arrangement captures some of the everyday ambiguities that fill the space between legality and illegality. It also speaks to the place-based specificity of expressions of political belonging, techniques of political exclusion, and the dynamic tension between them. The neighborhoods of Los Angeles traversed by Magic Cleaners, with their stark divides between rich and poor, embody the history of border crossings that has shaped the city's fortunes. A rapidly expanding Latino presence marks out certain spaces as its own and filters through the wider urban landscape in linguistic, aesthetic, and political forms that resist assimilation to standard tropes of U.S. citizenship. This global city is constituted by the movement of people across its freeways and subways, its bathrooms and lawns, its restaurants and office blocks—people who have traveled from south of the border and elsewhere to shape a new mobile service sector that accommodates demand from wealthy households, transnational corporations, and migrant communities alike. There is constant traffic on the roads and in the airwaves, in e-mails and phone calls, in minds and in memories, between origin and destination. The density of traffic gives life and weight to alternative border stories—not only the well-known adage "I didn't cross the border; the border crossed me," but also new ways of articulating being in places that are not understood as either side of a territorial divide. Los Angeles emerges as a translocal space in the sense of being made meaningful through place-to-place and person-to-person connections that are both narrower and broader than the nation-state territories to which our geopolitical imaginations have become accustomed. Its residents are positioned in unique scalar governance structures that make things possible (business forms, policing policies) at city and regional levels in ways that are inconceivable elsewhere.

All of this particular positioning plays into the reasons why Magic Cleaners was established in Los Angeles and not, say, in Sydney or Singapore. Although global flows constitute the spaces of all three cities, they manifest in distinctly localized ways. Community organizations now interested in copying the Magic Cleaners model (with Filipino caregivers and Latino gardeners, for instance) are embedded in longer-term disputes between anti- and pro-immigrant forces that have galvanized the Latino community in greater Los Angeles into a political force to be reckoned with and have forged what was never an automatic alliance between citizen and noncitizen migrants.[3] Each business transaction conducted by Magic Cleaners ties into the momentum generated by a vocal progressive movement that has mobilized across migrant and labor constituencies and is calling for legalization for the city's estimated one million undocumented residents.[4]

When pushed on the question of legalization, Magic Cleaners expressed thoroughly pragmatic concerns about what the transformation in status would mean and none of the *affect* (the "feeling like a citizen") that one senses in the claims of the Sans-Papiers, for instance. I had the distinct impression that papers alone, though essential to secure their future, could not so easily capture the legitimacy these women might feel about where and who they are in the world or the relations to places and people that provide them with the grounding to know where they belong. There was neither the urge to justify their "place" in these terms nor an attempt to articulate an alternative register of status—perhaps on account of what they recognized as my own implication in an analytics that was insufficient to the task of conveying multiple and everyday sovereignties. I was prompted to imagine a different starting point for political belonging that is not so fixated on positioning people with reference to fixed identities, administrative categories, and Cartesian reference points and that, on account of those qualities, is illusive and evasive to the social scientific–trained eye.

Each business transaction conducted by Magic Cleaners also intersects, therefore, with more radical assertions of political belonging that defy categorization in terms of either (il)legality or territorial space. Precisely because the women who run this business collective exert a daily presence that is hard to represent on prevailing mental maps, their public encounters *as* Magic Cleaners unsettle our registers of political belonging. Their daily interactions remind us that ways of living in political relation to others exceed and defy conventional modes of citizenship in social and spatial terms.

My brief interaction with Magic Cleaners cuts to the core of the citizenship dynamics that have been the subject of this book. As I moved with ease and speed from Melbourne to Los Angeles and into the office of irregular entrepreneurs whose mobility was far more circumscribed than mine, the transnational dimensions of neoliberal hierarchies were glaringly evident. Yet our conversation focused on the potential for business cooperatives run by irregular migrants to create real change in local civic spheres. Though the context was highly specific, the strategies deployed to carve out a space of belonging resonated strongly with acts of contestation in other corners of the globe and yet could not be pigeon-holed as part of a coherent social movement. Making sense of this specific case required a more creative sense of sociospatial relations than that which typically frames accounts of political subjectivity. In this brief conclusion, I reflect on the spatial dimensions of irregular migrants' acts of contestation, for in everyday places, such as the northern suburbs of Los Angeles, there are spaces that resist subordination to territorial norms and to neoliberal rationalities—spaces of excess that are located in the crevices and gaps of sovereign power and that shape solidarities across alternative grounds.

It takes a great deal of spatial work to render the subjects of citizenship beyond contestation as if their constitution were fixed and eternal rather than in process of becoming. Border policing is the spatial work through which the distinction between citizens and aliens is ordered and policed. It involves the discursive framing and material management of spaces through which we come to recognize our political relation to others. Borders literally give shape to hierarchies of belonging that buttress sovereign power, but the spatial dimensions of borders (and of sovereign power) are also dynamic. Territorial borders originally took form in conjunction with the centralization of power in the modern territorial state and continue to play a crucial role in the strategies through which populations are identified, audited, and controlled. Different kinds of borders have emerged in and through a new terrain of sovereign practice. Performative gestures that mark those borders also mark new neoliberal subjectivities that do not map directly onto territorial norms but instead generate cross-cutting and multilayered hierarchies of belonging. Borders that once seemed solid now seem highly ambiguous, shifting in time and space through offshore technologies that change a person's identity from refugee to "illegal," from tax-paying citizen to subsidy-eligible tourist dependent on mobile jurisdictions. Borders are virtual, arising differentially through administrative processes that fast-track some crossings and circumvent others. Borders are mapped onto bodies—fingerprints and retinas that alert authorities to "risky" subjects in a grand display of sovereign territorial defense. Borders are porous: the gaps in policing are wide enough so that all manner of traffic passes through, but not so wide as to annul the effects of *the threat* of border control. New technologies of border control generate "frequent flyers" and "citizens via investment" alongside "offshore entry persons," "'bogus' asylum seekers," and "fugitive aliens," and they legitimize enormously differential treatment across differently regulated zones.

Those who challenge the givenness of hierarchies so drawn also engage in performative space-making practices of citizenship. It seems unnecessary, even banal, to draw attention to the simple fact that each act of contestation occurs in a spatial setting. Yet doing so reminds us that each act also has the potential to change the associations we make about that space—its history and its future, whose space it is, who moves through it, and who has authority do so. All these ideas *make up* that space insofar as space is the product of social interaction and collective experience. Thus, irregular migrants' acts of contestation involve first and foremost a claim to be part of a collective space. The starting point, in other words, is simply *to be there*, in public space, to render visible a part of the public that demands its due on account of a shared claim to the space we call our own. When the Sans-Papiers occupy worksites, churches, and union and United Nations offices, they dramatically assert their presence in the everyday. They refuse invisibility and instead become embodied proof of the racial distinctions, labor networks, colonial histories, and illiberal orders that make access to the city possible for some but not for others. When undocumented students mobilize on Californian campuses, they ritualize those places in new ways, embedding their presence as "irregular citizens" in traditions of civil rights activism that become part and parcel of a powerful story of U.S. citizenship. This presence does more than express those students' immediate demands. It creates a spatial platform from which broader political claims can be made and from which counternarratives of "who we are" and "where we belong" can emerge and gain traction.

Is the transformation of political space implied by such acts, or do these acts merely "stretch" that space, more or less as it is, to include a broader public? Throughout this study, I have argued that both kinds of maneuvers are in play. I have made a case for a spectrum of acts of contestation and a complex interweaving of claims and frames that challenge us to think in terms of layered modes of political belonging, some of which reflect more familiar patterns of sociospatial relations and others that may well exceed what we are able to imagine in social or spatial terms as reference points for civic solidarities. The struggles of irregular migrants accordingly cannot be reduced to a coherent set of claims that works on any one sociospatial level. Rather, an array of strategies both resist *and* renew the spatial frames for conventional forms of citizenship as well as enact alternative spaces of political possibility.

Consider first the tendency to reinforce prevailing forms of citizenship. Calls for legalization work in part to reproduce the very same hierarchies and territorial maps that exclude so many prospective migrants and those seeking refuge in states that are not "their own." When "irregular citizens" are regularized, their transgression is resolved by reversion to the state/citizen/territory constellation, and proof of alternative forms of status *already in social circulation* is removed from visibility. Legalization programs reboot the system, tidying rough edges and anomalies that exposed its cracks and strains. Legitimate residence once again equates to legality and pathways to formal citizenship. Arguments for legalization can also confirm the spatial logics that separate citizens and territories from unwanted and unworthy outsiders. When the Sans-Papiers invoke the authority of the "rights of man" to justify their claims, they also invoke a specific tradition of French republican citizenship that is forged on the back of distinctions between a "civilized" space of unfolding human rights and a "backward" realm of corrupt political relations. This very same distinction plays into images of "African hordes" threatening to transfer to France and Europe their brutal conflicts and cultures. The distinction serves, in other words, to legitimize upscaled policing designed to prevent the arrival of undesirable people and politics. As citizenship norms are reconstituted on neoliberal lines, claims to legalization that are based on worker identity both reinvigorate national narratives of model citizen status and further entrench flexibility as a form of civic virtue. The audience to which such claims are directed likewise determines a circular effect. When asylum seekers in Australia address their protection claims to a bureaucratic order that is systematically operating to narrow the legally acceptable bases upon which such claims can be made, they reinforce the legal and symbolic power of that sovereign agent to allocate forms of status that effectively decide one's fate.

At a time when border policing has gained the added performative dimension of a first-order state security practice, when exorbitant budgets are assigned to deliver more innovative, invasive, and coordinated techniques of border control, and when market forces actively constitute border policing as a lucrative global industry, it is easy to interpret irregular migrants' acts of contestation in pessimistic terms. From this perspective, whatever successes might be achieved through modest changes to living and working conditions, informal modes of recognition, legalization programs, or guest-worker schemes only reflect the co-optation of irregular migrant struggles into the very governance regimes through which human traffic is regulated under conditions of contemporary global capitalism. Citizenship might be widened or deepened to incorporate new kinds of subjects, but only in ways that entrench existing and emerging hierarchies of status in line with the prerogatives of the globalizing state.

There is no denying that sovereign power is adept at changing strategies (from illegalization to legalization, for instance) in order to mitigate the destabilizing effects of the presence of irregular migrants. Yet conclusions that rest on the absolute triumph of sovereign power reduce irregular migrants' acts of contestation to purely reactive practices and fail to acknowledge their equally productive dimensions. They also tend to reproduce a spatially homogenous account of political belonging that buys into the totalizing story of neoliberal globalization. From this perspective, we yet again view the globe as a thoroughly colonized space of market relations where irregular migrants are universally cast as a global underclass. Such interpretations miss important subtleties and variations both in the exercise of neoliberal rationalities and in techniques of resistance, for as we have seen throughout this book, subjects of border control change in space and time on account of both sovereign power's creative use of geography and acts of contestation that generate momentum for alternative arrangements in one place rather than another.

Consider, by contrast, the transformative dimensions of acts that simultaneously reinforce conventional citizenship norms. When irregular migrants claim "to be" citizens of France or the United States in advance of legal status, they generate new narratives of citizenship. When the Sans-Papiers retell the story of French nation building as one that extends across wider spaces (geographies of colonialism) that state borders obscure, they rewrite the content of citizenship. I am here now, their claim proceeds, because of a specific spatial relation that links our histories together, and due to this relation's ongoing legacies I demand recognition as part of a shared future. The Sans-Papiers challenge the fiction of citizenship's territorial enclosure by mobilizing other spaces and times that have served, through their very exclusion, to mark the boundaries of what it means to be French. The conquest of the colonies and the labor and resources that shifted to the metropole to make it what it is are witnessed on the bodies of those who now claim their due. Though the claim reasserts the authority that being a citizen confers, citizenship is also framed in a way that captures the fuller spatial dimensions of its constitutive elements. The act of contestation through which that frame is articulated enlivens the potential for new modes of political belonging.

We can also reflect on the same mobilization across U.S. cities in 2006 that on one hand built momentum for legalization ("Legalize Now!") and on the other provided a forum to reject legal status as a legitimate measure of status allocation ("I'm illegal, so what?"). The latter provocation undermines prevailing registers of political belonging with a force that draws its legitimacy from sheer weight of numbers (eleven million irregular migrants across the United States) and from the common recognition of the central place of those who are "illegal" in the everyday workings of the cities through which they marched. The provocation resists proposing an alternative measure of status and instead asserts the power to be present *regardless* of status in general and of illegality in particular. There is a sentiment here that resonates with the autonomy expressed by irregular migrants in the European context who refuse recognition within the scope of existing categories (asylum seeker or otherwise forced migrant). They publicize an alternative account of autonomous choices to be on the move in defiance of state-centric identities. The resonance extends to Magic Cleaners members' sidestepping of status in their efforts to gain greater control of their working lives. It extends to the failure of existing status categories to capture alternative ways of knowing where and with whom one belongs. The social and spatial stretch of each of these practices is deliberately unspecified, and this nonspecificity is precisely what is troubling to citizenship norms. As acts of contestation, these practices produce indeterminacy, and this is a radical challenge to hierarchies that are normalized through the representation and performative repetition of solid borderlines and fixed identities.

In terms of citizenship dynamics, therefore, the successes and failures of acts of contestation cannot be reduced to immediate outcomes—legalization or successful asylum applications, for instance. Although these outcomes may remain the focus of the majority of irregular migrants' mobilizations, they do not reveal the full scope of subjectivities and solidarities that emerge through social struggle across new spatial terrains. Alternative subjectivities may not be directed toward recognition by the state's sovereign agents, and precisely for this reason they may well have the best chance of escaping the grasp of hegemonic sociospatial categories. In this relative space of freedom, we may yet witness new "ethical problematizations . . . [that] circumvent human rights or citizenship, coming to rest on resolutions that reflect contingent and ambiguous ethical horizons of the human."[5]

What I am suggesting is something different from the notion of a global social movement that rests on clearly articulated rights (say, to mobility) and ambitions (say, for open borders). Elements of such a movement may yet emerge in the face of a globally coordinated and locally enforced border-policing regime. Irregular migrants, however diverse their positioning may be, share an increasingly common struggle against illegalization on this global scale. But if we are to take seriously the notion of spatiality as plural spatial ontologies, and if we are to understand globalization as the reconstitution of political space via ontological encounters, then the social and spatial terms in which such struggles play out are likely to be more nuanced, contentious, and multifarious than a singular global cleavage can convey. This is why I have emphasized a spectrum of acts of contestation that counter the locally specific ways in which exclusion is sustained and that are in turn productive of new and diverse political relations. These acts work together *or in tension* in unpredictable ways and deploy a variety of spatial frames in the service of different claims. The cumulative momentum of such acts generates a shifting ground of political belonging, only some of which is perceptible through existing lenses. This shifting ground intersects with and transforms more taken-for-granted spatial frames for citizenship, and in the process new kinds of political subjects emerge. There is no sense, therefore, in which we should expect a wholesale transition to the new. Rather, we must learn to live with what Michael Peter Smith and Matt Bakker call "multipositional subjects" who "are engaged in an ever-changing, dialectical internal struggle over their personal and political identities in which conflicts between inclusion and transformation . . . are not generally viewed in either/or terms."[6]

Yet how should we begin to engage with new ethical horizons that remain obscured precisely on account of their imperceptibility or inarticulability? Here we confront the *political* limits of "staying underground" in communion with a world of alternative belongings that bypass direct confrontation with sovereign power. If an irregular migrant counterpublic is prepolitical in this sense, it is all the more reason for inquiry to proceed with the awareness that the social and spatial "excess" of human experience will outrun our current political imaginations. This is the creative moment—the frontier of the political— when the terms of social antagonism, subjectivities, and spaces that give form to social struggle are in process of becoming.

NOTES

INTRODUCTION

1. Alejandro (a pseudonym) in discussion with the author, May 4, 2009, Los Angeles. The bills referred to are the federal Development, Relief, and Education for Alien Minors (DREAM) Act and the California DREAM Act. After several unsuccessful attempts to pass the federal DREAM Act since 2001, the most recent versions are still under congressional review. HR 1751 and S 729 , 111th Cong., 1st sess., March 26, 2009. The California DREAM Act (S 1460, February 27, 2008, amended January 11, 2010) gained the approval of the Senate Education Committee on April 14, 2010.

2. Neil Brenner, *New State Spaces: Urban Governance and the Rescaling of State-hood* (Oxford, U.K.: Oxford University Press, 2004), 3.

3. Pheng Cheah, *Inhuman Conditions: On Cosmopolitanism and Human Rights* (Cambridge, Mass.: Harvard University Press, 2006), 92–93.

4. On the intersections of gender, race, nation, and neoliberal globalization, see Christine Chin, *In Service and Servitude: Foreign Domestic Workers and the Malaysian "Modernity Project"* (New York: Columbia University Press, 1998); V. Spike Peterson, *A Critical Rewriting of Global Political Economy: Integrating Repro-ductive, Productive, and Virtual Economies* (London: Routledge, 2003), Elisabeth Prügel, *The Global Construction of Gender: Home-Based Work in the Political Econ-omy of the 20th Century* (New York: Columbia University Press, 1999). On gen-der and immigration detention, see Gabriella Alberti, "Open Space Across the Borders of Lesvos: The Gendering of Migrants' Detention in the Aegean," *Femi-nist Review* 94, no. 1 (2010): 138–47. On the theme of race, see especially Nicho-las De Genova, *Working the Boundaries: Race, Space, and "Illegality" in Mexican Chicago* (Durham, N.C.: Duke University Press, 2005); and Adam M. McKeown, *Melancholy Order: Asian Migration and the Globalization of Borders* (New York: Columbia University Press, 2008).

1. IRREGULAR MIGRANTS AND NEW FRONTIERS OF THE POLITICAL

1. The United Nations Convention Relating to the Status of Refugees defines a refugee as a person who "owing to well-founded fear of being persecuted for reasons of race, religion, nationality, membership of a particular social group or political opinion, is outside the country of his nationality and is unable, or owing to such fear, is unwilling to avail himself of the protection of that country; or who, not having a nationality and being outside the country of his former habitual residence as a result of such events, is unable or, owing to such fear, is unwilling to return to it." United Nations General Assembly, "Convention Relating to the Status of Refugees," July 28, 1951, *United Nations Treaty Series* 189, p. 137, available at http://www.unhcr.org/refworld/docid/3be01b964.html.

2. The details of Asif and Jacob's journeys are virtually the same as those of these two real men. The precise details of Asif's boat passage to Australian territory and of the meeting between Asif and Jacob are fictitious but not unrealistic. The stories are adapted from personal communication with Asif and from the following sources: Penelope Debelle, "Detainee Free After 7 Years' Incarceration," *The Age*, July 18, 2005; Penelope Debelle, "Nearly Free, but Normal Life a Distant Dream," *The Age*, June 21, 2005; Greg Egan, "Australia's National Shame: Peter Qasim's 2191 Stolen Days," Project Safecom Inc., September 2, 2004, available at http://www.safecom.org/peter_qasim.htm; Andra Jackson, "Aladdin Sisalem Released from Manus Island," *The Age*, June 1, 2005; Andra Jackson, "Life in Detention, for Seven Years," *The Age*, March 5, 2005; Andra Jackson, "Refugee's Journey from the Depths to the Heights and Back Again," *The Age*, May 30, 2009; Andra Jackson, "Struggle for a Modern Crusoe on Manus Isle," *The Age*, November 25, 2003; Angie Latif, "Castaway," originally published in *Aramicia*, October 6–20, 2003, reprinted by NauruWire.org at http://www.nauruwire.org/manusarchives.htm. Asif and Jacob are pseudonyms.

3. Michael Walzer, *Spheres of Justice: A Defence of Pluralism and Equality* (New York: Basic Books, 1983), 32.

4. Engin F. Isin, *Being Political: Genealogies of Citizenship* (Minneapolis: University of Minnesota Press, 2002), 7–21.

5. Ibid., 3–7, 279–83.

6. Monica Varsanyi, "Interrogating 'Urban Citizenship' *Vis-à-Vis* Undocumented Migration," *Citizenship Studies* 10, no. 2 (2006), 243. Federal legislation (REAL ID Act of 2005) attempts to restrict the use of licenses as identification for official purposes. However, U.S. states (responsible for issuing licenses) have a mixed record of intention to comply with federal legislation. Enforcement of the act has been twice postponed in efforts to seek greater support from states.

7. Adam M. McKeown, *Melancholy Order: Asian Migration and the Globalization of Borders* (New York: Columbia University Press, 2008), 36.

8. For an overview of the rise of a crisis mentality in relation to irregular migration, see Aristide R. Zolberg, "Introduction: Beyond the Crisis," in *Global Migrants, Global Refugees: Problems and Solutions*, ed. Aristide R. Zolberg and Peter M. Benda (New York: Berghahn Books, 2001), 1–8.

9. Peter Andreas, "Redrawing the Line: Borders and Security in the Twenty-First Century," *International Security* 28, no. 2 (2003): 78–111; Stephen Castles and Mark J. Miller, *The Age of Migration*, 3rd ed. (New York: Guildford Press, 2003), 94–121; Michael Collyer, "Migrants, Migration, and the Security Paradigm: Constraints and Opportunities," *Mediterranean Politics* 11, no. 2 (2006), 257–66.

10. Zai Liang and Wenzhen Ye, "From Fujian to New York: Understanding the New Chinese Immigration," in *Global Human Smuggling: Comparative Perspectives*, ed. David Kyle and Rey Koslowski (Baltimore: Johns Hopkins University Press, 2001), 192–200; Susanne Schmeidl, "Conflict and Forced Migration: A Quantitative Review, 1964–1995," in *Global Migrants, Global Refugees*, ed. Zolberg and Benda, 75–83; Roberto Suro, Sergio Bendixen, B. Lindsay Lowell, and Dulce C. Benavides, *Billions in Motion: Latino Immigrants, Remittances, and Banking* (Washington, D.C.: Pew Hispanic Center and Multilateral Investment Fund, 2002), 14–16.

11. Michael Hoefer, Nancy Rytina, and Bryan C. Baker, "Estimates of the Unauthorized Immigrant Population Residing in the United States: January 2009," in *Population Estimates, January 2010*, 1–8 (Washington, D.C.: U.S. Department of Homeland Security, Office of Immigration Statistics, Policy Directorate, 2010), 1; Irina Ivakhnyuk, *The Russian Migration Policy and Its Impact on Human Development: The Historical Perspective*, Research Paper 2009/14, Human Development Reports (Paris: United Nations Development Program, 2009), 43, available at http://hdr.undp.org/en/reports/global/hdr2009/papers/HDRP_2009_14.pdf; Dita Vogel, *Size and Development of Irregular Migration to the EU*, European Commission, Clandestino Project Policy Briefing (Brussels: European Commission, October 2009), 4, available at http://clandestino.eliamep.gr/.

12. Greta Uehling, "Irregular and Illegal Migration Through Ukraine," *International Migration* 42, no. 3 (2004), 85.

13. United Nations High Commission for Refugees (UNHCR), *2008 Global Trends: Refugees, Asylum-Seekers, Returnees, Internally Displaced and Stateless Persons* (Geneva: UNHCR, June 16, 2009), 3, available at http://www.unhcr.org/ 4a375c426.html.

14. U.S. Committee for Refugees, *World Refugee Survey 2009* (Arlington, Va.: U.S. Committee for Refugees, 2010), available at http://www.refugees.org/survey.

15. Global Commission on International Migration, *Migration in an Interconnected World: New Directions for Action* (Geneva: Global Commission on International Migration, 2005), 16, available at http://www.gcim.org; Organization for Economic Cooperation and Development (OECD), *International Migration*

Outlook: Managing Labour Migration Beyond the Crisis, OECD Continuous Reporting System on Migration (SOPEMI) (Paris: OECD, 2009), 206.

16. Douglas S. Massey, *Backfire at the Border: Why Enforcement Without Legalization Cannot Stop Illegal Immigration*, Trade Policy Analysis no. 29 (Washington, D.C.: Center for Trade Policy Studies, June 13, 2005), 5–9.

17. See, for example, Australian Department of Immigration and Multicultural and Indigenous Affairs, *Refugee and Humanitarian Issues: Australia's Response* (Canberra: Commonwealth of Australia, 2002), 3–4. For evidence of this logic in official French discourse, see also Jane Freedman, "Mobilising Against Detention and Deportation: Collective Actions Against the Detention and Deportation of 'Failed' Asylum Seekers in France," *French Politics* 7, nos. 3–4 (2009), 345–46.

18. Sonia Sirtori and Patricia Coelho, *Defending Refugees' Access to Protection in Europe* (Brussels: European Council of Refugees and Exiles, 2007), 4–16; Matthew J. Gibney, *Outside the Protection of the Law: The Situation of Irregular Migrants in Europe*, Working Paper no. 6 (Oxford, U.K.: Refugee Studies Centre, University of Oxford, 2000), 13; Sile Reynolds and Helen Muggeridge, *Remote Controls: How UK Border Controls Are Endangering the Lives of Refugees* (London: Refugee Council, 2008), 4–6; Catherine Dauvergne, *Making People Illegal: What Globalization Means for Migration and Law* (Cambridge, U.K.: Cambridge University Press, 2008), 50–60.

19. Tony Blair, "New International Approaches to Asylum Processing and Protection," paper submitted for discussion at the European Council, Brussels, March 20–21, 2003; Otto Schily, "Effecktiver Schutz für Flüchtlinge, Wrikungsvolle Bekämpfung illegaler Migration," press statement, September 9, 2005, available at http://www.bmi.bund.de/cln_012/nn_662928/Internet/Content/Nachrichten/Archiv/Pressemitteilungen/2005/09/Fluechtlingsschutz.html.

20. Liza Schuster, *The Realities of a New Asylum Paradigm*, Working Paper no. 20 (Oxford, U.K.: Centre on Migration, Policy, and Society, University of Oxford, 2005), 11–16; Bernd Kasparek, "Frontex und die Europäische Außengrenze," in *Was Ist Frontex? Aufgaben und Strukturen der Europäischen Agentur für die Operative Zusammenarbeit an den Außengrenzen*, Materialien gegen Krieg, Repression und für andere Verhältnisse, no. 4 (brochure by order of Tobias Pflüger, Member of European Parliament, 2008), 13; Amnesty International (European Union Office), "Immigration Cooperation with Libya: The Human Rights Perspective," briefing ahead of the Justice and Home Affairs Council meeting, Brussels, April 14, 2005, 1–5; Rutvica Andrijasevic, "Deported: The Right to Asylum at EU's External Border of Italy and Libya," *International Migration* 48, no. 1 (2009), 154.

21. Jef Huysmans and Alessandra Buonfino, "Politics of Exception and Unease: Immigration, Asylum, and Terrorism in Parliamentary Debates in the UK," *Political Studies* 56 (2008), 782–83; Didier Bigo, "Security and Immigration:

Toward a Critique of the Governmentality of Unease," *Alternatives* 27, special issue (2002), 65–73.

22. Nicholas De Genova, "Migrant 'Illegality' and Deportability in Everyday Life," *Annual Review of Anthropology* 31 (2002), 422–23.

23. For discussions on these dilemmas, see *The Rights of Irregular Migrants*, special issue of *Ethics and International Relations* 22 (2008); and Ayelet Shachar, "Against Birthright Privilege: Redefining Citizenship as Property," in *Identities, Affiliations, and Allegiances*, ed. Seyla Benhabib, Ian Shapiro, and Danilo Petranović, 257–81 (Cambridge, U.K.: Cambridge University Press, 2007).

24. Jennifer Gordon, *Suburban Sweatshops: The Fight for Immigrant Rights* (Cambridge, Mass.: Belknap Press of Harvard University Press, 2005), chaps. 5 and 6.

25. Monica Varsanyi, "The Paradox of Contemporary Immigrant Political Mobilization: Organized Labor, Undocumented Migrants, and Electoral Participation in Los Angeles," *Antipode* 37, no. 4 (2005), 782–87.

26. See, for example, Andrew Linklater, *The Transformation of Political Community: Ethical Foundations of the Post-Westphalian Era* (Cambridge, U.K.: Polity Press, 1998); Daniele Archibugi, ed., *Debating Cosmopolitics* (London: Verso, 2003); Benhabib, Shapiro, and Petranović, *Identities, Affiliations, and Allegiances*; Ulf Hedetoft and Mette Hjort, eds., *The Postnational Self: Belonging and Identity* (Minneapolis: University of Minnesota Press, 2002); Wayne Hudson and Steven Slaughter, eds., *Globalization and Citizenship: The Transnational Challenge* (London: Routledge, 2007); Mike Savage, Gaynor Bagnall, and Brian Longhurst, *Globalization and Belonging* (London: Sage, 2005); Michael Lister, ed., *Europeanization and Migration: Challenging the Values of Citizenship in Europe?* special issue of *Citizenship Studies* 12, no. 6 (2008); Patricia Ehrkamp and Helga Leitner, eds., *Rethinking Immigration and Citizenship: New Spaces of Migrant Transnationalism and Belonging*, special issue of *Environment and Planning A* 38 (2006).

27. Michael Peter Smith, *Transnational Urbanism: Locating Globalization* (Malden, Mass.: Blackwell, 2001). Numerous others have focused on cities as key sites of contemporary citizenship transformation. See, for instance, the following edited collections: Soledad Garcia, ed., *Cities and Citizenship*, special issue of *International Journal of Urban and Regional Research* 20 (1996); James Holston and Arjun Appadurai, eds., *Cities and Citizenship*, special issue of *Public Culture* 8 (1996); Engin F. Isin, ed., *Democracy, Citizenship, and the Global City* (London: Routledge, 2000); Lynn A. Staeheli, ed., *Cities and Citizenship*, special issue of *Urban Geography* 24, no. 2 (2003).

28. Nevzat Soguk, "Transversal Communication, Diaspora, and the Euro-Kurds," *Review of International Studies* 34, no. 1 (2008), 174.

29. Aihwa Ong, *Flexible Citizenship: The Cultural Logics of Transnationality* (Durham, N.C.: Duke University Press, 1999).

30. See, for example, Michael Peter Smith and Matt Bakker, *Citizenship Across Borders: The Political Transnationalism of* El Migrante (Ithaca, N.Y.: Cornell University Press, 2008), esp. 208; Nina Glick Schiller and Georges Fouron, "Transnational Lives and National Identities: The Identity Politics of Haitian Immigrants," in *Transnationalism from Below*, ed. Michael Peter Smith and Luis E. Guarnizo, 112–40 (New Brunswick, N.J.: Transaction, 1998); Ninna Nyberg Sørensen, "Narrating Identity Across Dominican Worlds," in *Transnationalism from Below*, ed. Smith and Guarnizo, 196–217; Nadje Al-Ali, Richard Black, and Khalid Koser, "The Limits to 'Transnationalism': Bosnian and Eritrean Refugees in Europe as Emerging Transnational Communities," *Ethnic and Racial Studies* 24, no. 4 (2001): 578–600; Eva K. Østergaard-Nielsen, "The Politics of Migrants' Transnational Political Practices," *International Migration Review* 37, no. 3 (2003): 760–86. For notable exceptions that incorporate the experience of irregular migrants, see Carlos G. Vélez-Ibáñez and Anna Sampaio, eds., *Transnational Latina/o Communities* (Lanham, Md.: Rowman and Littlefield, 2002), 15, 21–23; María de los Angeles Torres, "Transnational Political and Cultural Identities: Crossing Theoretical Borders," in *Latino/a Thought: Culture, Politics, and Society*, ed. Francisco H. Vazquez and Rodolfo D. Torres (Lanham, Md.: Rowman and Littlefield, 2003), 371.

31. Smith, *Transnational Urbanism*, 150–52. See also Ruud Koopmans, Paul Statham, Marco Giugni, and Florence Passy, *Contested Citizenship: Immigration and Cultural Diversity in Europe* (Minneapolis: University of Minnesota Press, 2005). Although Koopmans and colleagues include irregular migrants within the scope of their study into migrant contestations of citizenship, they make little of the distinction between regular and irregular status.

32. Yasemin Nuhoglu Soysal, *Limits of Citizenship: Migrants and Postnational Membership in Europe* (Chicago: University of Chicago Press, 1994), 2.

33. Ibid., 3.

34. Koopmans et al., *Contested Citizenship*, 75–76; Rainer Bauböck, "Who Are the Citizens of Europe?" *Eurozine* (December 23, 2006), 1–2.

35. Soysal, *Limits of Citizenship*, 9.

36. Seyla Benhabib, *The Rights of Others: Aliens, Residents, and Citizens* (Cambridge, U.K.: Cambridge University Press, 2004), 178–79.

37. Ibid., 168.

38. Ibid., 173.

39. Ibid., 169, 181, emphasis in original.

40. Etienne Balibar, *Strangers as Enemies: Further Reflections on the Aporias of Transnational Citizenship*, Working Paper no. 06/4 (Hamilton, Canada: Institute on Globalization and the Human Condition, McMaster University, 2006); Cristina Beltrán, "Going Public: Hannah Arendt, Immigrant Action, and the Space of Appearance," *Political Theory* 37, no. 5 (2009): 595–622; Carolina Moulin and

Peter Nyers, "'We Live in a Country of UNHCR': Refugee Protests and Global Political Society," *International Political Sociology* 1, no. 4 (2007): 356–72; Peter Nyers, "Abject Cosmopolitanism: The Politics of Protection in the Anti-deportation Movement," *Third World Quarterly* 24, no. 6 (2003): 1069–93; Peter Nyers, "No One Is Illegal Between City and Nation," in *Acts of Citizenship*, ed. Engin F. Isin and Greg M. Nielson, 160–81 (London: Zed Books, 2008); Peter Nyers, *Rethinking Refugees: Beyond States of Emergency* (New York: Routledge, 2006); Vicki Squire, *The Exclusionary Politics of Asylum* (New York: Palgrave Macmillan, 2009); Varsanyi, "Interrogating 'Urban Citizenship' *Vis-à-Vis* Undocumented Migration"; Varsanyi, "The Paradox of Contemporary Immigrant Political Mobilization."

41. Ernesto Laclau and Chantal Mouffe, *Hegemony and Socialist Strategy: Towards a Radical Democratic Politics*, 2d ed. (London: Verso, 2001), x.

42. Ibid., 152–58.

43. Ibid., 159–71.

44. Chantal Mouffe, *The Return of the Political* (London: Verso, 1993), 1–4.

45. Manfred Steger, *The Rise of the Global Imaginary: Political Ideologies from the French Revolution to the Global War on Terror* (Oxford, U.K.: Oxford University Press, 2008).

46. In a classic management text of the early 1990s, for example, Kenichi Ohmae argues that companies must develop a set of values that abandon national identities in favor of a new orientation toward "global localization. . . . Before national identity, before local affiliation, before German ego or Italian ego or Japanese ego—before any of this comes the commitment to a single, unified global mission. You don't think any longer that the company you work for is a Japanese automaker trying to build and sell its products in the United States. You work for Honda or Nissan or Toyota. The customers you care about are the people who love your products everywhere in the world. . . . When you think of your colleagues, you think of people who share that mission. Country of origin does not matter. Location of headquarters does not matter. The products for which you are responsible and the company you serve have become denationalized." The role of government, Ohmae argues, is to "let in the light" that such companies represent, to facilitate their operation, and to cease resisting the global market through nationalized barriers. "These companies and their products do not represent the edge of exploitation. They represent the availability of greater choice and greater satisfaction." Kenichi Ohmae, *The Borderless World: Power and Strategy in the Interlinked Economy* (New York: Harper Perennial, 1991), 94, 194, 201. See also Gary Burtless, Robert Z. Lawrence, Robert E. Litan, and Robert J. Shapiro, *Globaphobia: Confronting Fears About Open Trade* (Washington, D.C.: Brookings Institution, Progressive Policy Institute, and Twentieth Century Fund, 1998), 6–10; Thomas L. Friedman, *The Lexus and the Olive Tree* (New York: Farrar, Straus and Giroux, 1999), 8–10, 197–98; John

Micklethwait and Adrian Wooldridge, eds., *A Future Perfect: The Challenge and Hidden Promise of Globalization* (New York: Crown Business, 2000), xii–xiii.

47. See, for example, Helga Leitner, Eric Sheppard, and Kristin M. Sziarto, "The Spatialities of Contentious Politics," *Transactions of the Institute of British Geographers* 33 (2008): 157–72; Bob Jessop, Neil Brenner, and Martin Jones, "Theorizing Sociospatial Relations," *Environment and Planning D: Society and Space* 26, no. 3 (2008): 389–401; Neil Brenner, Jamie Peck, and Nik Theodore, "After Neoliberalization?" *Globalizations* 7, no. 3 (2010): 327–45; Eric Sheppard, "The Spaces and Times of Globalization: Place, Scale, Networks, and Positionality," *Economic Geography* 78, no. 3 (2002): 307–30; Mimi Sheller and John Urry, "The New Mobilities Paradigm," *Environment and Planning A* 38 (2006): 207–26.

48. Michael J. Shapiro, "Jessop et Al's More Is Better: A Political Rejoinder," *Environment and Planning D: Society and Space* 26, no. 3 (2008), 413.

49. Ibid., 412.

50. Doreen Massey, *For Space* (London: Sage, 2005), 9–11. For a detailed account of the intersection and overlaying of multiple spatialities, see also Paul James, *Globalism, Nationalism, Tribalism: Bringing Theory Back In* (London: Sage, 2006), chap. 7.

51. Edward W. Soja, *Postmodern Geographies: The Reassertion of Space in Critical Social Theory* (London: Verso, 1989), 125.

52. Ibid.

2. THE GLOBALIZING STATE: REMAKING SOVEREIGNTY AND CITIZENSHIP

1. Rafael Alarcón, "The Role of States and Markets in Creating Global Professionals," in *Migration Between States and Markets*, ed. Han Entzinger, Marco Martiniello, and Catherine Wihtol de Wenden (Aldershot, U.K.: Ashgate, 2004), 28–29, 35–37; Peter van de Veer, "Virtual India: Indian IT Labor and the Nation-State," in *Sovereign Bodies: Citizens, Migrants, and States in the Postcolonial World*, ed. Thomas Blom Hansen and Finn Stepputat (Princeton, N.J.: Princeton University Press, 2005), 276–83.

2. Matthew B. Sparke, "A Neoliberal Nexus: Economy, Security, and the Biopolitics of Citizenship on the Border," *Political Geography* 25, no. 2 (2006), 169.

3. Peter Nyers, "Abject Cosmopolitanism: The Politics of Protection in the Anti-deportation Movement," *Third World Quarterly* 24, no. 6 (2003), 1071.

4. Compare Kenichi Ohmae, *The Borderless World: Power and Strategy in the Interlinked Economy* (New York: Harper Perennial, 1991), x–xiii, with Susan

Strange, *The Retreat of the State: The Diffusion of Power in the World Economy* (Cambridge, U.K.: Cambridge University Press, 1996), 4.

5. See, for example, Adam M. McKeown, *Melancholy Order: Asian Migration and the Globalization of Borders* (New York: Columbia University Press, 2008); Neil Brenner, *New State Spaces: Urban Governance and the Rescaling of Statehood* (Oxford, U.K.: Oxford University Press, 2004); Edward S. Cohen, "Globalization and the Boundaries of the State: A Framework for Analyzing the Changing Practice of Sovereignty," *Governance* 14, no. 1 (2001): 75–97; Saskia Sassen, *Territory, Authority, Rights: From Medieval to Global Assemblages* (Princeton, N.J.: Princeton University Press, 2006); Seán Patrick Eudaily and Steve Smith, "Seeing Through States: Sovereign Geopolitics? Uncovering the 'Sovereignty Paradox,'" *Geopolitics* 13, no. 2 (2008): 309–34; Hartmut Behr, "Deterritorialisation and the Transformation of Statehood: The Paradox of Globalisation," *Geopolitics* 13, no. 2 (2008): 359–82; John A. Agnew, *Globalization and Sovereignty* (Lanham, Md.: Rowman and Littlefield, 2009); John A. Agnew, "The Territorial Trap: The Geographical Assumptions of International Relations Theory," *Review of International Political Economy* 1, no. 1 (1994): 53–80.

6. Ravi K. Roy, Arthur T. Denzau, and Thomas D. Willett, "Introduction: Neoliberalism as a Shared Mental Model," in *Neoliberalism: National and Regional Experiments with Global Ideas*, ed. Ravi K. Roy, Arthur T. Denzau, and Thomas D. Willett (London: Routledge, 2007), 4.

7. See, for example, Joseph Stiglitz, *Globalization and Its Discontents* (New York: W. W. Norton, 2002); Joseph Stiglitz, *The Roaring Nineties: Seeds of Destruction* (London: Allen Lane, 2003).

8. See, for example, Gary Burtless, Robert Z. Lawrence, Robert E. Litan, and Robert J. Shapiro, *Globaphobia: Confronting Fears About Open Trade* (Washington, D.C.: Brookings Institution, Progressive Policy Institute, and Twentieth Century Fund, 1998), 6–10 and chap. 11; Thomas L. Friedman, *The Lexus and the Olive Tree* (New York: Farrar, Straus and Giroux, 1999), 8–10, 197–98; John Micklethwait and Adrian Wooldridge, eds., *A Future Perfect: The Challenge and Hidden Promise of Globalization* (New York: Crown Business, 2000), xii–xiii. For discussions of key neoliberal axioms, see Colin Hay, "The Genealogy of Neoliberalism," in *Neoliberalism*, ed. Roy, Denzau, and Willett, 51–70; Nancy Neiman Auerbach, "The Meanings of Neoliberalism," in *Neoliberalism*, ed. Roy, Denzau, and Willett, 26–50. For critical readings of the ideological content of neoliberal globalization, also known as "market globalism," see Stephen Gill, "Theorizing the Interregnum: The Dynamics and Dialectics of Globalization," in *International Political Economy: Understanding Global Disorder*, ed. Björn Hettne (Halifax, Canada: Fernwood Books, 1995), 67–78; Mark Rupert, *Ideologies of Globalization: Contending Visions of a New World Order* (London: Routledge, 2000),

42–64; Manfred Steger, *Globalism: Market Ideology Meets Terrorism* (Lanham, Md.: Rowman and Littlefield, 2005), 47–90.

9. Aihwa Ong, *Flexible Citizenship: The Cultural Logics of Transnationality* (Durham, N.C.: Duke University Press, 1999), 17–18, 227–28; Roy, Denzau, and Willett, *Neoliberalism*. The latter volume includes several chapters on diverse expressions of neoliberalism across different national, geographic, cultural, and religious milieus from the United States to Europe, the Middle East, India, East Asia, Ghana, and Latin America.

10. Barry Hindess, "Neo-liberal Citizenship," *Citizenship Studies* 6, no. 2 (2002): 127–30; Don Flynn, "New Borders, New Management: The Dilemmas of Modern Immigration Policies," *Ethnic and Racial Studies* 28, no. 3 (2005), 471–87; Henk Overbeek, "Neoliberalism and the Regulation of Global Labor Mobility," *Annals of the American Academy of Political and Social Science* 581, no. 1 (2002), 79–85; Rutvica Andrijasevic and William Walters, "The International Organization for Migration and the International Government of Borders," *Environment and Planning D: Society and Space* 28, no. 6 (2010): 977–99.

11. Cohen, "Globalization and the Boundaries of the State," 83, 85.

12. For critical readings of the idea of offshore centers as the natural expansion of the market, see Matthew Donaghy and Michael Clarke, "Are Offshore Financial Centres the Product of Global Markets? A Sociological Response," *Economy and Society* 32, no. 3 (2003), 383–89; Bill Maurer, "Complex Subjects: Offshore Finance, Complexity Theory, and the Dispersion of the Modern," *Socialist Review* 25, nos. 3–4 (1995), 113–17.

13. Heikki Patomäki, *Democratising Globalisation: The Leverage of the Tobin Tax* (London: Zed Books, 2001), 85–86; Tax Justice Network, "The Price of Offshore," March 14, 2005, available at http://www.taxjustice.net/cms/upload/pdf/Briefing_Paper_-_The_Price_of_Offshore_14_MAR_2005.pdf. On the size of the offshore economy, see also Ronen Palan, *The Offshore World: Sovereign Markets, Virtual Places, and Nomad Millionaires* (Ithaca, N.Y.: Cornell University Press, 2003), 7.

14. Jason Sharman, "Offshore and the New International Political Economy," *Review of International Political Economy* 17, no. 1 (2010), 2.

15. William Vlcek, "Behind an Offshore Mask: Sovereignty Games in the Global Political Economy," *Third World Quarterly* 30, no. 8 (2009), 1466.

16. Aihwa Ong, *Neoliberalism as Exception: Mutations in Citizenship and Sovereignty* (Durham, N.C.: Duke University Press, 2006), 75–96.

17. Ong, *Flexible Citizenship*, 217–24; William Milberg and Matthew Amengual, *Economic Development and Working Conditions in Export Processing Zones: A Survey of Trends* (Geneva: International Labour Organisation, 2008), 32–34; Jennifer Hurley, "Garment Industry Subcontracting Chains and Working Conditions: Research Overview," in *Core Labour Standards and the Rights of Women*

Workers in International Supply Chains: Garment Industry Subcontracting in Nine Countries (Manchester, U.K.: Women Working Worldwide, 2004), 24.

18. Tim Bunnell, Hamzah Muzaini, and James D. Sidaway, "Global City Frontiers: Singapore's Hinterland and the Contested Socio-political Geographies of Bintan, Indonesia," *International Journal of Urban and Regional Research* 30, no. 1 (2006), 4.

19. Sassen, *Territory, Authority, Rights*, 235.

20. For a critical discussion of the mixed development results of Mexico's maquiladora zones, for example, see Raúl Delgado Wise and James M. Cypher, "The Strategic Role of Mexican Labor Under NAFTA: Critical Perspectives on Current Economic Integration," *Annals of the American Academy of Political and Social Science* 610, no. 1 (2007), 125–29.

21. Saskia Sassen, *Cities in a World Economy*, 2d ed. (Thousand Oaks, Calif.: Pine Forge Press, 2000), 1, 4, 7.

22. Brenner, *New State Spaces*, 172–256.

23. Sharman, "Offshore and the New International Political Economy," 2.

24. Vlcek, "Behind an Offshore Mask," 1473–78; Sharman, "Offshore and the New International Political Economy," 1–3.

25. Sassen, *Territory, Authority, Rights*, 348–65.

26. Ibid., 362.

27. Oded Löwenheim, "Examining the State: A Foucauldian Perspective on International 'Governance Indicators,'" *Third World Quarterly* 29, no. 2 (2008): 255–74; Patomäki, *Democratising Globalisation*, 93–97; Saskia Sassen, "A New Cross-Border Field for Public and Private Actors," in *Political Space: Frontiers of Change and Governance in a Globalizing World*, ed. Yale H. Ferguson and R. J. Barry Jones (Albany: State University of New York Press, 2002), 179.

28. For a neoliberal perspective, see, for example, Friedman, *The Lexus and the Olive Tree*, 7–13. For a more critical perspective, see Strange, *The Retreat of the State*, 4.

29. Engin F. Isin, "Governing Cities Without Government," in *Democracy, Citizenship and the Global City*, ed. Engin F. Isin (London: Routledge, 2000), 162.

30. "The Global Plan for Recovery and Reform," G20 London Summit communiqué, April 2, 2009, available at http://www.londonsummit.gov.uk/en/.

31. Quoted in Edward Cody, "Sarkozy Advocates Systemic Change After Crisis," *Washington Post*, September 26, 2008.

32. Neil Brenner, Jamie Peck, and Nik Theodore, "After Neoliberalization?" *Globalizations* 7, no. 3 (2010): 327–45.

33. See, for example, the discussions of alternative political arrangements in Tim Bunnell and Neil M. Coe, "Re-fragmenting the 'Political': Globalization, Governmentality, and Malaysia's Multimedia Super Corridor," *Political Geography* 24, no. 7 (2005), 844–45, and in Reece Jones, "Sovereignty and Statelessness

in the Border Enclaves of India and Bangladesh," *Political Geography* 28, no. 6 (2009), 374–75.

34. Paul Bairoch and Richard Kozul-Wright, *Globalization Myths: Some Historical Reflections on Integration, Industrialization, and Growth in the World Economy*, United Nations Commission on Trade and Development (UNCTAD) Discussion Paper no. 113 (Geneva: UNCTAD, 1996), 25–26; Paul Hirst and Grahame Thompson, *Globalization in Question: The International Economy and the Possibility of Governance*, 2d ed. (Cambridge, U.K.: Polity Press, 1999), 2–3.

35. Raúl Delgado Wise and Humberto Márquez Covarrubias, "Capitalist Restructuring, Development, and Labour Migration: The Mexico–U.S. Case," *Third World Quarterly* 29, no. 7 (2008): 1359–74; Global Commission on International Migration, *Migration in an Interconnected World: New Directions for Action* (Geneva: Global Commission on International Migration, October 2005), 32–37, available at http://www.gcim.org; Madeleine Leonard, *Invisible Work, Invisible Workers: The Informal Economy in Europe and the United States* (Houndsmill, U.K.: Macmillan, 1998), 26–56; Bill Jordan and Franck Düvell, *Irregular Migration: The Dilemmas of Transnational Mobility* (Cheltenham, U.K.: Edward Elgar, 2002), 54–76.

36. Hurley, "Garment Industry Subcontracting Chains and Working Conditions," 10–18; Marta López-Garza, "A Study of the Informal Economy and Latina/o Immigrants in Greater Los Angeles," in *Asian and Latino Immigrants in a Restructuring Economy: The Metamorphosis of Southern California*, ed. Marta López-Garza and David R. Diaz (Stanford, Calif.: Stanford University Press, 2001), 144–45; Eric Florence, "Migrant Workers in Shenzhen: Between Discursive Inclusion and Exclusion," in *Migration Between States and Markets*, ed. Entzinger, Martiniello, and Wihtol de Wenden, 45; Ong, *Neoliberalism as Exception*, 106; Amnesty International, *China: Internal Migrants: Discrimination and Abuse. The Human Cost of an Economic "Miracle,"* AI Index: ASA 17/008/2007 (New York: Amnesty International, March 1, 2007), 1–40.

37. On the oil-producing states, see United Nations Population Division, *Levels and Trends of International Migration to Selected Countries in Asia* (New York: United Nations, 2003), 1, 61; Vaughan Robinson, "Security, Migration, and Refugees," in *Redefining Security: Population Movements and National Security*, ed. Nana Poku and David T. Graham (Westport, Conn.: Praeger, 1998), 73. On other locations, see Silvina Schammah Gesser, Rebeca Raijman, Adriana Kemp, and Julia Reznik, "'Making It' in Israel? Latino Undocumented Migrant Workers in the Holy Land," *Estudios Interdisciplinarios de America Latina y el Caribe* 11, no. 2 (2002), available at http://www1.tau.ac.il/eial/index.php?option=com_content&task=view&id=433&Itemid=206; Kamal Sadiq, "When States Prefer Non-citizens Over Citizens: Conflict Over Illegal Immigration Into Malaysia," *International Studies Quarterly* 49, no. 1 (2005): 101–22; Amy Gurowitz, "Migrant Rights and

Activism in Malaysia: Opportunities and Constraints," *Journal of Asian Studies* 59, no. 4 (2000), 865; Yasushi Igushi, "Illegal Migration, Overstay, and Illegal Working in Japan: Development of Policies and Their Evaluation," in *Combating the Illegal Employment of Foreign Workers*, 157–65 (Paris: Organization for Economic Cooperation and Development, 2000); Rochelle Ball and Nicola Piper, "Globalisation and Regulation of Citizenship: Filipino Migrant Workers in Japan," *Political Geography* 21, no. 8 (2002): 1013–34.

38. International Labour Organisation, "Changing Patterns in the World of Work," International Labour Conference, Report I(C), 95th sess., Geneva, 2006, 28; International Labour Organisation, "Towards a Fair Deal for Migrant Workers in the Global Economy," International Labour Conference, Report VI, 92d sess., Geneva, 2004, 11–12; Sassen, *Cities in a World Economy*, 124.

39. Sassen, *Cities in a World Economy*, 126–27.

40. Jennifer Gordon, *Suburban Sweatshops: The Fight for Immigrant Rights* (Cambridge, Mass.: Belknap Press of Harvard University Press, 2005), 10–66; Andrew Herod and Luis L. M. Aguiar, "Introduction: Cleaners and the Dirty Work of Neoliberalism," *Antipode* 38, no. 3 (2006): 425–34; Jon May, Jane Wills, Kavita Datta, Yara Evans, Joanna Herbert, and Cathy McIlwaine, "Keeping London Working: Global Cities, the British State, and London's New Migrant Division of Labour," *Transactions of the Institute of British Geographers* 32, no. 2 (2007): 151–67.

41. Sassen, *Cities in a World Economy*, 135; Norma Stoltz Chinchilla and Nora Hamilton, "Doing Business: Central American Enterprises in Los Angeles," in *Asian and Latino Immigrants in a Restructuring Economy*, ed. López-Garza and Diaz, 188–214; Matthew J. Gibney, *Outside the Protection of the Law: The Situation of Irregular Migrants in Europe*, Working Paper no. 6 (Oxford, U.K.: Refugee Studies Centre, University of Oxford, 2000), 7, 13, 16; Philip Martin, *Bordering on Control: Combating Irregular Migration in North America and Europe*, Migration Research Series no. 13 (Geneva: International Organization for Migration, 2003), 52; International Labour Organisation, "Towards a Fair Deal for Migrant Workers," 48–60; Organization for Economic Cooperation and Development (OECD) Secretariat, "Some Lessons from Recent Regularisation Programmes," in *Combating the Illegal Employment of Foreign Workers* (Paris: OECD, 2000), 61–62; Natasha Iskander, "Immigrant Workers in an Irregular Situation: The Case of the Garment Industry in Paris and Its Suburbs," in *Combating the Illegal Employment of Foreign Workers*, 46–49.

42. Pheng Cheah, *Inhuman Conditions: On Cosmopolitanism and Human Rights* (Cambridge, Mass.: Harvard University Press, 2006), 226.

43. Ibid., 178–229.

44. See, for example, Gurowitz, "Migrant Rights and Activism in Malaysia," 865–67; Claudia Sadowski-Smith, "Reading Across Diaspora: Chinese and Mexican Undocumented Immigration Across U.S. Land Borders," in *Globalization on*

the Line: Culture, Capital, and Citizenship at U.S. Borders, ed. Claudia Sadowski-Smith (New York: Palgrave, 2002), 82–84; Ball and Piper, "Globalisation and Regulation of Citizenship," 1015. For an uncritical reading, see Michael LeMay, *Illegal Immigration: A Reference Handbook* (Santa Barbara, Calif.: ABC-CLIO, 2007).

45. The *Wall Street Journal,* for example, has since 1984 advocated open borders for labor migration in line with the liberalization of trade. See Robert L. Bartley, "Open NAFTA Borders? Why Not?" *Wall Street Journal,* July 2, 2001. See also Julian Simon, "The Case for Greatly Increased Immigration," *The Public Interest* 102 (Winter 1991): 89–103; Thomas Straubhaar, "Why Do We Need a General Agreement on Movements of People (GAMP)?" in *Managing Migration: Time for a New International Regime?* ed. Bimal Ghosh, 110–36 (Oxford, U.K.: Oxford University Press, 2000); Philippe Legrain, *Immigrants: Your Country Needs Them* (London: Little, Brown, 2006).

46. Nicholas De Genova, "Race, Space, and the Reinvention of Latin America in Mexican Chicago," *Latin American Perspectives* 25, no. 5 (1998), 100.

47. Bayram Unal, "The New Patterns and the State: Construction of Illegality for Immigrants in Istanbul," in *Migration Between States and Markets,* ed. Entzinger, Martiniello, and Wihtol de Wenden, 67–78.

48. Stephen Castles and Mark J. Miller, *The Age of Migration,* 4th ed. (New York: Guildford Press, 2009), 67–70.

49. McKeown, *Melancholy Order,* 319.

50. Ibid., 320.

51. Ibid., 321.

52. Sassen provides a list of indicative statistics: "The worldwide (notional) value of traded derivatives, which accounts for most financial market transactions, was $30 trillion in 1994, over $65 trillion in 1999, over $80 trillion by 2000, $97 trillion by 2001, and $220 trillion by 2004, for a 120 percent increase as of 2001, pointing not only to higher levels in values traded but also to an increase in the growth rate. . . . To put this in perspective it is helpful to compare it to the value of other major components of the global economy, such as the value of cross-border trade ($11 trillion in 2004) and global foreign direct investment stock ($6 trillion in 2000 and $8.2 trillion in 2003)." Sassen, *Territory, Authority, Rights,* 250.

53. Mark Purcell and Joseph Nevins, "Pushing the Boundary: State Restructuring, State Theory, and the Case of U.S.–Mexico Border Enforcement in the 1990s," *Political Geography* 24, no. 2 (2005), 228–29; Peter Andreas, *Border Games: Policing the U.S.–Mexico Divide* (Ithaca, N.Y.: Cornell University Press, 2000), x, 9–12; Joseph Nevins, *Operation Gatekeeper: The Rise of the "Illegal Alien" and the Making of the U.S.–Mexico Boundary* (New York: Routledge, 2002), 12.

54. Xavier Ferrer-Gallardo, "The Spanish–Moroccan Border Complex: Processes of Geopolitical, Functional, and Symbolic Rebordering," *Political Geography*

27 (2008), 315. See also Douglas S. Massey, Joaquín Arango, Graeme Hugo, Ali Kouaouci, Adela Pellegrino, and J. Edward Taylor, *Worlds in Motion: Understanding International Migration at the End of the Millennium* (Oxford, U.K.: Clarendon Press, 1998), 6–7, 14, 288.

55. Jean Bethke Elshtain, *Women and War* (New York: Basic Books, 1987).

56. The citizen-warrior ideal has nevertheless been modified. Many militaries are now engaged in less obviously "warlike" activities such as development and peacekeeping; publics are less likely to accept the loss of their soldiers' lives on anything like the scale of wars half a century ago (notwithstanding the reinvigoration of security discourses in the post–September 11 context); and wars are subject to much more widespread critical public appraisal in terms of the justness of the cause (the case of public opposition in the United States and allied countries to the Vietnam War being a turning point in this regard).

57. Amada Root, *Market Citizenship: Experiments in Democracy and Globalization* (London: Sage, 2007); Ong, *Flexible Citizenship*; Hindess, "Neo-liberal Citizenship" 127–30; Engin F. Isin, *Being Political: Genealogies of Citizenship* (Minneapolis: University of Minnesota Press, 2002), 231–63; Margaret R. Somers, *Genealogies of Citizenship: Markets, Statelessness, and the Right to Have Rights* (Cambridge, U.K.: Cambridge University Press, 2008).

58. Ong, *Neoliberalism as Exception*, 11.

59. Ong, *Flexible Citizenship*, 112. See also Aihwa Ong, "Latitudes of Citizenship: Membership, Meaning, and Multiculturalism," in *People out of Place: Globalization, Human Rights and the Citizenship Gap*, ed. Alison Brysk and Gershon Shafir (London: York: Routledge, 2004), 57– 61.

60. Bill Maurer, "Cyberspatial Sovereignties: Offshore Finance, Digital Case, and the Limits of Liberalism," *Indiana Journal of Global Legal Studies* 5, no. 2 (1998), 494.

61. U.S. Citizenship and Immigration Services, *Green Card Through Investment* (Washington, D.C.: U.S. Department of Homeland Security, n.d.), available at http://www.uscis.gov/portal/site/uscis/menuitem.eb1d4c2a3e5b9ac89243 c6a7543f6d1a/?vgnextoid=cf54a6c515083210VgnVCM100000082ca60aRCRD &vgnextchannel=cf54a6c515083210VgnVCM100000082ca60aRCRD, current as of June 15, 2010.

62. John Tagliabue, "Pace of Change Too Slow to Keep Entrepreneurs in France," *New York Times*, March 11, 2008.

63. Van de Veer, "Virtual India," 277–78; Paula Chakravartty, "Symbolic Analysts of Indentured Servants? Indian High-Tech Migrants in America's Information Economy," in *The Human Face of Global Mobility*, ed. Michael Peter Smith and Adrian Favell (New Brunswick, N.J.: Transaction, 2006), 161.

64. On states' instrumental approach to overseas workers and remittances, see Gurowitz, "Migrant Rights and Activism in Malaysia," 870–71; Ball and

Piper, "Globalisation and Regulation of Citizenship," 1014, 1020–23; Katherine Gibson, Lisa Law, and Deidre McKay, "Beyond Heroes and Victims: Filipina Contract Migrants, Economic Activism, and Class Transformations," *International Feminist Journal of Politics* 3, no. 3 (2001), 366–69. On figures for workers' remittances, see Dilip Ratha, "Workers' Remittances: An Important and Stable Source of External Development Finance," in *Global Development Finance: Striving for Stability in Development Finance* (Washington, D.C.: World Bank, 2003), 1:161; Dilip Ratha, Sanket Mohapatra, and Ani Silwal, *Migration and Remittance Trends, 2009*, Migration and Development Brief no. 11 (Washington, D.C.: World Bank, November 3, 2009), 1–14.

65. Nicola Phillips, "Migration as Development Strategy? The New Political Economy of Dispossession and Inequality in the Americas," *Review of International Political Economy* 16, no. 2 (2009), 251. For an alternative view that identifies more progressive migrant-led outcomes of neoliberal development strategies based on migrant remittances, see Michael Peter Smith and Matt Bakker, *Citizenship Across Borders: The Political Transnationalism of El Migrante* (Ithaca, N.Y.: Cornell University Press, 2008), 79–105.

66. Steven Vertovec, "Conceiving and Researching Transnationalism," *Ethnic and Racial Studies* 22, no. 2 (1999), 455. On the case of Mexican ID cards, see Monica Varsanyi, *Rising Tensions Between National and Local Immigration and Citizenship Policy: Matrículas Consulares, Local Membership, and Documenting the Undocumented* Working Paper no. 140 (San Diego: Center for Comparative Immigration Studies, University of California, 2006), 8–11.

67. Peter Nyers, "Forms of Irregular Citizenship," in *The Contested Politics of Mobility: Borderzones and Irregularity*, ed. Vicki Squire (London: Routledge, 2010), 184–98.

68. Several unions have formed a "Change to Win" coalition on this basis. See http://www.changetowin.org/about-us.html. See also Richard L. Trumka, "Remarks by AFL-CIO President Richard L. Trumka at the City Club of Cleveland, Cleveland Ohio," June 18, 2010, available at: http://www.aflcio.org/mediacenter/prsptm/sp06182010.cfm.

69. On labor organizing around temporary migration in Australia, see Nicole Oke, "Working Transnationally: Australian Unions and Temporary Migrant Work," *Social Alternatives* 29, no. 3 (forthcoming). On a new "student-migrant-worker" subjectivity, see Brett Neilson, "The World Seen from a Taxi: Students-Migrants-Workers in the Global Multiplication of Labour," *Subjectivity*, no. 29 (2009), 427–41.

70. Özge Berber Ağtaş, Beate Amler, and Luciole Sauviat, "Between Organising and Exclusion: Trade Union Strategies and Undocumented Migrant Workers," in *Leben in der Illegalität: Ein Dossier* (Berlin: Heinrich-Böll-Stiftung [Schriften Zur Demokratie, Band 5], 2008), 73–76; Herod and Aguiar, "Introduction," 432;

Jane Wills, "Making Class Politics Possible: Organizing Contract Cleaners in London," *International Journal of Urban and Regional Research* 32, no. 2 (2008), 312–14.

71. May et al., "Keeping London Working," 151.

72. See the organization's Web site at http://www.women-ww.org/index .html.

73. See *Core Labour Standards and the Rights of Women Workers*, the collection published by Women Working Worldwide in 2004.

74. Angela Hale, "Introduction: Why Research International Subcontracting Chains?" in *Core Labour Standards and the Rights of Women Workers*, 5–6.

3. POLICING AUSTRALIA'S BORDERS: NEW TERRAINS
OF SOVEREIGN PRACTICE

1. Australian Broadcasting Corporation, "The Inside Story," *Four Corners*, ABC Television August 13, 2001.

2. That border policing in Australia has been carefully crafted and perfectly timed for cynical political purposes is now well established. For details of this chapter in Australian political history as well as its effects on those seeking asylum, see David Marr and Marian Wilkinson, *Dark Victory*, 2d ed. (Sydney: Allen & Unwin, 2004); Robert Manne and David Corlett, "Sending Them Home: Refugees and the New Politics of Indifference," *Quarterly Essay*, no. 13 (2004): 1–95; Kasimierz Bem, Nina Field, Nic Maclellan, Sarah Meyer, and Tony Morris, *A Price Too High: The Cost of Australia's Approach to Asylum Seekers* (Sydney: A Just Australia, Oxfam Australia, and Oxfam Novib, 2007); Human Rights and Equal Opportunity Commission, *A Last Resort? Report of the National Inquiry Into Children in Detention* (Sydney: Commonwealth of Australia, 2004); Phil Glendenning, Carmel Leavey, Margaret Hetherton, Mary Britt, and Tony Morris, *Deported to Danger: A Study of Australia's Treatment of 40 Rejected Asylum Seekers* (Sydney: Edmund Rice Centre for Justice and Community Education with the School of Education, Australian Catholic University, 2004); Greg Marston, *Temporary Protection, Permanent Uncertainty: The Experience of Refugees Living on Temporary Protection Visas* (Melbourne: Centre for Applied Social Research, RMIT University, 2003).

3. James F. Hollifield, "The Emerging Migration State," *International Migration Review* 38, no. 3 (2004), 886.

4. The former Howard government maintained a ban on work rights for asylum seekers on certain types of visas despite research showing the economic benefits of the entrance of asylum seekers to the labor market. The maintenance

of the ban was not so much a case of contradictory policies as the prioritization of being seen to be tough on asylum seekers—a performative territorial gesture in the greater service of legitimizing a broader neoliberal project. On the economic argument for asylum seekers' right to work, see Gwilym Croucher, "A Chance to Contribute: Some Remarks on the Potential Economic Impact of Allowing Asylum Seekers the Right to Work," *Just Policy: A Journal of Australian Social Policy*, no. 44 (2007): 37–43.

5. Michael Pusey, *Economic Rationalism in Canberra: A Nation-Building State Changes Its Mind* (Cambridge, U.K.: Cambridge University Press, 1991), 6; Lindy Edwards, *How to Argue with an Economist: Reopening Political Debate in Australia* (Cambridge, U.K.: Cambridge University Press, 2002), 6–7, 23–26.

6. The phrase became famous after it was used by former treasurer Paul Keating in a media conference in 1991. On the new role of the state, see Tom Conley, "The Domestic Politics of Globalisation," *Australian Journal of Political Science* 36, no. 2 (2001), 241.

7. John Edwards, Australia's Economic Revolution (Sydney: University of New South Wales Press, 2000), 10; Richard Blandy, "Australian Labour Market Reform: What Needs to Be Done?" Australian Bulletin of Labour 32, no. 1 (2006), 8. By early 2007, Australia had enjoyed a record of fifteen years of uninterrupted economic growth, and unemployment had been reduced to its lowest in thirty-two years. See Australian Bureau of Statistics, Australian National Accounts: National Income, Expenditure, and Product, Catalogue no. 5206.0 (Canberra: Commonwealth of Australia, 2006), and Australian Bureau of Statistics, Labour Force, Australia, March 2007, Catalogue no. 6202.0 (Canberra: Commonwealth of Australia, 2007), both available at http://www.abs.gov.au.

8. Edwards, *Australia's Economic Revolution*, 12–14, 50–52.

9. Francis Fukuyama, "The End of History," *The National Interest* 16 (Summer 1989), 3.

10. Thomas L. Friedman, *The Lexus and the Olive Tree*, 2d ed. (New York: Farrar, Straus and Giroux, 2000), 241.

11. Kevin Rudd, "The Global Financial Crisis," *The Monthly*, no. 42 (2009), 20.

12. Tim Colebatch, "To Reform or Not to Reform," *The Age*, December 7, 2004; John Burgess and Ian Campbell, "Casual Employment in Australia: Growth, Characteristics, a Bridge or a Trap?" *Economic and Labour Relations Review* 9, no. 1 (1998): 31–54.

13. "Income Distribution Trends," in *Advance Australia Where?* special feature in *The Australian*, June 17–22, 2000. See also Jeff Borland, Bob Gregory, and Paul Sheehan, "Inequality and Economic Change," in *Work Rich, Work Poor: Inequality and Economic Change in Australia*, ed. Jeff Borland, Bob Gregory, and Paul Sheehan, 1–20 (Melbourne: Centre for Strategic Economic Studies, Victoria University, 2001), as well as other essays in this volume.

14. Michael Pusey, *The Experience of Middle Australia: The Dark Side of Economic Reform* (Cambridge, U.K.: Cambridge University Press, 2003), 59–73; Ian McAllister and Clive Bean, "The Electoral Politics of Economic Reform in Australia: The 1998 Election," *Australian Journal of Political Science* 35, no. 3 (2000), 392. See also Alison McClelland and Susan St. John, "Social Policy Responses to Globalisation in Australia and New Zealand, 1980–2005," *Australian Journal of Political Science* 41, no. 2 (2006), 183.

15. On the issue of envy, see Clive Hamilton, "What's Left? The Death of Social Democracy," *Quarterly Essay* 21 (2006), 22. On government transfers, see David Johnson, Ian Manning, and Otto Hellwig, "Trends in the Distribution of Income in Australia," *Australian Journal of Labour Economics* 2, no. 1 (1998), 21–22; Ann Harding and Quoc Ngu Vu, "Income Inequality and Tax-Transfer Policy: Trends and Questions," presentation to the Economic and Social Outlook Conference, University of Melbourne, November 2, 2006.

16. James Jupp, *From White Australia to Woomera: The Story of Australian Immigration* (Cambridge, U.K.: Cambridge University Press, 2002), 129–30; McAllister and Bean, "The Electoral Politics of Economic Reform in Australia," 396–98; Rachel Gibson, Ian McAllister, and Tami Swenson, "The Politics of Race and Immigration in Australia: One Nation Voting in the 1998 Election," *Ethnic and Racial Studies* 25, no. 5 (2002), 823–38.

17. Katharine Betts, *The Great Divide: Immigration Politics in Australia* (Sydney: Duffy & Snellgrove, 1999). The first edition of this book was published in 1988 under the title *Ideology and Immigration: Australia 1976–1987*.

18. John Howard, "The Role of Government: A Modern Liberal Approach," Menzies Research Centre National Lecture Series, June 6, 1995, available on the Australian Politics Web site at http://australianpolitics.com/executive/howard/pre-2002/95-06-06role-of-government.shtml.

19. See, for example, the collected articles in Robert Manne, ed., *The New Intolerance*, special edition of *Quadrant* 35 (1990); Piers Ackerman, "Losers Left Behind," *Sunday Telegraph*, August 29, 1999.

20. Barry Hindess and Marian Sawer, "Introduction," in *Us and Them: Anti-elitism in Australia*, ed. Barry Hindess and Marian Sawer, 1–13 (Perth: API Network, 2004); Damien Cahill, "New-Class Discourse and the Construction of Left Wing Elites," in *Us and Them*, ed. Hindess and Sawer, 84–94.

21. Cited in Manne and Corlett, "Sending Them Home," 32.

22. Some two thousand persons arrived by boat compared with a total of more than sixty thousand Indo-Chinese who arrived by various means, fifty thousand of whom were Vietnamese. Most were accepted via refugee camps in Southeast Asia. See Nancy Viviani, *The Long Journey: Vietnamese Migration and Settlement in Australia* (Melbourne: University of Melbourne Press, 1984), 50–51.

23. Don McMaster, "Asylum-Seekers and the Insecurity of a Nation," *Australian Journal of International Affairs* 56, no. 2 (2002), 284–85.

24. Quoted in Anthony Burke, *In Fear of Security: Australia's Invasion Anxiety* (Sydney: Pluto Press, 2001), xxii. Asylum seekers arriving in Australia by boat increased in number from 921 in 1998–99 to 4,175 in 1999–2000 and 4,137 in 2000–2001; see Australian Department of Immigration and Multicultural and Indigenous Affairs, "Unauthorised Arrivals by Air and Sea," Fact Sheet no. 74, available at http://www.immi.gov.au/facts/74unauthorised.htm.

25. For a summary, see Penelope Mathew, "Australian Refugee Protection in the Wake of the *Tampa*," *American Journal of International Law* 96, no. 3 (2002): 661–76.

26. Amnesty International, *Offending Human Dignity: The "Pacific Solution,"* AI Index: ASA 12/009/2002 (New York: Amnesty International, 2002), 7; William Maley, "Asylum-Seekers in Australia's International Relations," *Australian Journal of International Affairs* 57, no. 1 (2003), 195; Tony Kevin, *A Certain Maritime Incident: The Sinking of SIEV X* (Melbourne: Scribe, 2004), 238–54.

27. Peter Reith, in an interview by Derryn Hinch, Radio 3AK, September 13, 2001, available on the Australian Department of Defence Web site, http://www.defence.gov.au/minister/2001/1309013.doc.

28. Howard quoted in Prem Kumar Rajaram and Carl Grundy-Warr, "The Irregular Migrant as Homo Sacer: Migration and Detention in Australia, Malaysia, and Thailand," *International Migration* 42, no. 1 (2004), 43–44.

29. This sentiment was reflected more generally as Muslim Australians became the subject of verbal and physical attacks and arguably of official discrimination after September 11, 2001. See New South Wales Anti-discrimination Board, *Race for the Headlines: Racism and Media Discourse* (Sydney: Government of New South Wales, August 24, 2003), 41–55; Suvendrini Perera, "A Line in the Sea," *Race & Class* 44, no. 2 (2002), 29; Chloe Saltau, "Call for Calm After Rise in Attacks on Muslims," *The Age*, September 15, 2001. It is no coincidence that Muslim Australians subsequently expressed concern that they might be used as a "new *Tampa*" in the context of a renewed government emphasis on defining Australian values in citizenship and education. See Barney Zwartz, "Muslim Leaders Feel Betrayed," *The Age*, September 18, 2006. Considering that some commentators have called for deportation of Australian Muslims who express objectionable views—regardless of their citizenship status—and others for a halt to all Muslim immigration to Australia, suggestions of fears of a "new *Tampa*" are not unrealistic. See, for example, "Deport Rape Comment Cleric, Says Goward," *The Age*, October 26, 2006; John Stone, "The Muslim Problem and What to Do About It," *Quadrant* 50, no. 9 (2006): 11–17.

30. Burke, *In Fear of Security*, 324; Ghassan Hage, *Against Paranoid Nationalism: Searching for Hope in a Shrinking Society* (Sydney: Pluto Press, 2003), 31–68.

31. John Howard, "Address at Community Morning Tea, Ocean Grove, Victoria," September 6, 2001, available at http://www.pm.gov.au/news/speeches/2001/speech1221.htm.

32. See, for example, Philip Ruddock, "Refugee Claims and Australian Migration Law: A Ministerial Perspective," *University of New South Wales Law Journal* 23, no. 3 (2000): 1–11; Australian Department of Immigration and Multicultural Affairs, *Protecting the Border: Immigration Compliance* (Canberra: Commonwealth of Australia, 2001); Howard, "Address at Community Morning Tea, Ocean Grove, Victoria."

33. On this topic, see chapter 1 in this volume, p. 22.

34. Human Rights Watch, *"By Invitation Only": Australian Asylum Policy* (New York: Human Rights Watch, December 2002), available at http://hrw.org/reports/2002/australia/.

35. Cited in Andrew West, "Asylum-Seeker Teenagers Join Lip Sewing Protest," *Sun Herald*, January 20, 2002.

36. Philip Ruddock, interviewed for Australian Broadcasting Corporation, "The Inside Story."

37. John Howard, interviewed by Phillip Clark, Radio 2GB, October 8, 2001, available at http://www.pm.gov.au/media/Interview/2001/interview1371.cfm.

38. In the wake of the *Tampa* affair, polling indicated that three-quarters of the Australian public supported the decision to refuse entry to the *Tampa*'s asylum seekers and approved of the government's handling of events. Graeme Hugo, "Australian Immigration Policy: The Significance of the Events of September 11," *International Migration Review* 36, no. 1 (2002), 38.

39. Mike Scrafton, "PM Told No Children Overboard" (letter), *The Australian*, August 16, 2004.

40. Ian McAllister, "Border Protection, the 2001 Australian Election, and the Coalition Victory," *Australian Journal of Political Science* 38, no. 3 (2003), 446.

41. For example, Robert Jovicic, born in France to Serbian parents, migrated with them to Australia in 1968 as a two-year-old. In 2004, Jovicic had his permanent residency status revoked and was deported to Serbia on character grounds as a result of a series of burglaries committed to support his heroin addiction. He was refused Serbian citizenship and effectively rendered stateless. After media attention in 2006 revealed that Jovicic was living on the streets in Serbia, the Australian government agreed to allow his return to Australia and granted a special-purpose visa that allowed for a temporary stay of two years. After coming to power in 2007, the Rudd Labor government finally granted Jovicic permanent residency.

42. Australian Commonwealth Ombudsman, *Inquiry Into the Circumstances of the Vivian Alvarez Matter* (Canberra: Commonwealth of Australia, 2005), ix–xvi;

Misha Schubert, "Identity Crisis: Eleven Ailing Australian Citizens or Residents Wrongly Detained," *The Age*, October 29, 2005.

43. Mick Palmer, *Inquiry Into the Circumstances of the Immigration Detention of Cornelia Rau* (Canberra: Commonwealth of Australia, 2005), 161.

44. In June 2005, five Liberal Party Backbenchers negotiated with Prime Minister Howard to achieve time limits on the processing of asylum applications, the release of all families with children into community (rather than remote and secure) detention, and greater oversight of detention arrangements by the Commonwealth Ombudsman.

45. GSL (Australia) Pty Ltd., *Corporate Profile* (Melbourne: GSL [Australia], 2006), 4.

46. From Logan's appearance in Australian Broadcasting Corporation, "The Detention Industry," *Background Briefing*, ABC Radio National, June 20, 2004, available at http://www.abc.net.au/rn/talks/bbing/stories/s1137813.htm.

47. George Zoley, president of GEO Group (a longtime player in the U.S. detention industry), cited in Tom Barry, *The National Imperative to Imprison Immigrants for Profit*, Americas Program Report (Washington, D.C.: Center for International Policy, March 10, 2009), 4.

48. Parliament of the Commonwealth of Australia, *Detention Centre Contracts: Review of Audit Report No. 1, 2005–2006, Management of the Detention Centre Contracts: Part B* (Canberra: Joint Standing Committee on Migration, 2005), 18.

49. Richard Harding, inspector of custodial services in Western Australia, cited in Australian Broadcasting Corporation, "The Detention Industry."

50. Michael Flynn and Cecilia Cannon, *The Privatization of Immigration Detention: Towards a Global View* (Geneva: Global Detention Project, Graduate Institute of International and Development Studies, 2009), 14–15.

51. Parliament of the Commonwealth of Australia, *Immigration Detention in Australia: Facilities, Services, and Transparency* (Canberra: Joint Standing Committee on Migration, 2009), 66–72.

52. Australian Human Rights Commission, *Immigration Detention and Offshore Processing on Christmas Island* (Sydney: Australian Human Rights Commission, 2009), 22.

53. Saskia Sassen, *Territory, Authority, Rights: From Medieval to Global Assemblages* (Princeton, N.J.: Princeton University Press, 2006), 222–71.

54. Anthony Bergin, John Azarias, and Don Williams, *Advancing Australian Homeland Security: Leveraging the Private Sector*, Australian Strategic Policy Institute (ASPI) Special Report, Issue 14 (Canberra: ASPI, 2008), 2, 5, emphasis added.

55. Parliament of the Commonwealth of Australia, *Immigration Detention in Australia*, 34.

56. Alexander Downer and Amanda Vanstone, "Minasa Bone Returns to Indonesia," joint media release from the Australian minister for foreign affairs and the minister for immigration, multicultural, and Indigenous affairs, November 9, 2003, available at http://www.foreignminister.gov.au/releases/2003/joint_Minasa_Bone.html.

57. Alexander Kirk, "Govt Maintains Kurds Didn't Seek Asylum," *The World Today,* ABC Radio National, November 11, 2003, available at http://www.abc.net.au/worldtoday/content/2003/s986708.htm. For a summary of the legislation regarding excision, see Mary Crock, Ben Saul, and Azadeh Dastyari, *Future Seekers II: Refugees and Irregular Migration in Australia* (Sydney: Federation Press, 2006), 117–20.

58. Commonwealth of Australia, *Securing Australia, Protecting Our Community: Counter-terrorism White Paper* (Canberra: Department of the Prime Minister and Cabinet, 2010), 39.

59. Bem et al., *A Price Too High,* 36–37.

60. Chris Evans, "Refugee Policy Under the Rudd Government: The First Year," address to the Refugee Council of Australia, Paramatta Town Hall, November 17, 2008, available at http://www.chrisevans.alp.org.au/news/1108/immispeeches17–01.php; Karin Fathimath Afeef, *The Politics of Extraterritorial Processing: Offshore Asylum Policies in Europe and the Pacific,* Working Paper no. 36 (Oxford, U.K.: Refugee Studies Centre, University of Oxford, 2006), 23. The cost of offshore detention and processing of asylum seekers in the six years following the *Tampa* affair amounted to more than one billion Australian dollars. Government estimates suggest that onshore detention for a maximum of three months would have reduced costs by a startling 96.5 percent. Bem et al., *A Price Too High,* 4.

61. On Australia's influence on European policy development, see Bem et al., *A Price Too High,* 48. On Italy's use of island territories, see Rutvica Andrijasevic, "Deported: The Right to Asylum at EU's External Border of Italy and Libya," *International Migration* 48, no. 1 (2009): 148–62. On the externalization of the European border in general, see Christoph Marischka, "Frontex: Die Vernetzungs-Maschine an den Randzonen des Rechtes und der Staaten," in *Was Ist Frontex? Aufgaben und Strukturen der Europäischen Agentur für die operative Zusammenarbeit an den Außengrenzen,* 16–23, Materialien gegen Krieg, Repression und für andere Verhältnisse, no. 4 (brochure by order of Tobias Pflüger, Member of European Parliament, 2008); Liza Schuster, *The Realities of a New Asylum Paradigm,* Working Paper no. 20 (Oxford, U.K.: Centre on Migration, Policy, and Society, University of Oxford, 2005), 11–16. On the growing role of African states in European border policing, see Hein de Haas, "The Myth of Invasion: The Inconvenient Realities of African Migration to Europe," *Third World Quarterly* 29, no. 7 (2008), 1305–19.

62. Bernd Kasparek, "Frontex und die Europäische Außengrenze," in *Was Ist Frontex?* 12.

63. Commonwealth of Australia, *Securing Australia*, 37.

64. Rudd, "The Global Financial Crisis," 29.

65. Kevin Rudd quoted in "People Smugglers Should Rot in Hell: Rudd," *PM*, ABC Radio National, April 17, 2009, available at http://www.abc.net.au/pm/content/2008/s2546098.htm.

66. Chris Evans, "New Directions in Detention: Restoring Integrity to Australia's Immigration System," address to the Centre for International and Public Law, Australian National University, Canberra, July 29, 2008, available at http://www.minister.immi.gov.au/media/speeches/2008/ce080729.htm.

67. "Pushing the border offshore" is an expression used in a government brochure explaining the logic behind administrative profiling of passengers at points of departure. Cited in Leanne Weber, "Policing the Virtual Border: Punitive Preemption in Australian Offshore Migration Control," *Social Justice* 34, no. 2 (2007), 84.

4. ACTS OF CONTESTATION: THE SANS-PAPIERS OF FRANCE

1. For a summary of the early phases of the movement, see Teresa Hayter, *Open Borders: The Case Against Immigration Controls* (London: Pluto Press, 2000), 142–48. Details of the occupation of the General Confederation of Labor and the Sans-Papiers' "ministry" can be found on the Coordination de Sans-Papiers 75 Web site, Occupation de la Bourse du Travail, at http://bourse.occupee.free.fr/. On the 2009–2010 strikes, see Antoine Boulangé, "No Let-up in French Strike," *The Commune*, no. 11 (February 2010): 5.

2. Laurent Dubois, "La République Métissée: Citizenship, Colonialism, and the Borders of French History," *Cultural Studies* 14, no. 1 (2000), 22.

3. Agamben's most cited work in this field is Giorgio Agamben, *Homo Sacer: Sovereign Power and Bare Life*, trans. Daniel Heller-Roazen (Stanford, Calif.: Stanford University Press, 1998). For examples of how his work is taken up in critical refugee studies, see Jenny Edkins and Véronique Pin-Fat, "Through the Wire: Relations of Power and Relations of Violence," *Millennium: Journal of International Studies* 34, no. 1 (2005): 1–24; Prem Kumar Rajaram and Carl Grundy-Warr, "The Irregular Migrant as Homo Sacer: Migration and Detention in Australia, Malaysia, and Thailand," *International Migration* 42, no. 1 (2004): 33–63; Bülent Diken, "From Refugee Camps to Gated Communities: Biopolitics and the End of the City," *Citizenship Studies* 8, no. 1 (2004): 83–106. For an excellent argument contra Agamben with respect to refugee activism, see Patricia Owens,

"Reclaiming 'Bare Life'? Against Agamben on Refugees," *International Relations* 23, no. 4 (2009): 567–82.

4. William Walters, "Acts of Demonstration: Mapping the Territory of (Non-) Citizenship," in *Acts of Citizenship*, ed. Engin F. Isin and Greg M. Nielson (London: Zed Books, 2008), 188.

5. Michael Hardt and Antonio Negri, *Empire* (Cambridge, Mass.: Harvard University Press, 2000), 13–19, 361–63, 95–400; Michael Hardt and Antonio Negri, *Multitude: War and Democracy in the Age of Empire* (New York: Penguin, 2004), 133–34.

6. Dimitris Papadopoulos, Niamh Stephenson, and Vassilis Tsianos, *Escape Routes: Control and Subversion in the 21st Century* (Ann Arbor, Mich.: Pluto Press, 2008), 220, 2–21.

7. Nevzat Soguk, "Border's Capture: Insurrectional Politics, Border-Crossing Humans, and the New Political," in *Borderscapes: Hidden Geographies and Politics at Territory's Edge*, ed. Prem Kumar Rajaram and Carl Grundy-Warr (Minneapolis: University of Minnesota Press, 2007), 291.

8. Prem Kumar Rajaram and Carl Grundy-Warr, "Introduction," in *Borderscapes*, ed. Rajaram and Grundy-Warr, xxiv.

9. Engin F. Isin, "Theorizing Acts of Citizenship," in *Acts of Citizenship*, ed. Isin and Nielson, 15–43.

10. Hannah Arendt, *Imperialism: Part Two of the Origins of Totalitarianism* (New York: Harcourt Brace Jovanovich, 1968), 176.

11. Henri Astier, "'We Want to Be French!'" *Open Democracy* (November 22, 2005), available at http://www.opendemocracy.net/articles/ViewPopUpArticle.jsp?id=6&articleId=3051; Catherine Wihtol de Wenden, "Urban Riots in France," *SAIS Review* 26, no. 2 (2006), 51.

12. Engin F. Isin, "Citizenship After Orientalism: Ottoman Citizenship," in *Challenges to Citizenship in a Globalizing World: European Questions and Turkish Experiences*, ed. Fuat Keyman and Ahmet Icduygu (London: Routledge, 2005), 31–48.

13. Sanjay Seth, "Historical Sociology and Postcolonial Theory: Two Strategies for Challenging Eurocentrism," *International Political Sociology* 3, no. 3 (2009), 337.

14. Judith Butler, "A Response to Ali, Beckford, Bhatt, Modood, and Woodhead," *British Journal of Sociology* 59, no. 2 (2008), 257.

15. Jane Freedman, *Immigration and Insecurity in France* (Hants, U.K.: Ashgate, 2004), 9–10.

16. Paul A. Silverstein, *Algeria in France: Transpolitics, Race, and Nation* (Bloomington: Indiana University Press, 2004), 194. For summaries of France's recent immigration history, see James F. Hollifield, "France: Republicanism and the Limits of Immigration Control," in *Controlling Immigration: A Global Perspective*, ed. Wayne A. Cornelius, Takeyuki Tsuda, Philip A. Martin, and James F. Hollifield (Stanford, Calif.: Stanford University Press, 2004), 191–211; Alec G. Hargreaves,

Multi-ethnic France: Immigration, Politics, Culture, and Society (London: Routledge, 2007), 141–61.

17. Carl Levy, *The European Union After 9/11: The Demise of a Liberal Democratic Asylum Regime?* Paper no. 109 (Canberra: National Europe Centre, Australian National University, 2003), 4–8; Freedman, *Immigration and Insecurity in France*, 31, 50.

18. For a detailed discussion of the changes in immigration law in France, see Freedman, *Immigration and Insecurity in France*, 34–53, and Hollifield, "France," 190–211.

19. Nick Hewlett, "Nicolas Sarkozy and the Legacy of Bonapartism: The French Presidential and Parliamentary Elections of 2007," *Modern and Contemporary France* 15, no. 4 (2008), 419–20. See also Meng-Hsuan Chou and Nicolas Baygert, *The 2006 French Immigration and Integration Law: Europeanisation or Nicolas Sarkozy's Presidential Keystone?* Working Paper no. 45 (Oxford, U.K.: Centre on Migration, Policy, and Society, University of Oxford, 2007), 15–19; Susan Ossman and Susan Terio, "The French Riots: Questioning Spaces of Surveillance and Sovereignty," *International Migration* 44, no. 2 (2006), 6–7.

20. *Manifesto of the Sans-Papiers*, in Hayter, *Open Borders*, 143.

21. Ababacar Diop, "The Struggle of the 'Sans-Papiers': Realities and Perspectives," trans. Iain Nappier, April 4, 1997, available at http://bok.net/pajol/sanspap/sptextes/ababacar2.en.html.

22. Madjiguène Cissé, *The Sans-Papiers: A Woman Draws the First Lessons*, trans. Selma James, Nina Lopez-Jones, and Helen West (London: Crossroads Books, 1997), 22.

23. *Manifesto of the Sans-Papiers*, in Hayter, *Open Borders*, 143. For details on the Paris occupations, see NoBorder Network, "Sans Papiers' Hunger-Strike Reaches 30th Day at UNICEF," April 18, 2005, available at http://www.noborder.org/news_index.php.

24. *Manifesto of the Sans-Papiers*, in Hayter, *Open Borders*, 143.

25. Ibid.

26. Freedman, *Immigration and Insecurity in France*, 10–15.

27. Hargreaves, *Multi-ethnic France*, 119.

28. For discussions of the head scarf affair, see Hargreaves, *Multi-ethnic France*, 114–19, and Seyla Benhabib, *The Claims of Culture: Equality and Diversity in the Global Era* (Princeton, N.J.: Princeton University Press, 2002), 94–100.

29. Cissé, *The Sans-Papiers*, 15.

30. Ababacar Diop, *Dans la peau d'un Sans-Papiers*, cited in Vincenzo Ruggiero, "The Fight to Reappear," *Social Justice* 27, no. 2 (2000), 55. See also Diop, "The Struggle of the 'Sans-Papiers.'"

31. Doreen Massey, "Spaces of Politics," in *Human Geography Today*, ed. Doreen Massey, John Allen, and Philip Sarre (Cambridge, U.K.: Polity Press, 1999),

283–84; Engin F. Isin, *Being Political: Genealogies of Citizenship* (Minneapolis: University of Minnesota Press, 2002), 42–50.

32. Natasha Iskander, "Immigrant Workers in an Irregular Situation: The Case of the Garment Industry in Paris and Its Suburbs," in *Combating the Illegal Employment of Foreign Workers*, 45–51 (Paris: Organization of Economic Co-operation and Development, 2000); Freedman, *Immigration and Insecurity in France*, 82–86. For a more general discussion of these labor market trends, see chapter 2, pp. 53–56.

33. Freedman, *Immigration and Insecurity in France*, 84–85.

34. *Manifesto of the Sans-Papiers*, in Hayter, *Open Borders*, 143.

35. Edward Maltby, "Defending Migrant Workers in France," *Workers' Liberty* (February 3, 2008), available at http://www.workersliberty.org/print/9973.

36. Cissé, *The Sans-Papiers*, 21.

37. Pierre-Henri Lab, "Hortefeux Is Playing It Tough," trans. Edward Lamb, *L'Humanite in English*, April 29, 2008, http://www.humaniteinenglish.com/article917.html.

38. "Where Is the Struggle Going?" October 20, 2008, available on the Coordination de Sans-Papiers 75 Web site, Occupation de la Bourse du Travail, at http://bourse.occupee.free.fr/index.php?option=com_content&view=article&id=60:struggle&catid=35:english&Itemid=56.

39. Cissé, *The Sans-Papiers*, 15–17; European Network of Migrants Refugees and Sans-Papiers, *European Manifesto* (2004), available at http://www.noborder.org/item.php?id=287.

40. Babacar Ndiaye, Bahija Benkouka, Bas M. Sene, Brahim Nadi, Sokhna Codou Sene, African Women Association, El Rapta Association of Egyptian Workers in Greece, Ethiopian Community in Athens, Nigerian Community in Greece, Sierra Leonean Association in Greece, and Sudanese Community of Greece, "To Our Sisters and Brothers in Africa: A Common Struggle for the Freedom of Movement and the Right to Stay," *Crossing Borders: Movements and Struggles of Migration*, no. 2 (January 2007), 1.

41. Ibid.

42. Hargreaves, *Multi-ethnic France*, 161–62.

43. Hayter, *Open Borders*, 145.

44. Elizabeth Collett, *The EU Immigration Pact: From Hague to Stockholm, Via Paris*, policy brief (Brussels: European Policy Centre, October 2008), 1–4.

45. United Nations Human Rights Committee, *International Covenant on Civil and Political Rights: Consideration of Reports Submitted by State Parties Under Article 40 of the Covenant: France*, CCPR/C/FRA/CO/4 (Geneva: United Nations Human Rights Committee, July 31, 2008), paras. 18–20; Council of Europe, *Memorandum by Thomas Hammarberg, Council of Europe Commissioner for Human Rights, Following His Visit to France from 21 to 23 May 2008*,

CommDH(2008)34 (Strasbourg: Council of Europe, November 20, 2008), paras. 92–125.

46. Özge Berber Ağtaş, Beate Amler, and Luciole Sauviat, "Between Organising and Exclusion: Trade Union Strategies and Undocumented Migrant Workers," in *Leben in der Illegalität: Ein Dossier* (Berlin: Heinrich-Böll-Stiftung [Schriften zur Demokratie, Band 5], 2008), 75; Angelique Chrisafis, "The Crackdown," *The Guardian*, October 3, 2007. See also the Education Without Borders Network Web site at http://www.educationsansfrontieres.org/.

47. Platform for International Cooperation on Undocumented Migrants (PICUM), "France," *PICUM Newsletter* (August–September 2009), 4.

48. Miriam Iris Ticktin, "Between Justice and Compassion: 'Les Sans Papiers' and the Political-Economy of Health, Human Rights, and Humanitarianism in France," Ph.D. diss., Stanford University, 2002, 3–9.

49. Etienne Balibar, "What We Owe to the *Sans-Papiers*," in *Social Insecurity*, ed. Len Guenther and Cornelius Heesters (Toronto: Anansi, 2000), 42.

50. Cissé, *The Sans-Papiers*, 17. Similar points are also made in Diop, "The Struggle of the 'Sans-Papiers.'"

51. Etienne Balibar, "Europe, an 'Unimagined' Frontier of Democracy," *Diacritics* 33, nos. 3–4 (2003), 42.

52. Ndiaye et al., "To Our Sisters and Brothers in Africa," 1.

5. FROM CITY TO CITIZEN: MODES OF BELONGING
IN THE UNITED STATES

1. Alan Weisman, *La Frontera: The United States Border with Mexico* (San Diego: Harcourt Brace Jovanovich, 1986), 173–74.

2. Michael Hoefer, Nancy Rytina, and Bryan C. Baker, "Estimates of the Unauthorized Immigrant Population Residing in the United States: January 2009," in *Population Estimates, February 2010* (Washington, D.C.: U.S. Department of Homeland Security, Office of Immigration Statistics, Policy Directorate, 2010), 1. This estimate corresponds with a figure given by the Pew Hispanic Center, which estimates a population of 11.9 million unauthorized immigrants in March 2008, allowing for subsequent decline due to the effects of the global financial crisis. See Jeffrey S. Passel, *Trends in Unauthorized Immigration: Undocumented Inflow Now Trails Legal Inflow* (Washington, D.C.: Pew Hispanic Center, October 2008), i.

3. Douglas S. Massey, *Backfire at the Border: Why Enforcement Without Legalization Cannot Stop Illegal Immigration*, Trade Policy Analysis no. 29 (Washington, D.C.: Center for Trade Policy Studies, June 13, 2005), 6–9.

4. Victor Davis Hanson, *Mexifornia: A State of Becoming*, 2d ed. (New York: Encounter Books, 2007); Samuel P. Huntington, "The Hispanic Challenge," *Foreign Policy* 141 (March–April 2004): 30–45.

5. Jeffrey S. Passel and D'Vera Cohn, *A Portrait of Unauthorized Immigrants in the United States* (Washington, D.C.: Pew Hispanic Center, April 2009), 2, 12.

6. See, for example, Peter Nicholas, "Senators Give Obama a Bipartisan Plan on Immigration," *Los Angeles Times*, March 12, 2010; "Pushing Back on Immigration" (editorial), *New York Times*, July 21, 2008.

7. Hoefer, Rytina, and Baker, "Estimates of the Unauthorized Immigrant Population, January 2009," 4.

8. Dilip Ratha, Sanket Mohapatra, and Ani Silwal, *Migration and Remittance Trends, 2009*, Migration and Development Brief no. 11 (Washington, D.C.: World Bank, 2009), 3. For a more critical take on the role of remittances and outward migration in development strategies, see Alejandro Portes, "Migration, Development, and Segmented Assimilation: A Conceptual Review of the Evidence," *Annals of the American Academy of Political and Social Science* 610, no. 1 (2007), 75–80.

9. Passel and Cohn, *A Portrait of Unauthorized Immigrants in the United States*, 16. On the relation among neoliberal restructuring, irregular migration, and demand for irregular migrant labor in the United States, see Madeleine Leonard, *Invisible Work, Invisible Workers: The Informal Economy in Europe and the United States* (Houndsmill, U..K: Macmillan, 1998), 26–56; Raúl Delgado Wise and Humberto Márquez Covarrubias, "Capitalist Restructuring, Development, and Labour Migration: The Mexico–U.S. Case," *Third World Quarterly* 29, no. 7 (2008), 1362–69; Raúl Delgado Wise and James M. Cypher, "The Strategic Role of Mexican Labor Under NAFTA: Critical Perspectives on Current Economic Integration," *Annals of the American Academy of Political and Social Science* 610, no. 1 (2007), 129–35; Patricia Fernández-Kelly and Douglas S. Massey, "Borders for Whom? The Role of NAFTA in Mexico–U.S. Migration," *Annals of the American Academy of Political and Social Science* 610, no. 1 (2007), 103–6; Joseph Nevins, "Dying for a Cup of Coffee? Migrant Deaths in the U.S.–Mexico Border Region in a Neoliberal Age," *Geopolitics* 12 (2007), 239–40.

10. Paul Rodriguez, comedian, at the Laugh Factory, Los Angeles, May 1, 2006, cited in "Taking the City's Pulse from the Pavement," *LATimes.com*, May 2, 2006.

11. Peter Andreas, "Redrawing the Line: Borders and Security in the Twenty-First Century," *International Security* 28, no. 2 (2003), 85–91; Joseph Nevins, *Operation Gatekeeper: The Rise of the "Illegal Alien" and the Making of the U.S.–Mexico Boundary* (New York: Routledge, 2002), 3–4. An outline of recent border-policing initiatives can be found in U.S. Customs and Border Protection, *Performance and Accountability Report: Fiscal Year 2009* (Washington, D.C.: U.S. Department of Homeland Security, March 9, 2010), 7–32.

12. In 2009, according to government sources, the number of unauthorized migrants dropped to 10.8 million, down from 11.6 million in 2008 and 11.8 million in 2007. Border-patrol agencies have claimed this figure as evidence for their success. However, given the general pattern of growth in irregular migration from 2000 onward, other commentators suggest that declining figures have more to do with changed labor-market conditions under the effects of the global financial crisis than with successful border control. Hoefer, Rytina, and Baker, "Estimates of the Unauthorized Immigrant Population," 2; "The Border Closes," *The Economist* (December 20, 2008): 61–62. For a critical appraisal of employer-focused enforcement strategies, see Philip Martin, *Bordering on Control: Combating Irregular Migration in North America and Europe*, Migration Research Series no. 13 (Geneva: International Organization for Migration, 2003), 27–28. For commentary critical of the Employee Verification Amendment Act of 2008 (HR 6633), see "Immigration, off the Books" (editorial), *New York Times*, April 17, 2008.

13. Joseph Nevins, *Dying to Live: A Story of U.S. Immigration in an Age of Global Apartheid* (San Francisco: Open Media/City Lights Books, 2008), 103.

14. A fuller account of this process is given in an essay by one of the interpreters who witnessed the court hearings in the Iowa case. The essay "Interpreting After the Largest ICE Raid in U.S. History: A Personal Account" by Professor Erik Camayd-Freias of Florida International University was made available via an article by Julia Preston, "An Interpreter Speaking Up for Migrants," *New York Times*, July 11, 2008. See also Spencer S. Hsu, "Expedited Trials of Illegal Immigrants Are Questioned," *Washington Post*, July 25, 2008; Adam Liptak and Julia Preston, "Justices Limit Use of Identity Theft Law in Immigration Cases," *New York Times*, May 5, 2009.

15. U.S. Immigration and Customs Enforcement, *ICE Fiscal Year 2007 Annual Report: Protecting National Security and Upholding Public Safety* (Washington, D.C.: U.S. Department of Homeland Security, 2008), iv.

16. Margot Mendelson, Shayna Strom, and Michael Wishnie, *Collateral Damage: An Examination of ICE's Fugitive Operations Program* (Washington, D.C.: Migration Policy Institute, 2009), 2, 10–11.

17. U.S. Immigration and Customs Enforcement, *ICE Fiscal Year 2007 Annual Report*, iii.

18. U.S. House of Representatives, *Border Protection, Anti-terrorism, and Illegal Immigration Control Act of 2005*, HR 4437, 109th Cong., 2d sess., December 6, 2005.

19. Victor Narro, Kent Wong, and Janna Shadduck-Hernández, "The 2006 Immigrant Uprising: Origins and Future," *New Labor Forum* 16, no. 1 (2007), 50–54; Jonathan Fox, *Mexican Migrant Civic Participation in the United States* (Brooklyn, N.Y.: Social Science Research Council, August 15, 2006), available at http://borderbattles.ssrc.org/Fox/; Jonathan Benjamin-Alvarado, Louis DeSipio, and

Celeste Montoya, "Latino Mobilization in New Immigrant Destinations: The Anti-H.R. 4437 Protest in Nebraska's Cities," *Urban Affairs Review* 44, no. 5 (2009), 718–19.

20. See, for example, Anna Gorman, "LA Mayor Chides ICE for Workplace Immigration Raids," *Los Angeles Times*, April 10, 2008; Police Foundation, *The Role of Local Police: Striking a Balance Between Immigration Enforcement and Civil Liberties* (Washington, D.C.: Police Foundation, 2008), 4. On employer groups in favor of legalization and guest-worker schemes, see David Bacon, *Illegal People: How Globalization Creates Migration and Criminalizes Immigrants* (Boston: Beacon Press, 2008), 105–18.

21. U.S. Senate, *Comprehensive Immigration Reform Act of 2006*, S 2611, 109th Cong., 2d sess., May 25, 2006.

22. U.S. House of Representatives, *Secure Fence Act of 2006*, HR 6061, 109th Cong., 1st sess., September 13, 2006. For a transcript of Bush's address, see George W. Bush, speech given at the Oval Office, May 15, 2006, at http://georgewbush-whitehouse.archives.gov/news/releases/2006/05/20060515-8.html. An earlier reform proposal that also offered pathways to legalization for existing irregular migrants was sponsored by Republican John McCain and Democrat Ted Kennedy, but it never passed: U.S. Senate, *Secure America and Orderly Immigration Act of 2005*, S 1033, 109th Cong., 1st sess., May 12, 2005. For an account of Republicans' response to the issue, see Jonathan Weisman and Jim VandeHei, "Debate on How to Reshape Law Has Divided Republicans," *Washington Post*, May 21, 2006.

23. Charles E. Schumer and Lindsey O. Graham, "The Right Way to Mend Immigration," *Washington Post*, March 19, 2010.

24. Bacon, *Illegal People*, 115, 233–38; Southern Poverty Law Center, *Close to Slavery: Guestworker Programs in the United States* (Montgomery, Ala.: Southern Poverty Law Center, 2007), 1–2.

25. Nicholas De Genova, "Conflicts of Mobility, and the Mobility of Conflict: Rightlessness, Presence, Subjectivity, Freedom," *Subjectivity*, no. 29 (2009), 460.

26. Dan Balz and Darryl Fears, " 'We Decided Not to Be Invisible Anymore,' " *Washington Post*, April 11, 2006.

27. Roberto Suro and Gabriel Escobar, *2006 National Survey of Latinos: The Immigration Debate* (Washington, D.C.: Pew Hispanic Center, 2006), 8. See also Matt A. Barreto, Sylvia Manzano, Ricardo Ramírez, and Kathy Rim, "Mobilization, Participation, and *Solidaridad*: Latino Participation in the 2006 Immigration Protest Rallies," *Urban Affairs Review* 44, no. 5 (2009), 757.

28. N. C. Aizenman, "From Latinos' Rally, Hopes for a Movement," *Washington Post*, April 9, 2006; Balz and Fears, " 'We Decided Not to Be Invisible Anymore' "; Maria L. Ontiveros, "Immigrant Rights and the Thirteenth Amendment," *New Labor Forum* 16, no. 2 (2007), 26.

29. Michael Muskal, "Cities Brace for Immigration Rallies," *Los Angeles Times*, May 1, 2006; Balz and Fears, "'We Decided Not to Be Invisible Anymore.'"

30. Quoted in Maria Newman, "Immigrants Stage Protests Across U.S.," *New York Times*, May 1, 2006.

31. Narro, Wong, and Shadduck-Hernández, "The 2006 Immigrant Uprising," 50, 54.

32. Leo R. Chavez, *The Latino Threat: Constructing Immigrants, Citizens, and the Nation* (Stanford, Calif.: Stanford University Press, 2008).

33. Aihwa Ong, *Neoliberalism as Exception: Mutations in Citizenship and Sovereignty* (Durham, N.C.: Duke University Press, 2006), 6–18.

34. Chavez, *The Latino Threat*, 176.

35. George W. Bush's speech at Yuma Sector Border Patrol Headquarters, May 18, 2006, is available at http://georgewbush-whitehouse.archives.gov/news/releases/2006/05/20060518-18.html.

36. Cited in Newman, "Immigrants Stage Protests Across U.S."

37. Laura Pulido, "A Day Without Immigrants: The Racial and Class Politics of Immigrant Exclusion," *Antipode* 39, no. 1 (2007), 2–3. On the role of work in narratives of entitlement and belonging in the U.S. context, see Jennifer Gordon and R. A. Lenhardt, "Rethinking Work and Citizenship," *UCLA Law Review* 55, no. 5 (2008), 1191–95.

38. Cristina Beltrán, "Going Public: Hannah Arendt, Immigrant Action, and the Space of Appearance," *Political Theory* 37, no. 5 (2009), 597–600.

39. Muskal, "Cities Brace for Immigration Rallies."

40. Suro and Escobar, *2006 National Survey of Latinos*, 6; Passel, *Trends in Unauthorized Immigration*, iii; Raphael J. Sonenshein and Mark H. Drayse, "Urban Electoral Coalitions in an Age of Immigration: Time and Place in the 2001 and 2005 Los Angeles Mayoral Primaries," *Political Geography* 25, no. 5 (2006), 571–75.

41. The details of this mobilization are taken from De Genova, "Conflicts of Mobility, and the Mobility of Conflict," 458–60.

42. Pulido, "A Day Without Immigrants," 2.

43. Quoted in Aizenman, "From Latinos' Rally, Hopes for a Movement."

44. Los Angeles City Council community worker in discussion with the author, May 20, 2009; Michael McGough, "So What's Illegal?" *Los Angeles Times*, May 3, 2007.

45. In many studies, for example, cities feature prominently as places in which national-territorial norms of citizenship are being spatially reconfigured. See, for example, David C. Earnest, "From Alien to Elector: Citizenship and Belonging in the Global City," *Globalizations* 4, no. 2 (2007): 137–55; Soledad Garcia, ed., *Cities and Citizenship*, special issue of *International Journal of Urban and Regional Research* 20 (1996); Lisa M. Hanley, Blair A. Ruble, and Allison

M. Garland, eds., *Immigration and Integration in Urban Communities: Renegotiating the City* (Washington, D.C., and Baltimore: Woodrow Wilson Center Press and Johns Hopkins University Press, 2008); James Holston and Arjun Appadurai, eds., *Cities and Citizenship*, special issue of *Public Culture* 8 (1996); Engin F. Isin, ed., *Democracy, Citizenship, and the Global City* (London: Routledge, 2000); Stephanie Pincetl, "Challenges to Citizenship: Latino Immigrants and Political Organizing in the Los Angeles Area," *Environment and Planning A* 26 (1994): 895–914; Saskia Sassen, "The Repositioning of Citizenship," in *People out of Place: Globalization, Human Rights, and the Citizenship Gap*, ed. Alison Brysk and Gershon Shafir, 191–208 (London: Routledge, 2004); Michael Peter Smith, *Transnational Urbanism: Locating Globalization* (Malden, Mass.: Blackwell, 2001); Lynn A. Staeheli, ed., *Cities and Citizenship*, special issue of *Urban Geography* 24, no. 2 (2003).

46. Nicholas De Genova, "Race, Space, and the Reinvention of Latin America in Mexican Chicago," *Latin American Perspectives* 25, no. 5 (1998): 87–116; Nicholas De Genova, *Working the Boundaries: Race, Space, and "Illegality" in Mexican Chicago* (Durham, N.C.: Duke University Press, 2005).

47. Monica Varsanyi, "Immigration Policing Through the Backdoor: City Ordinances, the 'Right to the City,' and the Exclusion of Undocumented Day Laborers," *Urban Geography* 29, no. 1 (2008), 35–38.

48. Kristina M. Campbell, "Local Illegal Immigration Relief Act Ordinances: A Legal, Policy, and Litigation Analysis," *Denver University Law Review* 84, no. 4 (2007), 1045–56.

49. See the information on Day Labor Program of the Institute of Popular Education of Southern California at http://idepsca.org/Programs/Day_Laborers/Day_Laborer.html and on the Community Organizing Program of the Coalition for Humane Immigrant Rights of Los Angeles at http://www.chirla.org/node/306. Similar initiatives have been undertaken in the Washington, D.C., metropolitan area: see Lorrie A. Frasure and Michael Jones-Correa, "The Logic of Institutional Interdependency: The Case of Day Labourer Policy in Suburbia," *Urban Affairs Review* 45, no. 4 (2010), 458–64.

50. Los Angeles City Council, *Permit Process / Day Laborer Operating Standards / Home Improvement Stores*, Ordinance no. 180174, introduced June 23, 2008, available at http://clkrep.lacity.org/onlinedocs/2008%5C08–1657_ord_180174.pdf.

51. Deborah M. Weissman, Rebecca C. Headen, and Katherine Lewis Parker, *The Policies and Politics of Local Immigration Enforcement Laws: 287(G) Program in North Carolina* (New York: American Civil Liberties Union and Immigration and Human Rights Policy Clinic, 2009).

52. Quoted in "The Reign of Sheriff Joe," *Washington Post*, July 28, 2008.

53. The legislation in question is SB 1070, State of Arizona Senate, 49th Leg., 2d sess., 2010. On the various government responses, see U.S. Department of

Justice, "Citing Conflict with Federal Law, Department of Justice Challenges Arizona Immigration Law," press release, Washington, D.C., July 6, 2010; "Mayor Newsom Targets 'Smart and Effective' Action Against Arizona's Punitive Anti-immigrant Law," press release, Office of the Mayor, City of San Francisco, April 27, 2010; U.S. Conference of Mayors, "BP Oil Spill in the Gulf of Mexico, Immigration, and Jobs Top Agenda at Annual Mayors Gathering in Oklahoma City," press release, Washington, D.C., June 14, 2010.

54. Peter Nyers, "No One Is Illegal Between City and Nation," in *Acts of Citizenship*, ed. Engin F. Isin and Greg M. Nielson (London: Zed Books, 2008), 172–73; Mathew Coleman, "Immigration Geopolitics Beyond the Mexico–U.S. Border," *Antipode* 39, no. 1 (2007), 66–67.

55. Tony Favro, "U.S. Cities Offer Very Different Ways of Dealing with Illegal Migration," *City Mayors Society*, May 31, 2007, available at http://www.citymayors .com/society/us-illegals.html; Wyatt Buchanan, "SF Supervisors Approve ID Cards for Residents," *San Francisco Chronicle*, November 14, 2007.

56. Monica Varsanyi, *Rising Tensions Between National and Local Immigration and Citizenship Policy: Matrículas Consulares, Local Membership, and Documenting the Undocumented*, Working Paper no. 140 (San Diego: Center for Comparative Immigration Studies, University of California, 2006), 8–14.

57. Monica Varsanyi, "Interrogating 'Urban Citizenship' *Vis-à-Vis* Undocumented Migration," *Citizenship Studies* 10, no. 2 (2006), 240–44; David C. Earnest, "From Alien to Elector: Citizenship and Belonging in the Global City," *Globalizations* 4, no. 2 (2007), 144–45. See also the Immigrant Voting Project Web site at http://www.immigrantvoting.org/.

58. "Mayor Villaraigosa Announces Opening of Over 40 'Cash for College' Financial Aid Workshops Throughout Los Angeles," press release, Office of the Mayor, City of Los Angeles, February 2, 2009.

59. Passel and Cohn, "A Portrait of Unauthorized Immigrants in the United States," 8.

60. Hightstown mayor Robert Patten quoted in Favro, "U.S. Cities Offer Very Different Ways of Dealing with Illegal Migration."

61. Varsanyi, *Rising Tensions Between National and Local Immigration and Citizenship Policy*, 9.

62. Nyers, "No One Is Illegal Between City and Nation," 178.

63. Nicola Phillips, "Migration as Development Strategy? The New Political Economy of Dispossession and Inequality in the Americas," *Review of International Political Economy* 16, no. 2 (2009), 251.

64. Fran Ansley, "Constructing Citizenship Without a Licence: The Struggle of Undocumented Immigrants in the USA for Livelihoods and Recognition," in *Inclusive Citizenship: Meanings and Expressions*, ed. Naila Kabeer (New Delhi: Zubaan, an imprint of Kali for Women, 2005), 210.

65. Monica Varsanyi, "The Paradox of Contemporary Immigrant Political Mobilization: Organized Labor, Undocumented Migrants, and Electoral Participation in Los Angeles," *Antipode* 37, no. 4 (2005), 789.

66. Jennifer Gordon, *Suburban Sweatshops: The Fight for Immigrant Rights* (Cambridge, Mass.: Belknap Press of Harvard University Press, 2005), 272.

67. Ibid., 270.

68. Veronica Valdez, "Walking Across the Stage," in *Underground Undergrads: UCLA Undocumented Immigrant Students Speak Out*, ed. Gabriela Madera, Angelo A. Mathay, Armin M. Najafi, Hector H. Saldívar, Stephanie Solis, Alyssa Jane M. Titony, Gaspar Rivera-Salgado, Janna Shadduck-Hernández, Kent Wong, Rebecca Frazier, and Julie Monroe (Los Angeles: UCLA Center for Labor Research and Education, 2008), 44.

69. See, for example, information on the Mexican American Legal Defense and Education Fund's Parent School Partnership Program at http://www.maldef.org/leadership/programs/psp/.

70. Manuel Pastor, "Common Ground at Ground Zero? The New Economy and the New Organizing in Los Angeles," *Antipode* 33, no. 2 (2001), 274–81; Lydia Savage, "Justice for Janitors: Scales of Organizing and Representing Workers," *Antipode* 38, no. 3 (2006), 653–54; Victor Narro, "Impacting Next Wave Organizing: Creative Campaign Strategies of the Los Angeles Worker Centers," *New York Law School Law Review* 50, no. 2 (2005–2006), 467–512; Victor Narro, "Finding the Synergy Between Law and Organizing: Experiences from the Streets of Los Angeles," *Fordham Urban Law Journal* 35, no. 2 (2008), 341–70.

71. Evelyn Nieves, "Domestic Workers Sue, Lobby, Organize for Workplace Rights," *WTOPnews.com*, June 4, 2008, available at http://www.wtop.com/?nid=104&sid=1415254. See also http://www.nationaldomesticworkeralliance.org/index.php.

72. Christina Beltrán argues that this association between irregular migrants and arduous labor remains constitutive of undocumented subjectivity in the United States and limits the transformative potential of a social movement for migrant rights. See Beltrán, "Going Public," 600.

73. Varsanyi, "Immigration Policing Through the Backdoor," 40.

CONCLUSION: CONTENTIOUS SPACES OF POLITICAL BELONGING

1. The documentation required to establish the business was two forms of identification (a passport and the worker ID card provided by the worker center) and an individual taxpayer identification number. The latter is issued by the Internal Revenue Service to those ineligible for a Social Security number, regardless of immigration status.

2. Manuela (a pseudonym), in discussion with the author, Los Angeles, May 6, 2009.

3. Plans to copy the business cooperative model were revealed by representatives from the Pilipino Workers' Center and the Instituto de Educación Popular del Sur de California (Institute for Popular Education of Southern California), in conversation with the author, May 4 and May 6, 2009, respectively.

4. The estimate of one million undocumented residents is from Manuel Pastor and Rhonda Ortiz, *Immigrant Integration in Los Angeles: Strategic Directions for Funders* (Los Angeles: Program for Environmental and Regional Equity and Center for the Study of Immigrant Integration, University of Southern California, commissioned by the California Community Foundation, January 2009), 36.

5. Aihwa Ong, *Neoliberalism as Exception: Mutations in Citizenship and Sovereignty* (Durham, N.C.: Duke University Press, 2006), 25.

6. Michael Peter Smith and Matt Bakker, *Citizenship Across Borders: The Political Transnationalism of* El Migrante (Ithaca, N.Y.: Cornell University Press, 2008), 199.

BIBLIOGRAPHY

Ackerman, Piers. "Losers Left Behind." *Sunday Telegraph*, August 29, 1999.

Afeef, Karin Fathimath. *The Politics of Extraterritorial Processing: Offshore Asylum Policies in Europe and the Pacific*. Working Paper no. 36. Oxford, U.K.: Refugee Studies Centre, University of Oxford, 2006.

Agamben, Giorgio. *Homo Sacer: Sovereign Power and Bare Life*. Trans. Daniel Heller-Roazen. Stanford, Calif.: Stanford University Press, 1998.

Agnew, John A. *Globalization and Sovereignty*. Lanham, Md.: Rowman and Littlefield, 2009.

——. "The Territorial Trap: The Geographical Assumptions of International Relations Theory." *Review of International Political Economy* 1, no. 1 (1994): 53–80.

Ağtaş, Özge Berber, Beate Amler, and Luciole Sauviat. "Between Organising and Exclusion: Trade Union Strategies and Undocumented Migrant Workers." In *Leben in der Illegalität: Ein Dossier*, 72–78. Berlin: Heinrich-Böll-Stiftung (Schriften zur Demokratie, Band 5), 2008.

Aizenman, N. C. "From Latinos' Rally, Hopes for a Movement." *Washington Post*, April 9, 2006.

Alarcón, Rafael. "The Role of States and Markets in Creating Global Professionals." In *Migration Between States and Markets*, ed. Han Entzinger, Marco Martiniello, and Catherine Wihtol de Wenden, 28–41. Aldershot, U.K.: Ashgate, 2004.

Alberti, Gabriella. "Open Space Across the Borders of Lesvos: The Gendering of Migrants' Detention in the Aegean." *Feminist Review* 94, no. 1 (2010): 138–47.

Al-Ali, Nadje, Richard Black, and Khalid Koser. "The Limits to 'Transnationalism': Bosnian and Eritrean Refugees in Europe as Emerging Transnational Communities." *Ethnic and Racial Studies* 24, no. 4 (2001): 578–600.

Amnesty International. *China: Internal Migrants: Discrimination and Abuse. The Human Cost of an Economic "Miracle."* AI Index: ASA 17/008/2007. New York: Amnesty International, March 1, 2007.

——. *Offending Human Dignity: The "Pacific Solution."* AI Index: ASA 12/009/2002. New York: Amnesty International, 2002.

Amnesty International, European Union Office. "Immigration Cooperation with Libya: The Human Rights Perspective." Briefing ahead of the Justice and Home Affairs Council meeting, Brussels, April 14, 2005.

Andreas, Peter. *Border Games: Policing the U.S.–Mexico Divide.* Ithaca, N.Y.: Cornell University Press, 2000.

——. "Redrawing the Line: Borders and Security in the Twenty-First Century." *International Security* 28, no. 2 (2003): 78–111.

Andrijasevic, Rutvica. "Deported: The Right to Asylum at EU's External Border of Italy and Libya." *International Migration* 48, no. 1 (2009): 148–74.

Andrijasevic, Rutvica, and William Walters. "The International Organization for Migration and the International Government of Borders." *Environment and Planning D: Society and Space* 28, no. 6 (2010): 977–99.

Ansley, Fran. "Constructing Citizenship Without a Licence: The Struggle of Undocumented Immigrants in the USA for Livelihoods and Recognition." In *Inclusive Citizenship: Meanings and Expressions*, ed. Naila Kabeer, 199–215. New Delhi: Zubaan, an imprint of Kali for Women, 2005.

Archibugi, Daniele, ed. *Debating Cosmopolitics.* London: Verso, 2003.

Arendt, Hannah. *Imperialism: Part Two of the Origins of Totalitarianism.* New York: Harcourt Brace Jovanovich, 1968.

Astier, Henri. "'We Want to Be French!'" *Open Democracy* (November 22, 2005). Available at http://www.opendemocracy.net/articles/ViewPopUpArticle.jsp?id=6&articleId=3051.

Auerbach, Nancy Neiman. "The Meanings of Neoliberalism." In *Neoliberalism: National and Regional Experiments with Global Ideas*, ed. Ravi K. Roy, Arthur T. Denzau, and Thomas D. Willett, 26–50. London: Routledge, 2007.

Australian Broadcasting Corporation. "The Detention Industry." *Background Briefing*, ABC Radio National, June 20, 2004. Available at http://www.abc.net.au/rn/talks/bbing/stories/s1137813.htm.

——. "The Inside Story." *Four Corners*, ABC Television, August 13, 2001.

Australian Bureau of Statistics. *Australian National Accounts: National Income, Expenditure, and Product.* Catalogue no. 5206.0. Canberra: Commonwealth of Australia, 2006.

——. *Labour Force, Australia, March 2007.* Catalogue no. 6202.0. Canberra: Commonwealth of Australia, 2007.

Australian Commonwealth Ombudsman. *Inquiry Into the Circumstances of the Vivian Alvarez Matter.* Canberra: Commonwealth of Australia, 2005.

Australian Department of Immigration and Multicultural Affairs. *Protecting the Border: Immigration Compliance.* Canberra: Commonwealth of Australia, 2001.

Australian Department of Immigration and Multicultural and Indigenous Affairs. *Refugee and Humanitarian Issues: Australia's Response.* Canberra: Commonwealth of Australia, 2002.

———. "Unauthorised Arrivals by Air and Sea." Fact Sheet no. 74. Available at http://www.immi.gov.au/facts/74unauthorised.htm.

Australian Human Rights Commission. *Immigration Detention and Offshore Processing on Christmas Island.* Sydney: Australian Human Rights Commission, 2009.

Bacon, David. *Illegal People: How Globalization Creates Migration and Criminalizes Immigrants.* Boston: Beacon Press, 2008.

Bairoch, Paul, and Richard Kozul-Wright. *Globalization Myths: Some Historical Reflections on Integration, Industrialization, and Growth in the World Economy.* United Nations Commission on Trade and Development (UNCTAD) Discussion Paper no. 113. Geneva: UNCTAD, 1996.

Balibar, Etienne. "Europe, an 'Unimagined' Frontier of Democracy." *Diacritics* 33, nos. 3–4 (2003): 36–44.

———. *Strangers as Enemies: Further Reflections on the Aporias of Transnational Citizenship.* Globalization Working Paper 06/4. Hamilton, Canada: Institute on Globalization and the Human Condition, McMaster University, 2006.

———. "What We Owe to the *Sans-Papiers.*" In *Social Insecurity,* ed. Len Guenther and Cornelius Heesters, 42–43. Toronto: Anansi, 2000.

Ball, Rochelle, and Nicola Piper. "Globalisation and Regulation of Citizenship: Filipino Migrant Workers in Japan." *Political Geography* 21, no. 8 (2002): 1013–34.

Balz, Dan, and Darryl Fears. "'We Decided Not to Be Invisible Anymore.'" *Washington Post,* April 11, 2006.

Barreto, Matt A., Sylvia Manzano, Ricardo Ramírez, and Kathy Rim. "Mobilization, Participation, and *Solidaridad*: Latino Participation in the 2006 Immigration Protest Rallies." *Urban Affairs Review* 44, no. 5 (2009): 736–64.

Barry, Tom. *The National Imperative to Imprison Immigrants for Profit.* Americas Program Report. Washington, D.C.: Center for International Policy, March 10, 2009.

Bartley, Robert L. "Open NAFTA Borders? Why Not?" *Wall Street Journal,* July 2, 2001.

Bauböck, Rainer. "Who Are the Citizens of Europe?" *Eurozine* (December 23, 2006): 1–7.

Behr, Hartmut. "Deterritorialisation and the Transformation of Statehood: The Paradox of Globalisation." *Geopolitics* 13, no. 2 (2008): 359–82.

Beltrán, Cristina. "Going Public: Hannah Arendt, Immigrant Action, and the Space of Appearance." *Political Theory* 37, no. 5 (2009): 595–622.

Bem, Kasimierz, Nina Field, Nic Maclellan, Sarah Meyer, and Tony Morris. *A Price Too High: The Cost of Australia's Approach to Asylum Seekers*. Sydney: A Just Australia, Oxfam Australia, and Oxfam Novib, 2007.

Benhabib, Seyla. *The Claims of Culture: Equality and Diversity in the Global Era*. Princeton, N.J.: Princeton University Press, 2002.

——. *The Rights of Others: Aliens, Residents, and Citizens*. Cambridge, U.K.: Cambridge University Press, 2004.

Benhabib, Seyla, Ian Shapiro, and Danilo Petranović, eds. *Identities, Affiliations, and Allegiances*. Cambridge, U.K.: Cambridge University Press, 2007.

Benjamin-Alvarado, Jonathan, Louis DeSipio, and Celeste Montoya. "Latino Mobilization in New Immigrant Destinations: The Anti–H.R. 4437 Protest in Nebraska's Cities." *Urban Affairs Review* 44, no. 5 (2009): 718–35.

Bergin, Anthony, John Azarias, and Don Williams. *Advancing Australian Homeland Security: Leveraging the Private Sector*. Australian Strategic Policy Institute (ASPI) Special Report, Issue 14. Canberra: ASPI, 2008.

Betts, Katharine. *The Great Divide: Immigration Politics in Australia*. Sydney: Duffy & Snellgrove, 1999.

Bigo, Didier. "Security and Immigration: Toward a Critique of the Governmentality of Unease." *Alternatives* 27, special issue (2002): 63–92.

Blair, Tony. "New International Approaches to Asylum Processing and Protection." Paper submitted for discussion at the European Council, Brussels, March 20–21, 2003.

Blandy, Richard. "Australian Labour Market Reform: What Needs to Be Done?" *Australian Bulletin of Labour* 32, no. 1 (2006): 1–17.

"The Border Closes." *The Economist* (December 20, 2008): 61–62.

Borland, Jeff, Bob Gregory, and Paul Sheehan. "Inequality and Economic Change." In *Work Rich, Work Poor: Inequality and Economic Change in Australia*, ed. Jeff Borland, Bob Gregory, and Paul Sheehan, 1–20. Melbourne: Centre for Strategic Economic Studies, Victoria University, 2001.

Boulangé, Antoine. "No Let-up in French Strike." *The Commune*, no. 11 (February 2010): 5.

Brenner, Neil. *New State Spaces: Urban Governance and the Rescaling of Statehood*. Oxford, U.K.: Oxford University Press, 2004.

Brenner, Neil, Jamie Peck, and Nik Theodore. "After Neoliberalization?" *Globalizations* 7, no. 3 (2010): 327–45.

Buchanan, Wyatt. "SF Supervisors Approve ID Cards for Residents." *San Francisco Chronicle*, November 14, 2007.

Bunnell, Tim, and Neil M. Coe. "Re-fragmenting the 'Political': Globalization, Governmentality, and Malaysia's Multimedia Super Corridor." *Political Geography* 24, no. 7 (2005): 831–49.

Bunnell, Tim, Hamzah Muzaini, and James D. Sidaway. "Global City Frontiers: Singapore's Hinterland and the Contested Socio-political Geographies of Bintan, Indonesia." *International Journal of Urban and Regional Research* 30, no. 1 (2006): 3–22.

Burgess, John, and Ian Campbell. "Casual Employment in Australia: Growth, Characteristics, a Bridge or a Trap?" *Economic and Labour Relations Review* 9, no. 1 (1998): 31–54.

Burke, Anthony. *In Fear of Security: Australia's Invasion Anxiety.* Sydney: Pluto Press, 2001.

Burtless, Gary, Robert Z. Lawrence, Robert E. Litan, and Robert J. Shapiro. *Globaphobia: Confronting Fears About Open Trade.* Washington, D.C.: Brookings Institution, Progressive Policy Institute, and Twentieth Century Fund, 1998.

Bush, George W. Speech given at the Oval Office, May 15, 2006. Available at http://georgewbush-whitehouse.archives.gov/news/releases/2006/05/20060518-18.html.

——. Speech given at Yuma Sector Border Patrol Headquarters, May 18, 2006. Available at http://georgewbush-whitehouse.archives.gov/news/releases/2006/05/20060518-18.html.

Butler, Judith. "A Response to Ali, Beckford, Bhatt, Modood, and Woodhead." *British Journal of Sociology* 59, no. 2 (2008): 255–60.

Cahill, Damien. "New-Class Discourse and the Construction of Left Wing Elites." In *Us and Them: Anti-elitism in Australia*, ed. Barry Hindess and Marian Sawer, 77–95. Perth: API Network, 2004.

Campbell, Kristina M. "Local Illegal Immigration Relief Act Ordinances: A Legal, Policy, and Litigation Analysis." *Denver University Law Review* 84, no. 4 (2007): 1041–60.

Castles, Stephen, and Mark J. Miller. *The Age of Migration.* 3rd ed. New York: Guildford Press, 2003; 4th ed., 2009.

Chakravartty, Paula. "Symbolic Analysts of Indentured Servants? Indian High-Tech Migrants in America's Information Economy." In *The Human Face of Global Mobility*, ed. Michael Peter Smith and Adrian Favell, 159–80. New Brunswick, N.J.: Transaction, 2006.

Chavez, Leo R. *The Latino Threat: Constructing Immigrants, Citizens, and the Nation.* Stanford, Calif.: Stanford University Press, 2008.

Cheah, Pheng. *Inhuman Conditions: On Cosmopolitanism and Human Rights.* Cambridge, Mass.: Harvard University Press, 2006.

Chin, Christine. *In Service and Servitude: Foreign Domestic Workers and the Malaysian "Modernity Project."* New York: Columbia University Press, 1998.

Chinchilla, Norma Stoltz, and Nora Hamilton. "Doing Business: Central American Enterprises in Los Angeles." In *Asian and Latino Immigrants in a*

Restructuring Economy: The Metamorphosis of Southern California, ed. Marta López-Garza and David R. Diaz, 188–214. Stanford, Calif.: Stanford University Press, 2001.

Chou, Meng-Hsuan, and Nicolas Baygert. *The 2006 French Immigration and Integration Law: Europeanisation or Nicolas Sarkozy's Presidential Keystone?* Working Paper no. 45. Oxford, U.K.: Centre on Migration, Policy, and Society, University of Oxford, 2007.

Chrisafis, Angelique. "The Crackdown." *The Guardian*, October 3, 2007.

Cissé, Madjiguène. *The Sans-Papiers: A Woman Draws the First Lessons*. Trans. Selma James, Nina Lopez-Jones, and Helen West. London: Crossroads Books, 1997.

Cody, Edward. "Sarkozy Advocates Systemic Change After Crisis." *Washington Post*, September 26, 2008.

Cohen, Edward S. "Globalization and the Boundaries of the State: A Framework for Analyzing the Changing Practice of Sovereignty." *Governance* 14, no. 1 (2001): 75–97.

Colebatch, Tim. "To Reform or Not to Reform." *The Age*, December 7, 2004.

Coleman, Mathew. "Immigration Geopolitics Beyond the Mexico–U.S. Border." *Antipode* 39, no. 1 (2007): 54–76.

Collett, Elizabeth. *The EU Immigration Pact: From Hague to Stockholm, Via Paris.* Policy brief. Brussels: European Policy Centre, October 2008.

Collyer, Michael. "Migrants, Migration, and the Security Paradigm: Constraints and Opportunities." *Mediterranean Politics* 11, no. 2 (2006): 255–70.

Commonwealth of Australia. *Securing Australia, Protecting Our Community: Counter-terrorism White Paper.* Canberra: Department of the Prime Minister and Cabinet, 2010.

Conley, Tom. "The Domestic Politics of Globalisation." *Australian Journal of Political Science* 36, no. 2 (2001): 223–46.

Core Labour Standards and the Rights of Women Workers in International Supply Chains: Garment Industry Subcontracting in Nine Countries. Manchester, U.K.: Women Working Worldwide, 2004.

Council of Europe. *Memorandum by Thomas Hammarberg, Council of Europe Commissioner for Human Rights, Following His Visit to France from 21 to 23 May 2008.* CommDH(2008)34. Strasbourg: Council of Europe, November 20, 2008.

Crock, Mary, Ben Saul, and Azadeh Dastyari. *Future Seekers II: Refugees and Irregular Migration in Australia.* Sydney: Federation Press, 2006.

Croucher, Gwilym. "A Chance to Contribute: Some Remarks on the Potential Economic Impact of Allowing Asylum Seekers the Right to Work." *Just Policy: A Journal of Australian Social Policy*, no. 44 (2007): 37–43.

Dauvergne, Catherine. *Making People Illegal: What Globalization Means for Migration and Law.* Cambridge, U.K.: Cambridge University Press, 2008.

Debelle, Penelope. "Detainee Free After 7 Years' Incarceration." *The Age*, July 18, 2005.

———. "Nearly Free, but Normal Life a Distant Dream." *The Age*, June 21, 2005.

De Genova, Nicholas. "Conflicts of Mobility and the Mobility of Conflict: Rightlessness, Presence, Subjectivity, Freedom." *Subjectivity*, no. 29 (2009): 445–66.

———. "Migrant 'Illegality' and Deportability in Everyday Life." *Annual Review of Anthropology* 31 (2002): 419–47.

———. "Race, Space, and the Reinvention of Latin America in Mexican Chicago." *Latin American Perspectives* 25, no. 5 (1998): 87–116.

———. *Working the Boundaries: Race, Space, and "Illegality" in Mexican Chicago*. Durham, N.C.: Duke University Press, 2005.

De Haas, Hein. "The Myth of Invasion: The Inconvenient Realities of African Migration to Europe." *Third World Quarterly* 29, no. 7 (2008): 1305–22.

Delgado Wise, Raúl, and James M. Cypher. "The Strategic Role of Mexican Labor Under NAFTA: Critical Perspectives on Current Economic Integration." *Annals of the American Academy of Political and Social Science* 610, no. 1 (2007): 120–42.

Delgado Wise, Raúl, and Humberto Márquez Covarrubias. "Capitalist Restructuring, Development, and Labour Migration: The Mexico–U.S. Case." *Third World Quarterly* 29, no. 7 (2008): 1359–74.

De los Angeles Torres, María. "Transnational Political and Cultural Identities: Crossing Theoretical Borders." In *Latino/a Thought: Culture, Politics, and Society*, ed. Francisco H. Vazquez and Rodolfo D. Torres, 370–85. Lanham, Md.: Rowman and Littlefield, 2003.

"Deport Rape Comment Cleric, Says Goward." *The Age*, October 26, 2006.

Diken, Bülent. "From Refugee Camps to Gated Communities: Biopolitics and the End of the City." *Citizenship Studies* 8, no. 1 (2004): 83–106.

Diop, Ababacar. "The Struggle of the 'Sans-Papiers': Realities and Perspectives." Trans. Iain Nappier. April 4, 1997. Available at http://bok.net/pajol/sanspap/sptextes/ababacar2.en.html.

Donaghy, Matthew, and Michael Clarke. "Are Offshore Financial Centres the Product of Global Markets? A Sociological Response." *Economy and Society* 32, no. 3 (2003): 381–409.

Downer, Alexander, and Amanda Vanstone. "Minasa Bone Returns to Indonesia." Joint media release from the Australian minister for foreign affairs and the minister for immigration, multicultural, and indigenous affairs, November 9, 2003. Available at http://www.foreignminister.gov.au/releases/2003/joint_Minasa_Bone.html.

Dubois, Laurent. "La République Métissée: Citizenship, Colonialism, and the Borders of French History." *Cultural Studies* 14, no. 1 (2000): 15–34.

Earnest, David C. "From Alien to Elector: Citizenship and Belonging in the Global City." *Globalizations* 4, no. 2 (2007): 137–55.

Edkins, Jenny, and Véronique Pin-Fat. "Through the Wire: Relations of Power and Relations of Violence." *Millennium: Journal of International Studies* 34, no. 1 (2005): 1–24.

Edwards, John. *Australia's Economic Revolution.* Sydney: University of New South Wales Press, 2000.

Edwards, Lindy. *How to Argue with an Economist: Reopening Political Debate in Australia.* Cambridge, U.K.: Cambridge University Press, 2002.

Egan, Greg. "Australia's National Shame: Peter Qasim's 2191 Stolen Days." Project Safecom Inc., September 2, 2004. Available at http://www.safecom.org.au/peter-qasim.htm.

Ehrkamp, Patricia, and Helga Leitner, eds. *Rethinking Immigration and Citizenship: New Spaces of Migrant Transnationalism and Belonging.* Special issue of *Environment and Planning A* 38 (2006).

Elshtain, Jean Bethke. *Women and War.* New York: Basic Books, 1987.

Eudaily, Seán Patrick, and Steve Smith. "Seeing Through States: Sovereign Geopolitics? Uncovering the 'Sovereignty Paradox.'" *Geopolitics* 13, no. 2 (2008): 309–34.

European Network of Migrants Refugees and Sans-Papiers. *European Manifesto.* 2004. Available at http://www.noborder.org/item.php?id=287.

Evans, Chris. "New Directions in Detention: Restoring Integrity to Australia's Immigration System." Address to the Centre for International and Public Law, Australian National University, Canberra, July 29, 2008. Available at http://www.minister.immi.gov.au/media/speeches/2008/ce080729.htm.

——. "Refugee Policy Under the Rudd Government: The First Year." Address to the Refugee Council of Australia, Paramatta Town Hall, November 17, 2008. Available at http://www.chrisevans.alp.org.au/news/1108/immispeeches17-01.php.

Favro, Tony. "U.S. Cities Offer Very Different Ways of Dealing with Illegal Migration." *City Mayors Society,* May 31, 2007. Available at http://www.citymayors.com/society/us-illegals.html.

Fernández-Kelly, Patricia, and Douglas S. Massey. "Borders for Whom? The Role of NAFTA in Mexico–U.S. Migration." *Annals of the American Academy of Political and Social Science* 610, no. 1 (2007): 98–118.

Ferrer-Gallardo, Xavier. "The Spanish–Moroccan Border Complex: Processes of Geopolitical, Functional, and Symbolic Rebordering." *Political Geography* 27 (2008): 301–21.

Florence, Eric. "Migrant Workers in Shenzhen: Between Discursive Inclusion and Exclusion." In *Migration Between States and Markets,* ed. Han Entzinger,

Marco Martiniello, and Catherine Wihtol de Wenden, 42–62. Aldershot, U.K.: Ashgate, 2004.

Flynn, Don. "New Borders, New Management: The Dilemmas of Modern Immigration Policies." *Ethnic and Racial Studies* 28, no. 3 (2005): 463–90.

Flynn, Michael, and Cecilia Cannon. *The Privatization of Immigration Detention: Towards a Global View.* Geneva: Global Detention Project, Graduate Institute of International and Development Studies, 2009.

Fox, Jonathan. *Mexican Migrant Civic Participation in the United States.* Brooklyn, N.Y.: Social Science Research Council, August 15, 2006. Available at http://borderbattles.ssrc.org/Fox/.

Frasure, Lorrie A., and Michael Jones-Correa. "The Logic of Institutional Interdependency: The Case of Day Labourer Policy in Suburbia." *Urban Affairs Review* 45, no. 4 (2010): 451–82.

Freedman, Jane. *Immigration and Insecurity in France.* Hants, U.K.: Ashgate, 2004.

——. "Mobilising Against Detention and Deportation: Collective Actions Against the Detention and Deportation of 'Failed' Asylum Seekers in France." *French Politics* 7, nos. 3–4 (2009): 342–58.

Friedman, Thomas L. *The Lexus and the Olive Tree.* New York: Farrar, Straus and Giroux, 1999; 2d ed., 2000.

Fukuyama, Francis. "The End of History." *The National Interest* 16 (Summer 1989): 3–18.

Garcia, Soledad, ed. *Cities and Citizenship.* Special issue of *International Journal of Urban and Regional Research* 20 (1996).

Gesser, Silvina Schammah, Rebeca Raijman, Adriana Kemp, and Julia Reznik. "'Making It' in Israel? Latino Undocumented Migrant Workers in the Holy Land." *Estudios Interdisciplinarios de America Latina y el Caribe* 11, no. 2 (2002). Available at http://www1.tau.ac.il/eial/index.php?option=com_content&task=view&id=433&Itemid=206.

Gibney, Matthew J. *Outside the Protection of the Law: The Situation of Irregular Migrants in Europe.* Working Paper no. 6. Oxford, U.K.: Refugee Studies Centre, University of Oxford, 2000.

Gibson, Katherine, Lisa Law, and Deidre McKay. "Beyond Heroes and Victims: Filipina Contract Migrants, Economic Activism, and Class Transformations." *International Feminist Journal of Politics* 3, no. 3 (2001): 365–86.

Gibson, Rachel, Ian McAllister, and Tami Swenson. "The Politics of Race and Immigration in Australia: One Nation Voting in the 1998 Election." *Ethnic and Racial Studies* 25, no. 5 (2002): 823–44.

Gill, Stephen. "Theorizing the Interregnum: The Dynamics and Dialectics of Globalization." In *International Political Economy: Understanding Global Disorder*, ed. Björn Hettne, 65–99. Halifax, Canada: Fernwood Books, 1995.

Glendenning, Phil, Carmel Leavey, Margaret Hetherton, Mary Britt, and Tony Morris. *Deported to Danger: A Study of Australia's Treatment of 40 Rejected Asylum Seekers*. Sydney: Edmund Rice Centre for Justice and Community Education with the School of Education, Australian Catholic University, 2004.

Global Commission on International Migration. *Migration in an Interconnected World: New Directions for Action*. Geneva: Global Commission on International Migration, October 2005. Available at http://www.gcim.org.

"The Global Plan for Recovery and Reform." G20 London Summit communiqué, April 2, 2009. Available at http://www.londonsummit.gov.uk/en/.

Gordon, Jennifer. *Suburban Sweatshops: The Fight for Immigrant Rights*. Cambridge, Mass.: Belknap Press of Harvard University Press, 2005.

Gordon, Jennifer, and R. A. Lenhardt. "Rethinking Work and Citizenship." *UCLA Law Review* 55, no. 5 (2008): 1161–238.

Gorman, Anna. "LA Mayor Chides ICE for Workplace Immigration Raids." *Los Angeles Times*, April 10, 2008.

GSL (Australia) Pty Ltd. *Corporate Profile*. Melbourne: GSL (Australia), 2006.

Gurowitz, Amy. "Migrant Rights and Activism in Malaysia: Opportunities and Constraints." *Journal of Asian Studies* 59, no. 4 (2000): 863–88.

Hage, Ghassan. *Against Paranoid Nationalism: Searching for Hope in a Shrinking Society*. Sydney: Pluto Press, 2003.

Hale, Angela. "Introduction: Why Research International Subcontracting Chains?" In *Core Labour Standards and the Rights of Women Workers in International Supply Chains: Garment Industry Subcontracting in Nine Countries*, 5–6. Manchester, U.K.: Women Working Worldwide, 2004.

Hamilton, Clive. "What's Left? The Death of Social Democracy." *Quarterly Essay* 21 (2006): 1–69.

Hanley, Lisa M., Blair A. Ruble, and Allison M. Garland, eds. *Immigration and Integration in Urban Communities: Renegotiating the City*. Washington, D.C., and Baltimore: Woodrow Wilson Center Press and Johns Hopkins University Press, 2008.

Hanson, Victor Davis. *Mexifornia: A State of Becoming*. 2d ed. New York: Encounter Books, 2007.

Harding, Ann, and Quoc Ngu Vu. "Income Inequality and Tax-Transfer Policy: Trends and Questions." Presentation to the Economic and Social Outlook Conference, University of Melbourne, November 2, 2006.

Hardt, Michael, and Antonio Negri. *Empire*. Cambridge, Mass.: Harvard University Press, 2000.

——. *Multitude: War and Democracy in the Age of Empire*. New York: Penguin, 2004.

Hargreaves, Alec G. *Multi-ethnic France: Immigration, Politics, Culture, and Society*. London: Routledge, 2007.

Hay, Colin. "The Genealogy of Neoliberalism." In *Neoliberalism: National and Regional Experiments with Global Ideas*, ed. Ravi K. Roy, Arthur T. Denzau, and Thomas D. Willett, 51–70. London: Routledge, 2007.

Hayter, Teresa. *Open Borders: The Case Against Immigration Controls*. London: Pluto Press, 2000.

Hedetoft, Ulf, and Mette Hjort, eds. *The Postnational Self: Belonging and Identity*. Minneapolis: University of Minnesota Press, 2002.

Herod, Andrew, and Luis L. M. Aguiar. "Introduction: Cleaners and the Dirty Work of Neoliberalism." *Antipode* 38, no. 3 (2006): 425–34.

Hewlett, Nick. "Nicolas Sarkozy and the Legacy of Bonapartism: The French Presidential and Parliamentary Elections of 2007." *Modern and Contemporary France* 15, no. 4 (2008): 405–22.

Hindess, Barry. "Neo-liberal Citizenship." *Citizenship Studies* 6, no. 2 (2002): 127–43.

Hindess, Barry, and Marian Sawer. "Introduction." In *Us and Them: Anti-elitism in Australia*, ed. Barry Hindess and Marian Sawer, 1–13. Perth: API Network, 2004.

Hirst, Paul, and Grahame Thompson. *Globalization in Question: The International Economy and the Possibility of Governance*. 2d ed. Cambridge, U.K.: Polity Press, 1999.

Hoefer, Michael, Nancy Rytina, and Bryan C. Baker. "Estimates of the Unauthorized Immigrant Population Residing in the United States: January 2009." In *Population Estimates, February 2010*, 1–8. Washington, D.C.: U.S. Department of Homeland Security, Office of Immigration Statistics, Policy Directorate, 2010.

Hollifield, James F. "The Emerging Migration State." *International Migration Review* 38, no. 3 (2004): 885–912.

———. "France: Republicanism and the Limits of Immigration Control." In *Controlling Immigration: A Global Perspective*, ed. Wayne A. Cornelius, Takeyuki Tsuda, Philip A. Martin, and James F. Hollifield, 183–214. Stanford, Calif.: Stanford University Press, 2004.

Holston, James, and Arjun Appadurai, eds. *Cities and Citizenship*. Special issue of *Public Culture* 8 (1996).

Howard, John. "Address at Community Morning Tea, Ocean Grove, Victoria." September 6, 2001. Available at http://www.pm.gov.au/news/speeches/2001/speech1221.htm.

———. Interview by Phillip Clark. Radio 2GB, October 8, 2001. Available at http://www.pm.gov.au/media/Interview/2001/interview1371.cfm.

———. "The Role of Government: A Modern Liberal Approach." Menzies Research Centre National Lecture Series, June 6, 1995. Available on the Australian Politics Web site at http://australianpolitics.com/executive/howard/pre-2002/95-06-06role-of-government.shtml.

Hsu, Spencer S. "Expedited Trials of Illegal Immigrants Are Questioned." *Washington Post*, July 25, 2008.

Hudson, Wayne, and Steven Slaughter, eds. *Globalization and Citizenship: The Transnational Challenge*. London: Routledge, 2007.

Hugo, Graeme. "Australian Immigration Policy: The Significance of the Events of September 11." *International Migration Review* 36, no. 1 (2002): 37–40.

Human Rights and Equal Opportunity Commission. *A Last Resort? Report of the National Inquiry Into Children in Detention*. Sydney: Commonwealth of Australia, 2004.

Human Rights Watch. *"By Invitation Only": Australian Asylum Policy*. New York: Human Rights Watch, December 2002. Available at http://hrw.org/reports/2002/australia/.

Huntington, Samuel P. "The Hispanic Challenge." *Foreign Policy* 141 (March–April 2004): 30–45.

Hurley, Jennifer. "Garment Industry Subcontracting Chains and Working Conditions: Research Overview." In *Core Labour Standards and the Rights of Women Workers in International Supply Chains: Garment Industry Subcontracting in Nine Countries*, 9–26. Manchester, U.K.: Women Working Worldwide, 2004.

Huysmans, Jef, and Alessandra Buonfino. "Politics of Exception and Unease: Immigration, Asylum ,and Terrorism in Parliamentary Debates in the UK." *Political Studies* 56 (2008): 766–88.

Igushi, Yasushi. "Illegal Migration, Overstay, and Illegal Working in Japan: Development of Policies and Their Evaluation." In *Combating the Illegal Employment of Foreign Workers*, 157–65. Paris: Organization for Economic Cooperation and Development, 2000.

"Immigration, off the Books" (editorial). *New York Times*, April 17, 2008.

"Income Distribution Trends." In *Advance Australia Where?* Special feature in *The Australian*, June 17–22, 2000.

International Labour Organisation. "Changing Patterns in the World of Work." International Labour Conference, Report I(C), 95th sess., Geneva, 2006.

——. "Towards a Fair Deal for Migrant Workers in the Global Economy." International Labour Conference, Report VI, 92d sess., Geneva, 2004.

Isin, Engin F. *Being Political: Genealogies of Citizenship*. Minneapolis: University of Minnesota Press, 2002.

——. "Citizenship After Orientalism: Ottoman Citizenship." In *Challenges to Citizenship in a Globalizing World: European Questions and Turkish Experiences*, ed. Fuat Keyman and Ahmet Icduygu, 31–51. London: Routledge, 2005.

——, ed. *Democracy, Citizenship, and the Global City*. London: Routledge, 2000.

——. "Governing Cities Without Government." In *Democracy, Citizenship, and the Global City*, ed. Engin F. Isin, 148–68. London: Routledge, 2000.

———. "Theorizing Acts of Citizenship." In *Acts of Citizenship*, ed. Engin F. Isin and Greg M. Nielson, 15–43. London: Zed Books, 2008.

Iskander, Natasha. "Immigrant Workers in an Irregular Situation: The Case of the Garment Industry in Paris and Its Suburbs." In *Combating the Illegal Employment of Foreign Workers*, 45–51. Paris: Organization of Economic Co-operation and Development, 2000.

Ivakhnyuk, Irina. *The Russian Migration Policy and Its Impact on Human Development: The Historical Perspective.* Research Paper 2009/14, Human Development Reports. Paris: United Nations Development Program, 2009. Available at http://hdr.undp.org/en/reports/global/hdr2009/papers/HDRP_2009_14 .pdf.

Jackson, Andra. "Aladdin Sisalem Released from Manus Island." *The Age*, June 1, 2005.

———. "Life in Detention, for Seven Years." *The Age*, March 5, 2005.

———. "Refugee's Journey from the Depths to the Heights and Back Again." *The Age*, May 30, 2009.

———. "Struggle for a Modern Crusoe on Manus Isle." *The Age*, November 25, 2003.

James, Paul. *Globalism, Nationalism, Tribalism: Bringing Theory Back In.* London: Sage, 2006.

Jessop, Bob, Neil Brenner, and Martin Jones. "Theorizing Sociospatial Relations." *Environment and Planning D: Society and Space* 26, no. 3 (2008): 389–401.

Johnson, David, Ian Manning, and Otto Hellwig. "Trends in the Distribution of Income in Australia." *Australian Journal of Labour Economics* 2, no. 1 (1998): 1–27.

Jones, Reece. "Sovereignty and Statelessness in the Border Enclaves of India and Bangladesh." *Political Geography* 28, no. 6 (2009): 373–81.

Jordan, Bill, and Franck Düvell. *Irregular Migration: The Dilemmas of Transnational Mobility.* Cheltenham, U.K.: Edward Elgar, 2002.

Jupp, James. *From White Australia to Woomera: The Story of Australian Immigration.* Cambridge, U.K.: Cambridge University Press, 2002.

Kasparek, Bernd. "Frontex und die Europäische Außengrenze." In *Was Ist Frontex? Aufgaben und Strukturen der Europäischen Agentur für die Operative Zusammenarbeit an den Außengrenzen*, 9–15. Materialien gegen Krieg, Repression und für andere Verhältnisse, no. 4. Brochure by order of Tobias Pflüger, Member of European Parliament, 2008.

Kevin, Tony. *A Certain Maritime Incident: The Sinking of SIEV X.* Melbourne: Scribe, 2004.

Kirk, Alexander. "Govt Maintains Kurds Didn't Seek Asylum." *The World Today*, ABC Radio National, November 11, 2003. Available at http://www.abc.net .au/worldtoday/content/2003/s986708.htm.

Koopmans, Ruud, Paul Statham, Marco Giugni, and Florence Passy. *Contested Citizenship: Immigration and Cultural Diversity in Europe*. Minneapolis: University of Minnesota Press, 2005.

Lab, Pierre-Henri. "Hortefeux Is Playing It Tough." Trans. Edward Lamb. *L'Humanite in English*, April 29, 2008. Available at http://www.humaniteinenglish.com/article917.html.

Laclau, Ernesto, and Chantal Mouffe. *Hegemony and Socialist Strategy: Towards a Radical Democratic Politics*. 2d ed. London: Verso, 2001.

Latif, Angie. "Castaway." Originally published in *Aramica*, October 6–20, 2003. Reprinted by NauruWire.org at http://www.nauruwire.org/manusarchives.htm.

Legrain, Philippe. *Immigrants: Your Country Needs Them*. London: Little, Brown, 2006.

Leitner, Helga, Eric Sheppard, and Kristin M. Sziarto. "The Spatialities of Contentious Politics." *Transactions of the Institute of British Geographers* 33 (2008): 157–72.

LeMay, Michael. *Illegal Immigration: A Reference Handbook*. Santa Barbara, Calif.: ABC-CLIO, 2007.

Leonard, Madeleine. *Invisible Work, Invisible Workers: The Informal Economy in Europe and the United States*. Houndsmill, U.K.: Macmillan, 1998.

Levy, Carl. *The European Union After 9/11: The Demise of a Liberal Democratic Asylum Regime?* Paper no. 109. Canberra: National Europe Centre, Australian National University, 2003.

Liang, Zai, and Wenzhen Ye. "From Fujian to New York: Understanding the New Chinese Immigration." In *Global Human Smuggling: Comparative Perspectives*, ed. David Kyle and Rey Koslowski, 187–215. Baltimore: Johns Hopkins University Press, 2001.

Linklater, Andrew. *The Transformation of Political Community: Ethical Foundations of the Post-Westphalian Era*. Cambridge, U.K.: Polity Press, 1998.

Liptak, Adam, and Julia Preston. "Justices Limit Use of Identity Theft Law in Immigration Cases." *New York Times*, May 5, 2009.

Lister, Michael, ed. *Europeanization and Migration: Challenging the Values of Citizenship in Europe?* Special issue of *Citizenship Studies* 12, no. 6 (2008).

López-Garza, Marta. "A Study of the Informal Economy and Latina/o Immigrants in Greater Los Angeles." In *Asian and Latino Immigrants in a Restructuring Economy: The Metamorphosis of Southern California*, ed. Marta López-Garza and David R. Diaz, 141–68. Stanford, Calif.: Stanford University Press, 2001.

Los Angeles City Council. *Permit Process / Day Laborer Operating Standards / Home Improvement Stores*. Ordinance no. 180174, introduced June 23, 2008. Available at http://clkrep.lacity.org/onlinedocs/2008%5C08-1657_ord_180174.pdf.

Löwenheim, Oded. "Examining the State: A Foucauldian Perpsective on International 'Governance Indicators.'" *Third World Quarterly* 29, no. 2 (2008): 255–74.

Madera, Gabriela, Angelo A. Mathay, Armin M. Najafi, Hector H. Saldívar, Stephanie Solis, Alyssa Jane M. Titony, Gaspar Rivera-Salgado, Janna Shadduck-Hernández, Kent Wong, Rebecca Frazier, and Julie Monroe, eds. *Underground Undergrads: UCLA Undocumented Immigrant Students Speak Out.* Los Angeles: Center for Labor Research and Education, University of California at Los Angeles, 2008.

Maley, William. "Asylum-Seekers in Australia's International Relations." *Australian Journal of International Affairs* 57, no. 1 (2003): 187–202.

Maltby, Edward. "Defending Migrant Workers in France." *Workers' Liberty* (February 3, 2008). Available at http://www.workersliberty.org/print/9973.

Manne, Robert, ed. *The New Intolerance.* Special issue of *Quadrant* 35 (1990).

Manne, Robert, and David Corlett. "Sending Them Home: Refugees and the New Politics of Indifference." *Quarterly Essay,* no. 13 (2004): 1–95.

Marischka, Christoph. "Frontex: Die Vernetzungs-Maschine an den Randzonen des Rechtes und der Staaten." In *Was Ist Frontex? Aufgaben und Strukturen der Europäischen Agentur für die operative Zusammenarbeit an den Außengrenzen,* 16–23. Materialien gegen Krieg, Repression und für andere Verhältnisse, no. 4. Brochure by order of Tobias Pflüger, Member of European Parliament, 2008.

Marr, David, and Marian Wilkinson. *Dark Victory.* 2d ed. Sydney: Allen & Unwin, 2004.

Marston, Greg. *Temporary Protection, Permanent Uncertainty: The Experience of Refugees Living on Temporary Protection Visas.* Melbourne: Centre for Applied Social Research, RMIT University, 2003.

Martin, Philip. *Bordering on Control: Combating Irregular Migration in North America and Europe.* Migration Research Series, no. 13. Geneva: International Organization for Migration, 2003.

Massey, Doreen. *For Space.* London: Sage, 2005.

——. "Spaces of Politics." In *Human Geography Today,* ed. Doreen Massey, John Allen, and Philip Sarre, 279–94. Cambridge, U.K.: Polity Press, 1999.

Massey, Douglas S. *Backfire at the Border: Why Enforcement Without Legalization Cannot Stop Illegal Immigration.* Trade Policy Analysis no. 29. Washington, D.C.: Center for Trade Policy Studies, June 13, 2005.

Massey, Douglas S., Joaquín Arango, Graeme Hugo, Ali Kouaouci, Adela Pellegrino, and J. Edward Taylor. *Worlds in Motion: Understanding International Migration at the End of the Millennium.* Oxford, U.K.: Clarendon Press, 1998.

Mathew, Penelope. "Australian Refugee Protection in the Wake of the *Tampa.*" *American Journal of International Law* 96, no. 3 (2002): 661–76.

Maurer, Bill. "Complex Subjects: Offshore Finance, Complexity Theory, and the Dispersion of the Modern." *Socialist Review* 25, nos. 3–4 (1995): 113–45.

——. "Cyberspatial Sovereignties: Offshore Finance, Digital Case, and the Limits of Liberalism." *Indiana Journal of Global Legal Studies* 5, no. 2 (1998): 493–519.

May, Jon, Jane Wills, Kavita Datta, Yara Evans, Joanna Herbert, and Cathy McIlwaine. "Keeping London Working: Global Cities, the British State, and London's New Migrant Division of Labour." *Transactions of the Institute of British Geographers* 32, no. 2 (2007): 151–67.

"Mayor Newsom Targets 'Smart and Effective' Action Against Arizona's Punitive Anti-immigrant Law." Press release, Office of the Mayor, City of San Francisco, April 27, 2010. Available at http://www.sfmayor.org/press-room/press-releases/.

"Mayor Villaraigosa Announces Opening of Over 40 'Cash for College' Financial Aid Workshops Throughout Los Angeles." Press release, Office of the Mayor, City of Los Angeles, February 2, 2009.

McAllister, Ian. "Border Protection, the 2001 Australian Election, and the Coalition Victory." *Australian Journal of Political Science* 38, no. 3 (2003): 445–63.

McAllister, Ian, and Clive Bean. "The Electoral Politics of Economic Reform in Australia: The 1998 Election." *Australian Journal of Political Science* 35, no. 3 (2000): 383–99.

McClelland, Alison, and Susan St. John. "Social Policy Responses to Globalisation in Australia and New Zealand, 1980–2005." *Australian Journal of Political Science* 41, no. 2 (2006): 177–91.

McGough, Michael. "So What's Illegal?" *Los Angeles Times*, May 3, 2007.

McKeown, Adam M. *Melancholy Order: Asian Migration and the Globalization of Borders*. New York: Columbia University Press, 2008.

McMaster, Don. "Asylum-Seekers and the Insecurity of a Nation." *Australian Journal of International Affairs* 56, no. 2 (2002): 279–90.

Mendelson, Margot, Shayna Strom, and Michael Wishnie. *Collateral Damage: An Examination of ICE's Fugitive Operations Program*. Washington, D.C.: Migration Policy Institute, 2009.

Micklethwait, John, and Adrian Wooldridge, eds. *A Future Perfect: The Challenge and Hidden Promise of Globalization*. New York: Crown Business, 2000.

Milberg, William, and Matthew Amengual. *Economic Development and Working Conditions in Export Processing Zones: A Survey of Trends*. Geneva: International Labour Organisation, 2008.

Mouffe, Chantal. *The Return of the Political*. London: Verso, 1993.

Moulin, Carolina, and Peter Nyers. "'We Live in a Country of UNHCR': Refugee Protests and Global Political Society." *International Political Sociology* 1, no. 4 (2007): 356–72.

Muskal, Michael. "Cities Brace for Immigration Rallies." *Los Angeles Times*, May 1, 2006.

Narro, Victor. "Finding the Synergy Between Law and Organizing: Experiences from the Streets of Los Angeles." *Fordham Urban Law Journal* 35, no. 2 (2008): 339–72.

———. "Impacting Next Wave Organizing: Creative Campaign Strategies of the Los Angeles Worker Centers." *New York Law School Law Review* 50, no. 2 (2005–2006): 465–513.

Narro, Victor, Kent Wong, and Janna Shadduck-Hernández. "The 2006 Immigrant Uprising: Origins and Future." *New Labor Forum* 16, no. 1 (2007): 49–56.

Ndiaye, Babacar, Bahija Benkouka, Bas M. Sene, Brahim Nadi, Sokhna Codou Sene, African Women Association, El Rapta Association of Egyptian Workers in Greece, Ethiopian Community in Athens, Nigerian Community in Greece, Sierra Leonean Association in Greece, and Sudanese Community of Greece. "To Our Sisters and Brothers in Africa: A Common Struggle for the Freedom of Movement and the Right to Stay." *Crossing Borders: Movements and Struggles of Migration*, no. 2 (January 2007): 1.

Neilson, Brett. "The World Seen from a Taxi: Students-Migrants-Workers in the Global Multiplication of Labour." *Subjectivity*, no. 29 (2009): 425–44.

Nevins, Joseph. "Dying for a Cup of Coffee? Migrant Deaths in the U.S.–Mexico Border Region in a Neoliberal Age." *Geopolitics* 12 (2007): 228–47.

———. *Dying to Live: A Story of U.S. Immigration in an Age of Global Apartheid.* San Francisco: Open Media/City Lights Books, 2008.

———. *Operation Gatekeeper: The Rise of the "Illegal Alien" and the Making of the U.S.–Mexico Boundary.* New York: Routledge, 2002.

Newman, Maria. "Immigrants Stage Protests Across U.S." *New York Times*, May 1, 2006.

New South Wales Anti-discrimination Board. *Race for the Headlines: Racism and Media Discourse.* Sydney: Government of New South Wales, August 24, 2003.

Nicholas, Peter. "Senators Give Obama a Bipartisan Plan on Immigration." *Los Angeles Times*, March 12, 2010.

Nieves, Evelyn. "Domestic Workers Sue, Lobby, Organize for Workplace Rights." *WTOPnews.com*, June 4, 2008. Available at http://www.wtop.com/?nid=104&sid=1415254.

NoBorder Network. "Sans Papiers' Hunger-Strike Reaches 30th Day at UNICEF." April 18, 2005. Available at http://www.noborder.org/news_index.php.

Nyers, Peter. "Abject Cosmopolitanism: The Politics of Protection in the Anti-deportation Movement." *Third World Quarterly* 24, no. 6 (2003): 1069–93.

———. "Forms of Irregular Citizenship." In *The Contested Politics of Mobility: Borderzones and Irregularity*, ed. Vicki Squire, 184–98. London: Routledge, 2010.

——. "No One Is Illegal Between City and Nation." In *Acts of Citizenship*, ed. Engin F. Isin and Greg M. Nielson, 160–81. London: Zed Books, 2008.

——. *Rethinking Refugees: Beyond States of Emergency.* New York: Routledge, 2006.

Ohmae, Kenichi. *The Borderless World: Power and Strategy in the Interlinked Economy.* New York: Harper Perennial, 1991.

Oke, Nicole. "Working Transnationally: Australian Unions and Temporary Migrant Work." *Social Alternatives* 29, no. 3 (forthcoming).

Ong, Aihwa. *Flexible Citizenship: The Cultural Logics of Transnationality.* Durham, N.C.: Duke University Press, 1999.

——. "Latitudes of Citizenship: Membership, Meaning, and Multiculturalism." In *People out of Place: Globalization, Human Rights, and the Citizenship Gap*, ed. Alison Brysk and Gershon Shafir, 53–70. London: Routledge, 2004.

——. *Neoliberalism as Exception: Mutations in Citizenship and Sovereignty.* Durham, N.C.: Duke University Press, 2006.

Ontiveros, Maria L. "Immigrant Rights and the Thirteenth Amendment." *New Labor Forum* 16, no. 2 (2007): 26–33.

Organization for Economic Cooperation and Development (OECD). *International Migration Outlook: Managing Labour Migration Beyond the Crisis.* OECD Continuous Reporting System on Migration (SOPEMI). Paris: OECD, 2009.

Organization for Economic Cooperation and Development (OECD) Secretariat. "Some Lessons from Recent Regularisation Programmes." In *Combating the Illegal Employment of Foreign Workers*, 53–69. Paris: OECD, 2000.

Ossman, Susan, and Susan Terio. "The French Riots: Questioning Spaces of Surveillance and Sovereignty." *International Migration* 44, no. 2 (2006): 5–21.

Østergaard-Nielsen, Eva K. "The Politics of Migrants' Transnational Political Practices." *International Migration Review* 37, no. 3 (2003): 760–86.

Overbeek, Henk. "Neoliberalism and the Regulation of Global Labor Mobility." *Annals of the American Academy of Political and Social Science* 581, no. 1 (2002): 74–90.

Owens, Patricia. "Reclaiming 'Bare Life'? Against Agamben on Refugees." *International Relations* 23, no. 4 (2009): 567–82.

Palan, Ronen. *The Offshore World: Sovereign Markets, Virtual Places, and Nomad Millionaires.* Ithaca, N.Y.: Cornell University Press, 2003.

Palmer, Mick. *Inquiry Into the Circumstances of the Immigration Detention of Cornelia Rau.* Canberra: Commonwealth of Australia, 2005.

Papadopoulos, Dimitris, Niamh Stephenson, and Vassilis Tsianos. *Escape Routes: Control and Subversion in the 21st Century.* Ann Arbor, Mich.: Pluto Press, 2008.

Parliament of the Commonwealth of Australia. *Detention Centre Contracts: Review of Audit Report No. 1, 2005–2006, Management of the Detention Centre Contracts: Part B.* Canberra: Joint Standing Committee on Migration, 2005.

——. *Immigration Detention in Australia: Facilities, Services, and Transparency.* Canberra: Joint Standing Committee on Migration, 2009.

Passel, Jeffrey S. *Trends in Unauthorized Immigration: Undocumented Inflow Now Trails Legal Inflow.* Washington, D.C.: Pew Hispanic Center, October 2008.

Passel, Jeffrey S., and D'Vera Cohn. *A Portrait of Unauthorized Immigrants in the United States.* Washington, D.C.: Pew Hispanic Center, April 2009.

Pastor, Manuel. "Common Ground at Ground Zero? The New Economy and the New Organizing in Los Angeles." *Antipode* 33, no. 2 (2001): 260–89.

Pastor, Manuel, and Rhonda Ortiz. *Immigrant Integration in Los Angeles: Strategic Directions for Funders.* Los Angeles: Program for Environmental and Regional Equity and Center for the Study of Immigrant Integration, University of Southern California, commissioned by the California Community Foundation, January 2009.

Patomäki, Heikki. *Democratising Globalisation: The Leverage of the Tobin Tax.* London: Zed Books, 2001.

"People Smugglers Should Rot in Hell: Rudd." *PM,* ABC Radio National, April 17, 2009. Available at http://www.abc.net.au/pm/content/2008/s2546098.htm.

Perera, Suvendrini. "A Line in the Sea." *Race & Class* 44, no. 2 (2002): 23–39.

Peterson, V. Spike. *A Critical Rewriting of Global Political Economy: Integrating Reproductive, Productive, and Virtual Economies.* London: Routledge, 2003.

Phillips, Nicola. "Migration as Development Strategy? The New Political Economy of Dispossession and Inequality in the Americas." *Review of International Political Economy* 16, no. 2 (2009): 231–59.

Pincetl, Stephanie. "Challenges to Citizenship: Latino Immigrants and Political Organizing in the Los Angeles Area." *Environment and Planning A* 26 (1994): 895–914.

Platform for International Cooperation on Undocumented Migrants (PICUM). "France." *PICUM Newsletter* (August–September 2009): 4.

Police Foundation. *The Role of Local Police: Striking a Balance Between Immigration Enforcement and Civil Liberties.* Washington, D.C.: Police Foundation, 2008.

Portes, Alejandro. "Migration, Development, and Segmented Assimilation: A Conceptual Review of the Evidence." *Annals of the American Academy of Political and Social Science* 610, no. 1 (2007): 73–97.

Preston, Julia. "An Interpreter Speaking Up for Migrants." *New York Times,* July 11, 2008.

Prügel, Elisabeth. *The Global Construction of Gender: Home-Based Work in the Political Economy of the 20th Century.* New York: Columbia University Press, 1999.

Pulido, Laura. "A Day Without Immigrants: The Racial and Class Politics of Immigrant Exclusion." *Antipode* 39, no. 1 (2007): 1–7.

Purcell, Mark, and Joseph Nevins. "Pushing the Boundary: State Restructuring, State Theory, and the Case of U.S.–Mexico Border Enforcement in the 1990s." *Political Geography* 24, no. 2 (2005): 211–35.

Pusey, Michael. *Economic Rationalism in Canberra: A Nation-Building State Changes Its Mind.* Cambridge, U.K.: Cambridge University Press, 1991.

——. *The Experience of Middle Australia: The Dark Side of Economic Reform.* Cambridge, U.K.: Cambridge University Press, 2003.

"Pushing Back on Immigration" (editorial). *New York Times*, July 21, 2008.

Rajaram, Prem Kumar, and Carl Grundy-Warr. "Introduction." In *Borderscapes: Hidden Geographies and Politics at Territory's Edge*, ed. Prem Kumar Rajaram and Carl Grundy-Warr, ix–xl. Minneapolis: University of Minnesota Press, 2007..

——. "The Irregular Migrant as Homo Sacer: Migration and Detention in Australia, Malaysia, and Thailand." *International Migration* 42, no. 1 (2004): 33–63.

Ratha, Dilip. "Workers' Remittances: An Important and Stable Source of External Development Finance." In *Global Development Finance: Striving for Stability in Development Finance*, 1:157–70. Washington, D.C.: World Bank, 2003.

Ratha, Dilip, Sanket Mohapatra, and Ani Silwal. *Migration and Remittance Trends, 2009.* Migration and Development Brief no. 11. Washington, D.C.: World Bank, November 3, 2009.

"The Reign of Sheriff Joe." *Washington Post*, July 28, 2008.

Reith, Peter. Interviewed by Derryn Hinch. Radio 3AK, September 13, 2001. Available on the Australian Department of Defence Web site at http://www.defence.gov.au/minister/2001/1309013.doc.

Reynolds, Sile, and Helen Muggeridge. *Remote Controls: How UK Border Controls Are Endangering the Lives of Refugees.* London: Refugee Council, 2008.

The Rights of Irregular Migrants. Special issue of *Ethics and International Relations* 22 (2008).

Robinson, Vaughan. "Security, Migration, and Refugees." In *Redefining Security: Population Movements and National Security*, ed. Nana Poku and David T. Graham, 67–90. Westport, Conn.: Praeger, 1998.

Root, Amada. *Market Citizenship: Experiments in Democracy and Globalization.* London: Sage, 2007.

Roy, Ravi K., Arthur T. Denzau, and Thomas D. Willett. "Introduction: Neoliberalism as a Shared Mental Model." In *Neoliberalism: National and Regional Experiments with Global Ideas*, ed. Ravi K. Roy, Arthur T. Denzau, and Thomas D. Willett, 3–13. London: Routledge, 2007.

——, eds. *Neoliberalism: National and Regional Experiments with Global Ideas.* London: Routledge, 2007.

Rudd, Kevin. "The Global Financial Crisis." *The Monthly*, no. 42 (2009): 20–29.

Ruddock, Philip. "Refugee Claims and Australian Migration Law: A Ministerial Perspective." *University of New South Wales Law Journal* 23, no. 3 (2000): 1–11.

Ruggiero, Vincenzo. "The Fight to Reappear." *Social Justice* 27, no. 2 (2000): 45–60.

Rupert, Mark. *Ideologies of Globalization: Contending Visions of a New World Order.* London: Routledge, 2000.

Sadiq, Kamal. "When States Prefer Non-citizens Over Citizens: Conflict Over Illegal Immigration Into Malaysia." *International Studies Quarterly* 49, no. 1 (2005): 101–22.

Sadowski-Smith, Claudia. "Reading Across Diaspora: Chinese and Mexican Undocumented Immigration Across U.S. Land Borders." In *Globalization on the Line: Culture, Capital, and Citizenship at U.S. Borders*, ed. Claudia Sadowski-Smith, 69–97. New York: Palgrave, 2002.

Saltau, Chloe. "Call for Calm After Rise in Attacks on Muslims." *The Age*, September 15, 2001.

Sassen, Saskia. *Cities in a World Economy.* 2d ed. Thousand Oaks, Calif.: Pine Forge Press, 2000.

——. "A New Cross-Border Field for Public and Private Actors." In *Political Space: Frontiers of Change and Governance in a Globalizing World*, ed. Yale H. Ferguson and R. J. Barry Jones, 173–88. Albany: State University of New York Press, 2002.

——. "The Repositioning of Citizenship." In *People out of Place: Globalization, Human Rights, and the Citizenship Gap*, ed. Alison Brysk and Gershon Shafir, 191–208. London: Routledge, 2004.

——. *Territory, Authority, Rights: From Medieval to Global Assemblages.* Princeton, N.J.: Princeton University Press, 2006.

Savage, Lydia. "Justice for Janitors: Scales of Organizing and Representing Workers." *Antipode* 38, no. 3 (2006): 645–66.

Savage, Mike, Gaynor Bagnall, and Brian Longhurst. *Globalization and Belonging.* London: Sage, 2005.

Schiller, Nina Glick, and Georges Fouron. "Transnational Lives and National Identities: The Identity Politics of Haitian Immigrants." In *Transnationalism from Below*, ed. Michael Peter Smith and Luis E. Guarnizo, 112–40. New Brunswick, N.J.: Transaction, 1998.

Schily, Otto. "Effecktiver Schutz für Flüchtlinge, Wrikungsvolle Bekämpfung illegaler Migration." Press statement, September 9, 2005. Available at http://www.bmi.bund.de/cln_012/nn_662928/Internet/Content/Nachrichten/Archiv/Pressemitteilungen/2005/09/Fluechtlingsschutz.html.

Schmeidl, Susanne. "Conflict and Forced Migration: A Quantitative Review, 1964–1995." In *Global Migrants, Global Refugees: Problems and Solutions*, ed. Aristide R. Zolberg and Peter M. Benda, 62–94. New York: Berghahn Books, 2001.

Schubert, Misha. "Identity Crisis: Eleven Ailing Australian Citizens or Residents Wrongly Detained." *The Age*, October 29, 2005.

Schumer, Charles E., and Lindsey O. Graham. "The Right Way to Mend Immigration." *Washington Post*, March 19, 2010.

Schuster, Liza. *The Realities of a New Asylum Paradigm*. Working Paper no. 20. Oxford, U.K.: Centre on Migration, Policy, and Society, University of Oxford, 2005.

Scrafton, Mike. "PM Told No Children Overboard" (letter). *The Australian*, August 16, 2004.

Seth, Sanjay. "Historical Sociology and Postcolonial Theory: Two Strategies for Challenging Eurocentrism." *International Political Sociology* 3, no. 3 (2009): 334–38.

Shachar, Ayelet. "Against Birthright Privilege: Redefining Citizenship as Property." In *Identities, Affiliations, and Allegiances*, ed. Seyla Benhabib, Ian Shapiro, and Danilo Petranović, 257–81. Cambridge, U.K.: Cambridge University Press, 2007.

Shapiro, Michael J. "Jessop et Al's More Is Better: A Political Rejoinder." *Environment and Planning D: Society and Space* 26, no. 3 (2008): 411–13.

Sharman, Jason. "Offshore and the New International Political Economy." *Review of International Political Economy* 17, no. 1 (2010): 1–19.

Sheller, Mimi, and John Urry. "The New Mobilities Paradigm." *Environment and Planning A* 38 (2006): 207–26.

Sheppard, Eric. "The Spaces and Times of Globalization: Place, Scale, Networks, and Positionality." *Economic Geography* 78, no. 3 (2002): 307–30.

Silverstein, Paul A. *Algeria in France: Transpolitics, Race, and Nation*. Bloomington: Indiana University Press, 2004.

Simon, Julian. "The Case for Greatly Increased Immigration." *The Public Interest* 102 (Winter 1991): 89–103.

Sirtori, Sonia, and Patricia Coelho. *Defending Refugees' Access to Protection in Europe*. Brussels: European Council of Refugees and Exiles, 2007.

Smith, Michael Peter. *Transnational Urbanism: Locating Globalization*. Malden, Mass.: Blackwell, 2001.

Smith, Michael Peter, and Matt Bakker. *Citizenship Across Borders: The Political Transnationalism of El Migrante*. Ithaca, N.Y.: Cornell University Press, 2008.

Soguk, Nevzat. "Border's Capture: Insurrectional Politics, Border-Crossing Humans, and the New Political." In *Borderscapes: Hidden Geographies and Politics at Territory's Edge*, ed. Prem Kumar Rajaram and Carl Grundy-Warr, 283–308. Minneapolis: University of Minnesota Press, 2007.

——. "Transversal Communication, Diaspora, and the Euro-Kurds." *Review of International Studies* 34, no. 1 (2008): 173–92.

Soja, Edward W. *Postmodern Geographies: The Reassertion of Space in Critical Social Theory.* London: Verso, 1989.

Somers, Margaret R. *Genealogies of Citizenship: Markets, Statelessness, and the Right to Have Rights.* Cambridge, U.K.: Cambridge University Press, 2008.

Sonenshein, Raphael J., and Mark H. Drayse. "Urban Electoral Coalitions in an Age of Immigration: Time and Place in the 2001 and 2005 Los Angeles Mayoral Primaries." *Political Geography* 25, no. 5 (2006): 570–95.

Sørensen, Ninna Nyberg. "Narrating Identity Across Dominican Worlds." In *Transnationalism from Below,* ed. Michael Peter Smith and Luis E. Guarnizo, 196–217. New Brunswick, N.J.: Transaction, 1998.

Southern Poverty Law Center. *Close to Slavery: Guestworker Programs in the United States.* Montgomery, Ala.: Southern Poverty Law Center, 2007.

Soysal, Yasemin Nuhoglu. *Limits of Citizenship: Migrants and Postnational Membership in Europe.* Chicago: University of Chicago Press, 1994.

Sparke, Matthew B. "A Neoliberal Nexus: Economy, Security, and the Biopolitics of Citizenship on the Border." *Political Geography* 25, no. 2 (2006): 151–80.

Squire, Vicki. *The Exclusionary Politics of Asylum.* New York: Palgrave Macmillan, 2009.

Staeheli, Lynn A., ed. *Cities and Citizenship.* Special issue of *Urban Geography* 24, no. 2 (2003).

Steger, Manfred. *Globalism: Market Ideology Meets Terrorism.* Lanham, Md.: Rowman and Littlefield, 2005.

———. *The Rise of the Global Imaginary: Political Ideologies from the French Revolution to the Global War on Terror.* Oxford, U.K.: Oxford University Press, 2008.

Stiglitz, Joseph. *Globalization and Its Discontents.* New York: W. W. Norton, 2002.

———. *The Roaring Nineties: Seeds of Destruction.* London: Allen Lane, 2003.

Stone, John. "The Muslim Problem and What to Do About It." *Quadrant* 50, no. 9 (2006): 11–17.

Strange, Susan. *The Retreat of the State: The Diffusion of Power in the World Economy.* Cambridge, U.K.: Cambridge University Press, 1996.

Straubhaar, Thomas. "Why Do We Need a General Agreement on Movements of People (GAMP)?" In *Managing Migration: Time for a New International Regime?* ed. Bimal Ghosh, 110–36. Oxford, U.K.: Oxford University Press, 2000.

Suro, Roberto, Sergio Bendixen, B. Lindsay Lowell, and Dulce C. Benavides. *Billions in Motion: Latino Immigrants, Remittances, and Banking.* Washington, D.C.: Pew Hispanic Center and Multilateral Investment Fund, 2002.

Suro, Roberto, and Gabriel Escobar. *2006 National Survey of Latinos: The Immigration Debate.* Washington, D.C.: Pew Hispanic Center, 2006.

Tagliabue, John. "Pace of Change Too Slow to Keep Entrepreneurs in France." *New York Times*, March 11, 2008.

"Taking the City's Pulse from the Pavement." *LATimes.com*, May 2, 2006.

Tax Justice Network. "The Price of Offshore." March 14, 2005. Available at http://www.taxjustice.net/cms/upload/pdf/Briefing_Paper_-_The_Price_of_Offshore_14_MAR_2005.pdf.

Ticktin, Miriam Iris. "Between Justice and Compassion: 'Les Sans Papiers' and the Political-Economy of Health, Human Rights, and Humanitarianism in France." Ph.D. diss., Stanford University, 2002.

Trumka, Richard L. "Remarks by AFL-CIO President Richard L. Trumka at the City Club of Cleveland, Cleveland Ohio." June 18, 2010. Available at http://www.aflcio.org/mediacenter/prsptm/sp06182010.cfm.

Uehling, Greta. "Irregular and Illegal Migration Through Ukraine." *International Migration* 42, no. 3 (2004): 77–107.

Unal, Bayram. "The New Patterns and the State: Construction of Illegality for Immigrants in Istanbul." In *Migration Between States and Markets*, ed. Han Entzinger, Marco Martiniello, and Catherine Wihtol de Wenden, 65–80. Aldershot, U.K.: Ashgate, 2004.

United Nations General Assembly. "Convention Relating to the Status of Refugees." July 28, 1951. *United Nations Treaty Series* 189, p. 137. Available at http://www.unhcr.org/refworld/docid/3be01b964.html.

United Nations High Commission for Refugees (UNHCR). *2008 Global Trends: Refugees, Asylum-Seekers, Returnees, Internally Displaced, and Stateless Persons*. Geneva: UNHCR, June 16, 2009. Available at http://www.unhcr.org/4a375c426.html.

United Nations Human Rights Committee. *International Covenant on Civil and Political Rights: Consideration of Reports Submitted by State Parties Under Article 40 of the Covenant: France*. CCPR/C/FRA/CO/4. Geneva: United Nations Human Rights Committee, July 31, 2008.

United Nations Population Division. *Levels and Trends of International Migration to Selected Countries in Asia*. New York: United Nations, 2003.

U.S. Citizenship and Immigration Services. *Green Card Through Investment*. Washington, D.C.: U.S. Department of Homeland Security, n.d. Available at http://www.uscis.gov/portal/site/uscis/menuitem.eb1d4c2a3e5b9ac89243c6 a7543f6d1a/?vgnextoid=cf54a6c515083210VgnVCM100000082ca60aRC RD&vgnextchannel=cf54a6c515083210VgnVCM100000082ca60aRCRD. Current as of June 15, 2010.

U.S. Committee for Refugees. *World Refugee Survey 2009*. Arlington, Va.: U.S. Committee for Refugees, 2010. Available at http://www.refugees.org/survey.

U.S. Conference of Mayors. "BP Oil Spill in the Gulf of Mexico, Immigration, and Jobs Top Agenda at Annual Mayors Gathering in Oklahoma City." Press release, Washington, D.C., June 14, 2010.

U.S. Customs and Border Protection. *Performance and Accountability Report: Fiscal Year 2009*. Washington, D.C.: U.S. Department of Homeland Security, March 9, 2010.

U.S. Department of Justice. "Citing Conflict with Federal Law, Department of Justice Challenges Arizona Immigration Law." Press release, Washington, D.C., July 6, 2010.

U.S. House of Representatives. *Border Protection, Anti-terrorism, and Illegal Immigration Control Act of 2005*. HR 4437, 109th Cong., 2d sess., December 6, 2005.

———. *Secure Fence Act of 2006*. HR 6061, 109th Cong., 1st sess., September 13, 2006.

U.S. Immigration and Customs Enforcement. *ICE Fiscal Year 2007 Annual Report: Protecting National Security and Upholding Public Safety*. Washington, D.C.: U.S. Department of Homeland Security, 2008.

U.S. Senate. *Comprehensive Immigration Reform Act of 2006*. S 2611, 109th Cong., 2d sess., May 25, 2006.

———. *Secure America and Orderly Immigration Act of 2005*. S 1033, 109th Cong., 1st sess., May 12, 2005.

Valdez, Veronica. "Walking Across the Stage." In *Underground Undergrads: UCLA Undocumented Immigrant Students Speak Out*, ed. Gabriela Madera, Angelo A. Mathay, Armin M. Najafi, Hector H. Saldívar, Stephanie Solis, Alyssa Jane M. Titony, Gaspar Rivera-Salgado, Janna Shadduck-Hernández, Kent Wong, Rebecca Frazier, and Julie Monroe, 41–44. Los Angeles: UCLA Center for Labor Research and Education, 2008.

Van de Veer, Peter. "Virtual India: Indian IT Labor and the Nation-State." In *Sovereign Bodies: Citizens, Migrants, and States in the Postcolonial World*, ed. Thomas Blom Hansen and Finn Stepputat, 276–90. Princeton, N.J.: Princeton University Press, 2005.

Varsanyi, Monica. "Immigration Policing Through the Backdoor: City Ordinances, the 'Right to the City,' and the Exclusion of Undocumented Day Laborers." *Urban Geography* 29, no. 1 (2008): 29–52.

———. "Interrogating 'Urban Citizenship' *Vis-à-Vis* Undocumented Migration." *Citizenship Studies* 10, no. 2 (2006): 229–49.

———. "The Paradox of Contemporary Immigrant Political Mobilization: Organized Labor, Undocumented Migrants, and Electoral Participation in Los Angeles." *Antipode* 37, no. 4 (2005): 775–95.

———. *Rising Tensions Between National and Local Immigration and Citizenship Policy: Matrículas Consulares, Local Membership, and Documenting the Undocumented*. Working Paper no. 140. San Diego: Center for Comparative Immigration Studies, University of California, 2006.

Vélez-Ibáñez, Carlos G., and Anna Sampaio, eds. *Transnational Latina/o Communities*. Lanham, Md.: Rowman and Littlefield, 2002.

Vertovec, Steven. "Conceiving and Researching Transnationalism." *Ethnic and Racial Studies* 22, no. 2 (1999): 447–62.

Viviani, Nancy. *The Long Journey: Vietnamese Migration and Settlement in Australia*. Melbourne: University of Melbourne Press, 1984.

Vlcek, William. "Behind an Offshore Mask: Sovereignty Games in the Global Political Economy." *Third World Quarterly* 30, no. 8 (2009): 1465–81.

Vogel, Dita. *Size and Development of Irregular Migration to the EU*. European Commission, Clandestino Project Policy Briefing. Brussels: European Commission, October 2009. Available at http://clandestino.eliamep.gr/.

Walters, William. "Acts of Demonstration: Mapping the Territory of (Non-)Citizenship." In *Acts of Citizenship*, ed. Engin F. Isin and Greg M. Nielson, 182–206. London: Zed Books, 2008.

Walzer, Michael. *Spheres of Justice: A Defence of Pluralism and Equality*. New York: Basic Books, 1983.

Weber, Leanne. "Policing the Virtual Border: Punitive Preemption in Australian Offshore Migration Control." *Social Justice* 34, no. 2 (2007): 77–92.

Weisman, Alan. *La Frontera: The United States Border with Mexico*. San Diego: Harcourt Brace Jovanovich, 1986.

Weisman, Jonathan, and Jim VandeHei. "Debate on How to Reshape Law Has Divided Republicans." *Washington Post*, May 21, 2006.

Weissman, Deborah M., Rebecca C. Headen, and Katherine Lewis Parker. *The Policies and Politics of Local Immigration Enforcement Laws: 287(G) Program in North Carolina*. New York: American Civil Liberties Union and Immigration and Human Rights Policy Clinic, 2009.

West, Andrew. "Asylum-Seeker Teenagers Join Lip Sewing Protest." *Sun Herald*, January 20, 2002.

"Where Is the Struggle Going?" October 20, 2008. Available at the Coordination de Sans-Papiers 75 Web site, Occupation de la Bourse du Travail, at http://bourse.occupee.free.fr/index.php?option=com_content&view=article&id=60:struggle&catid=35:english&Itemid=56.

Wihtol de Wenden, Catherine. "Urban Riots in France." *SAIS Review* 26, no. 2 (2006): 47–53.

Wills, Jane. "Making Class Politics Possible: Organizing Contract Cleaners in London." *International Journal of Urban and Regional Research* 32, no. 2 (2008): 305–23.

Zolberg, Aristide R. "Introduction: Beyond the Crisis." In *Global Migrants, Global Refugees: Problems and Solutions*, ed. Aristide R. Zolberg and Peter M. Benda, 1–25. New York: Berghahn Books, 2001.

Zwartz, Barney. "Muslim Leaders Feel Betrayed." *The Age*, September 18, 2006.

and Customs Enforcement (ICE), 123-124; immigration reform, 1, 27, 125–126, 129–130; localized immigration enforcement, 135–136; localized recognition of undocumented migrants, 9, 135, 136–139
United States-Mexico border, 8, 59, 118-119, 123,132

Unpaid Wages Prohibition Act, 26, 140–141

Walters, William, 96
Weisman, Alan, 118
Westphalia, Treaty of, 16, 52
Westphalian state system, 25

Vasanyi, Monica, 140, 143

CPSIA information can be obtained at www.ICGtesting.com
Printed in the USA
LVOW11*0843050916

503254LV00001B/1/P